6 Practice Tests for IELTS

Academic and General Training

Special thanks to the team who made this book possible:

Sumi Aktar, Kim Bowers, Matthew Callan, Louise Cook, Scarlet Edmonds, Sarah Graham, Brian Holmes, Abigail Kafka, Shannon O'Brien, Traci Shackelford, Nimesh Shah

*IELTS® is a registered trademark of University of Cambridge ESOL Examinations, British Council and IDP Education Australia, which neither sponsor nor endorse this product.

This publication is designed to provide accurate information in regard to the subject matter covered as of its publication date, with the understanding that knowledge and best practice constantly evolve. The publisher is not engaged in rendering medical, legal, accounting, or other professional service. If medical or legal advice or other expert assistance is required, the services of a competent professional should be sought. This publication is not intended for use in clinical practice or the delivery of medical care. To the fullest extent of the law, neither the Publisher nor the Editors assume any liability for any injury and/or damage to persons or property arising out of or related to any use of the material contained in this book.

Published by Kaplan Publishing, a division of Kaplan, Inc.
750 Third Avenue
New York, NY 10017

ISBN: 978-1-5062-5017-5

10 9 8 7 6 5 4 3 2 1

Kaplan Publishing print books are available at special quantity discounts to use for sales promotions, employee premiums, or educational purposes. For more information or to purchase books, please call the Simon & Schuster special sales department at 866-506-1949.

TABLE OF CONTENTS

How To Use This Book

WELCOME TO KAPLAN'S 6 PRACTICE TESTS FOR IELTS ACADEMIC AND GENERAL TRAINING

Congratulations on your decision to improve your English proficiency, and thank you for choosing Kaplan for your IELTS preparation. You've made the right choice in acquiring this book—you're now armed with six IELTS practice tests, which can be used for the Academic or General Training test, produced as a result of decades of researching the IELTS and similar tests and teaching many thousands of students the skills they need to succeed.

This book is guaranteed to help you to score higher—let's start by walking through what you need to know to take advantage of this book and the Online Study Plan.

Your Book

This book contains six IELTS practice tests, which include full-length Listening, Reading, Writing and Speaking subtests. If you are preparing for IELTS Academic, please used the Academic Reading and Writing sections of the test, while if you are preparing for IELTS General Training, please use the General Training Reading and Writing sections, located at the end of each test. IELTS Academic should be taken if you are applying for higher education (such as university) or professional registration in an English speaking environment. IELTS General Training can be taken for general visa purposes.

Both IELTS Academic and General Training follow the same format for the Listening and Speaking sections. As such, the Listening and Speaking sections of the Academic tests within this book can also be used by people studying for both IELTS Academic and IELTS General Training.

Review the listening scripts, answers and explanations at the back of this book to better understand your performance. Look for patterns in the questions you answered correctly and incorrectly. Were you stronger in some areas than others? This analysis will help you to target specific areas when you practice and prepare for IELTS.

Your Online Study Plan

Your Online Study Plan lets you access additional instruction and practice materials to reinforce key concepts and sharpen your IELTS skills. Resources include:

- Printable answer sheets to use when taking IELTS practice tests.
- Online answer grids for the practice tests in this book.
- Detailed answers and model Writing responses.
- Mock Speaking interviews with expert feedback.
- Self-assessment rubrics for Writing and Speaking.
- Listening tracks that accompany the practice tests in this book.

Register your book at **kaptestglobal.com/resources** to access your Online Study Plan. Select this book from the list and follow the instructions.

IELTS Practice Test 1

LISTENING MODULE

🎧 **Practice Test 1, Track 1**

Section 1   Questions 1–10

Questions 1–10

Complete the notes below.

*Write **NO MORE THAN TWO WORDS AND/OR A NUMBER** for each answer.*

<table>
<tr><td colspan="3" align="center">***Swing With Us – Swing Dancing Classes***
BOOKING FORM</td></tr>
<tr><td colspan="3">**CUSTOMER DETAILS**

Name: **1** ....
Phone Number: Landline × Mobile ✔ 0780 976 2942
School: **2** ....</td></tr>
<tr><td colspan="3" align="center">**COURSES**</td></tr>
<tr><td align="center">**Beginners**</td><td align="center">**Intermediate**</td><td align="center">**Advanced**</td></tr>
<tr><td>Start Date: 14th February</td><td>Start Date: **3** ....</td><td>Start Date: 24th February</td></tr>
<tr><td colspan="3">Form of course: **4** ....</td></tr>
<tr><td>Duration: **5** ....</td><td>Duration: 8 weeks</td><td>Duration: 8 weeks</td></tr>
<tr><td colspan="3">Frequency of all courses: **6** .... a week</td></tr>
<tr><td>£10 per lesson, or
7 .... for full programme</td><td>£10 per lesson, or £70 for full programme</td><td>£10 per lesson, or £70 for full programme</td></tr>
<tr><td colspan="3" align="center">**Extra Information**
Bringing a partner is **8** ....
Please wear **9** .... shoes.
10 .... accepted only in person or over the phone.</td></tr>
</table>

Practice Test 1, Track 2

Section 2   Questions 11–20

Questions 11–16

Label the plan below.

Choose **SIX** answers from the box and write the correct letters **A–K** next to questions 11–16.

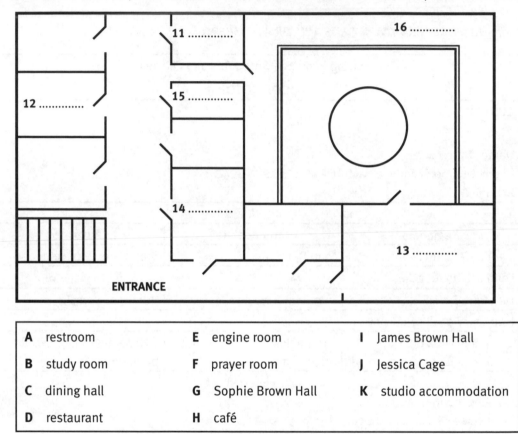

A restroom	**E** engine room	**I** James Brown Hall
B study room	**F** prayer room	**J** Jessica Cage
C dining hall	**G** Sophie Brown Hall	**K** studio accommodation
D restaurant	**H** café	

Questions 17–20

Choose the correct letter, **A, B or C**.

17   To join a society, you need to

    A   independently organise your submission.

    B   send them an email.

    C   add your personal information online and pay a fee.

18   There is a new volunteering opportunity for

    A   PR students.

    B   English Literature graduates.

    C   Marketing teachers.

19 One of Lincoln Hall's fortnightly activities is

    A the wine and cheese night.

    B organised trips.

    C language exchange.

20 The college campus currently has no

    A theatre.

    B football pitch.

    C supermarket.

🎧 **Practice Test 1, Track 3**

Section 3   Questions 21–30

Questions 21–24

Complete the table below.

*Write **NO MORE THAN TWO WORDS OR A NUMBER** for each answer.*

	Nadiya	Ian
Forum	**21** .... film forum	**22** .... music
Total number of members	62	**23** ....
Number of moderators	4	**24** ....

Questions 25–30

Complete the notes below.

*Write **NO MORE THAN TWO WORDS** for each answer.*

Write your answers in boxes 25–30 on your answer sheet.

Presentation Notes

The members in Ian's forum were initially apprehensive, but in Nadiya's forum they were immediately **25** .... Ian was surprised to learn that two of his forum members who lived across the world from each other **26** .... after flying to meet each other. The music forum members often discussed the **27** .... of organising a meet-up event, which was also the case with the members of the film forum. 'The Traveller' flew from country to country; unfortunately, the contents can't be shared for **28** .... reasons. Nadiya compared communication in online forums to the concept of **29** .... in the past, but argued that technology has transformed the way we are able to connect with others. One notable difference between the two forums is that trolls tended to be more **30** .... in Nadiya's forum than in Ian's.

Practice Test 1, Track 4

Section 4   Questions 31–40

Questions 31–36

Complete the summary below.

*Write **NO MORE THAN TWO WORDS** for each answer.*

The **31** .... dictates what employers are legally expected to do in the UK if one of their employees becomes disabled. According to the law, an employer should make reasonable adjustments to remove any **32** .... to their disabled employee's daily work life. This effectively means that discriminatory **33** .... will need to be changed. For example, an employer might have to offer a **34** .... nearer the company's building to a disabled member of staff, or they might have to make their doors automatic and install **35** .... for wheelchair access. In addition, the employer might have to **36** .... some of the disabled employee's responsibilities to another employee.

Questions 37–40

*Answer the questions in **NO MORE THAN TWO WORDS OR A NUMBER**.*

37   How does the lecturer describe the legislation surrounding disabilities?

38   What reasonable adjustment do most disabled members of staff ask for?

39   How much of the total cost of adjustments does an average company normally have to pay?

40   What will the adjustments need to be in order to be implemented?

ACADEMIC READING MODULE

Reading Passage 1   Questions 1–14

*You should spend about 20 minutes on **Questions 1–14**, which are based on Passage 1 below.*

Some 230 years ago, Scottish poet Robert Burns wrote his 'Address to the Toothache' in which he described the malady as the 'hell of all diseases'. For some, this description will still ring painfully true, but it should also emphasise how far we've come in dentistry and dental hygiene in Europe over the centuries.

In our modern world, we deal with toothache by picking up the phone, ringing the local dentist and booking an appointment. Granted, appointments might be scarce, and for some the cost of a simple procedure can be crippling, but neither the physical pain nor the inconvenience inflicted through modern practices can compare with what our ancestors would have had to face when one of their teeth decayed.

There are actually more instances of tooth decay now than ever before, probably due to our high-sugar diets, but evidence of tooth decay dates back to some of the earliest written texts. In fact, a reference to tooth decay can be found in a Sumerian text (circa 5,000 BC), which attributed the disease to 'tooth worms'. Scientists have even found evidence of dental decay in the skulls of the Cro-Magnon people, who lived 25,000 years ago.

When you consider the oral hygiene practices of the past, it's surprising that we don't have more instances of ancient tooth decay. The common toothbrush, for example, was patented in 1857, and collapsible tubes of toothpaste, which were introduced in the 1890s, didn't become popular until the early 1900s. Prior to this, most people either rinsed their mouths with plain water, or sometimes vinegar, which, any modern dentist will tell you, is highly acidic and can weaken your tooth enamel. Others used frayed sticks or cloths to remove food particles from between their teeth, occasionally in conjunction with primitive forms of toothpaste consisting of pulverised brick, charcoal and other dubious ingredients. Even after the invention of the common toothbrush, there were still several discrepancies in what was seen as proper dental hygiene. The book *Rules of Etiquette and Home Culture*, for example, which was published in 1889, advocated the use of toothbrushes with stiff bristles, which we now know not only damages tooth enamel but also hurts sensitive gum tissue.

Our ancestors did eventually do some things right: peppermint and chalk became toothpaste ingredients in the late 19th century—both of which are still used in modern toothpastes. Cinnamon, bay leaves, nutmeg and cloves were also used, as they were found to combat bad breath. The world's first dental society, the American Society of Dental Surgeons, was founded in 1840, and by 1896, not only had the manufacturing process of silver fillings been standardised, but the x-ray had also been adapted for use in dentistry by G.V. Black and Edmund Kells.

Still, modern dentistry was in its infancy for most of the 18th and the beginning of the 19th century and for the average person, the only solution to tooth decay would be extraction, the process being much more painful and less sterile than it is today. As renowned dentistry historian and Academy of General Dentistry spokesperson Eric Curtis explains, such procedures would be performed, somewhat informally, by 'barber-surgeons' using turnkeys, a tool that resembles a ratchet wrench. Barber-surgeons didn't just remove teeth: they also doled out detrimental advice on how to care for teeth and relieve toothache, suggesting, for instance, that patients pick their gums with the beak of an osprey bird.

In addition, the practice of selling one's teeth to wealthy people in exchange for a meager amount of money wasn't uncommon in the Victorian era. Human teeth were the preferred choice for the production of dentures, though ivory and the teeth of cattle were also used. Though the thought of having healthy teeth removed with pliers and with no anaesthetic may seem alarming and incredibly unwise to modern readers, for many desperately poor Victorians, including children, this was often one of the few ways to provide for themselves or their families.

Thankfully, dentistry rapidly developed in the 20th century with the emergence of tools such as composite fillings, the reclining dental chair, and of course, penicillin. Even inventions not directly linked to dentistry drove change, such as the invention of electricity, which allowed dentists to use electric drills. The last three or four generations have been the first in the history of humanity to live all their lives with the majority of their teeth intact, a trend set to continue, as advances in dental health continue into the 21st century. Next time you get a toothache so distracting you feel like you can't concentrate, remember this: had you been born just a hundred years ago, the results of tooth decay would've been much more serious.

Questions 1–6

Do the following statements reflect the claims of the writer in Reading Passage 1?

In boxes 1–6 on your answer sheet, write

> **YES** if the statement agrees with the claims of the writer
>
> **NO** if the statement contradicts the claims of the writer
>
> **NOT GIVEN** if it is impossible to say what the writer thinks about this

1 Toothache was once described as the 'hell of all diseases' by an English dentist.

2 Our ancestors' diets were better than ours.

3 Charcoal and pulverised brick were used to clean teeth.

4 Picking one's gums with the bill of an osprey was an effective method of pain relief in the 19th century.

5 Healthy individuals in the Victorian Era generally did not have their decayed teeth extracted.

6 Recent years have seen a drop in innovation in the dental hygiene world.

Questions 7–10

Complete the sentences below.

*Write **NO MORE THAN TWO WORDS** for each answer.*

7   ………….. in dentistry are not nearly as bad as they were in the past.

8   Tooth decay was described as the result of ………….. by the Sumerians.

9   Stiff bristles on a toothbrush and ………….. can be damaging to enamel.

10   Turnkeys and ………….. were used to pull out teeth, either due to decay or to be sold.

Questions 11–14

*Complete the summary below using the list of words, **A–I**, below.*

*Write the correct letter, **A–I**, in boxes 11–14 on your answer sheet.*

Scientific developments in the last 100 years have changed the way we view dental hygiene and healthy oral practices. **11** ………….. wasn't available in its current packaging until the 19th century, while water and vinegar were used as mouthwash. Different spices were popular in the fight against **12** ………….. It wasn't until the end of the 19th century that the **13** ………….. started being used in dentistry, thanks to Black and Kells. **14** ………….. was common practice in Victorian times for various reasons—both hygienic and financial. Thankfully, the 20th century brought with it major developments in dentistry, meaning that today our teeth can enjoy a long, healthy life.

A	toothbrush
B	tooth decay
C	extraction
D	x-ray
E	fillings
F	bad breath
G	toothpaste
H	denture
I	toothache

Reading Passage 2   Questions 15–28

*You should spend about 20 minutes on **Questions 15–28**, which are based on Passage 2 below.*

Living in the Dark: A WWII Story

A   Imagine this: it's six in the evening and you've just finished work. The sun has set, and instead of making your way home under the guidance of streetlights, you find yourself squinting to see on a road engulfed in total darkness. You can't switch your car's headlights on, you're not allowed to smoke a cigarette, and you have to fumble for cash in the dark to pay for your fare on the unlit bus. When you finally manage to get home, you can't watch TV, or turn on any of the lights, and you have to make sure all your windows have been covered with thick drapes. Although this may sound like a scene from science fiction, these rules were actually imposed on a daily basis to citizens of London during the Second World War.

B   The blackout was, without a doubt, one of the most intrusive measures of self defense on the home front by the UK, Germany, France and many more European countries during the war. It is also one of the lesser taught aspects of WWII, although it was one of the more successful methods employed to protect British civilians and their homes from German air raids by effectively making it more difficult for night bombers to navigate and pinpoint targets in the dark.

C   The blackout came into effect in Britain on the 1 September 1939, two days before the country joined the war. It was absolute and applied not just to households, but also to cars, factories, shops, office blocks and shipyards. Surprisingly, the measure was initially met with curiosity and excitement, and many civilians took to stargazing. It didn't take long for the novelty to wear off, however, as people soon realised the difficulties involved in making sure no lights were visible by measures such as hanging thick black cotton fabric and sealing any gaps with brown paper every single night.

D   To make matters worse, most people had to pay for their own black-out material (although the government made sure prices were low enough even for the poorest families), and if one of the Air Raid Patrol wardens who monitored the streets saw even the smallest hint of light slipping through their covers, the owners were subject to hefty fines and, less often, court appearances. To contend with this, many shops had to install a second door in order to prevent light from being visible outside when customers entered.

E   Though the blackout was a necessary measure for the protection of many homes and families, it didn't come without a price: crime rates soared during the blackout. Thieves and burglars soon discovered that the dark offered them the perfect opportunity to operate, they often targeted homes that belonged to evacuees or that had been damaged by bombs.

F   Gangs such as the infamous Billy Hill's raided jewellery shops and stores. As the men took to wearing Air Raid Patrol helmets and armbands to disguise themselves, they sometimes even received help from the public, who thought they were assisting ARP officials. Some people even attempted to use the bombings to cover up murder, as occurred in the case of the infamous Harry Dobkin, a man who murdered his wife then buried her under the floorboards of the recently bombed Vauxhall Baptist Chapel in hope that when her body was found she would be assumed to be an air raid victim.

G   Occurrences of sexual assault also rose during the blackout. Several accounts from the *Mass Observation* journals (a sociological research project that sought to record everyday human activity during this period) suggest that women were often followed home by strange men in the dark, who would attempt to attack them, using the darkness to protect their own identities. Such was the concern that women began to avoid travelling alone on the street at night, while public spaces such as train stations experienced a marked separation between men and women, with the latter congregating in the better-lit areas. According to figures collected by the Home Office, the reported cases of indecent assault on women in Britain almost doubled from 1935 to 1944—while cases of rape nearly quadrupled, growing from 104 to 416.

H   Crime wasn't the only unfortunate consequence of the blackout. Accidents on the road also increased, at least during the first two winters of the war, forcing the government to reduce the speed limit to 20 mph and paint white lines on the streets to guide pedestrians and drivers. People navigating the city in the dark sometimes fell off bridges into rivers and ponds. *The Daily Sketch*, a now defunct Manchester tabloid newspaper, reported a case of a man stepping out of a train and falling through an 80 foot viaduct. Serious injuries and fatalities became commonplace during the blackout, which, as can be expected, did not do much to improve the increasingly negative view of the measure among British citizens.

I   The blackout ended in 1944, when it was replaced by the dimout, which allowed lighting that was of roughly the brightness of moonlight. Full lighting did not return until April 1945—more than five years after the blackout was first introduced—with the symbolic illumination of Big Ben in London. This marked the end of an extremely unpopular but also necessary measure that had affected daily life and business not just in the UK, but throughout Europe.

Questions 15–20

*Reading Passage 2 has nine paragraphs labelled **A–I**. Which paragraph contains the following information?*

15 how the blackout provided self defense to the countries that adopted it

16 a measure taken by the government to fix a problem caused by the blackout

17 a pastime that gained popularity when the blackout was introduced

18 how long the blackout lasted

19 one of the sources of information regarding life during the blackout

20 the name of a religious place which was damaged during the war

Questions 21–24

Complete the sentences below.

*Write **NO MORE THAN TWO WORDS** for each answer.*

Write your answers in boxes 21–24 on your answer sheet.

21 People used .... to cover the parts of their windows that the blackout material didn't manage to cover.

22 Blackout infractions were usually met with ....

23 Some stores had a .... fitted to comply with blackout regulations.

24 Criminals often sported official .... and .... to trick the public.

Questions 25–28

Do the following statements agree with the information given in Reading Passage 2?

In boxes 25–28 on your answer sheet, write

> **TRUE**　　　　　*if the statement agrees with the information*
>
> **FALSE**　　　　*if the statement contradicts the information*
>
> **NOT GIVEN**　　*if there is no information on this*

25 Daily preparation for the blackout soon became a chore for people.

26 Indecent assault numbers in the UK were almost four times higher in 1944 compared with 1935.

27 A lot of people died falling off bridges during the blackout.

28 Big Ben was the last building to be lit in London in April 1945.

Reading Passage 3   Questions 29–40

You should spend about 20 minutes on ***Questions 29–40****, which are based on Passage 3 below.*

Digital Life after Death

The concept of life after death is a central notion in most major religions around the world, from Christianity to Islam, Judaism, Hinduism and Buddhism. It's also an idea that has been thoroughly explored by philosophers throughout history such as Plato, Descartes and Kant. Fear of death is at the core of human societies worldwide, and has been throughout our recorded history; recent technological developments, however, are beginning to change the way we view death. These changes can be divided into three distinct fields: virtual afterlife, digital reconnection, and digital immortality. As these technological emergences are still in a relative state of infancy, terminology and commentary is not at this point fixed or established; that is to say, at this point we are not quite sure how to talk about these different phenomena. As such, there is often a lack of distinction between the three fields. This passage will attempt to give a more concrete definition of each of the three distinct concepts.

To begin, let's look at virtual afterlife, that is, the personal information and online presence that remains on the internet after a person has died. It is estimated that there are currently about five million Facebook accounts belonging to people who have passed away—that number can only keep growing. The law, due to the relative newness of the issue as well as the murky and often contradictory online user agreements we are asked to sign when we join a website, is not clear on what we are allowed to do with a loved one's online accounts if they die. This is probably why online afterlife services such as *The Digital Beyond, Legacy Locker* and *If I Die* have sprung up. It's also why websites such as Google, Twitter, and Facebook are drawing up afterlife policies that offer options such as deletion, memorialisation or, as Facebook now offer, the ability to choose what happens with your account and nominate an executor of your wishes.

We are already experiencing the repercussions of living digital lives, yet we are only just starting to test the possibilities when it comes to digital reconnection, or the option to keep in touch with our loved ones after they pass. A hundred years ago, we would have been largely limited to photographs, paintings and writing as a source for remembering those who have passed away. Now, projects such as Eterni.me offers the possibility to leave behind a 3D avatar version of ourselves after we've gone, equipped with knowledge taken directly from our social media accounts and trained to emulate our speech patterns on a basic level so that our loved ones will have something to help them grieve or commemorate us after our death. And that's just the start: Project Elysium, headed by developers Nick Stavrou and Steve Koutsouliotas, aims to offer people the chance to meet and talk to deceased loved ones in a virtual-reality setting replicating a place with special significance to the deceased, adjusted in order to present a 'dreamscape look'.

Perhaps the aspect of a digital life after death with the most repercussions, however, is that of digital immortality. In recent decades, several films, novels and TV series have already considered this, to the extent that it is an established notion in the science fiction genre.

But it's not just fiction: the Terasem movement, founded by Martine Rothblatt, the CEO of United Therapeutics, is a religious group that believes digital immortality will become a reality in the not too distant future. As such, the memories and personalities, or 'mindfiles' of its members are stored in a server in its Florida headquarters in eager preparation. As Rothblatt explains, 'the end goal of Terasem is similar to other religions, [...] but for us it's not simply a spiritual concept, it's a mechanical challenge. Technology could one day make this a reality through digital backups.' When this day comes, Rohtblatt and his team plan to be immortalised online as realistically as possible.

Michael Graziano, professor of neuroscience at Princeton University in New Jersey, agrees with Rothblatt's seemingly optimistic aims. He explains that 'it is tempting to ignore these ideas as just another science fiction trope, a nerd fantasy. But I find myself asking, given what we know about the brain, whether we really could upload someone's mind to a computer. And my best guess is: yes, almost certainly.' For Graziano, this raises a host of ethical questions that will have to be considered not only by the developers of such software, but also by the future users of this technology. Among the questions which emerge are: how will we treat life and death? Will the sense of immortality provided by such technology cause people to act more recklessly with their natural lives? Will we contemptuously dismiss what we now call the 'sanctity' of life? What kind of human rights will we ascribe to digital humans? Will digital humans be protected by the same human rights as physical humans? Could atrocious crimes be punished with a ban from the digital beyond? How will digital afterlives affect the way we view religion and religious afterlives?

Of course, unlike with virtual afterlife and digital reconnection, digital afterlives remain simply speculation for now. Currently, we've only managed to map the brain of a roundworm and small parts of a mouse brain so far, and Graziano admits we've got a long way to go before we're able to map an entire human brain. Still, there will probably come a day when we will need to consider these aforementioned issues, much like we are currently doing with the issues related to virtual afterlife. When that day arrives, our understanding and view of death may change significantly.

Questions 29–34

Answer the questions below with words taken from the passage.

*Write **NO MORE THAN THREE WORDS** for each answer.*

29   What's currently altering our understanding of what it means to pass away?

30   What's described as inconsistent and obscure in the text?

31   *Legacy Locker* provides what to its customers?

32   What source of information does Eterni.me use to make its avatars more believable?

33   How does the Terasem leader describe his movement's object?

34   According to Michael Graziano, what will be an immediate consequence of digital immigration?

Questions 35–40

Complete the table below with words from the passage.

*Write **NO MORE THAN TWO WORDS** for each answer.*

Digital Life after Death	
Virtual Afterlife	This focuses on a person's **35** .... after death. The law remains unclear on what is acceptable in this field. Online 'afterlife' services promise to deal with digital legacy.
Digital Reconnection	This focuses on the possibility of reconnecting with deceased loved ones online. Websites like Eterni.me allow people to create a **36** .... to help their loved ones. Project Elysium aims to create VR settings with a **37** .... to talk to dead loved ones.
Digital Immortality	This focuses on the idea that human consciousness can be uploaded to computers. The Terasem movement is currently taking precautions by making **38** .... of its members' memories. This movement will probably lead to legislation aimed at defining the rights of **39** .... Remains **40** .... for the time being.

ACADEMIC WRITING MODULE

Task 1

You should spend about 20 minutes on this task.

The flow chart below illustrates the typical stages of a traditionally published novel. Write a report for a university lecturer describing the process.

Write at least 150 words.

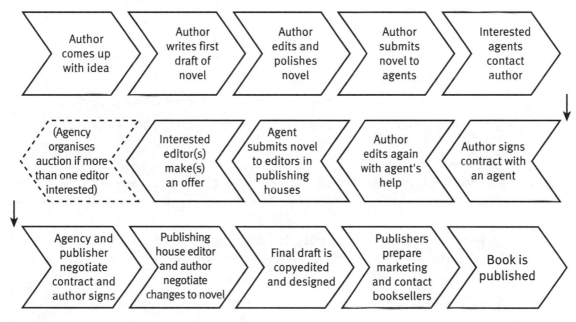

Task 2

You should spend about 40 minutes on this task.

A staggering amount of food is wasted every year, both in businesses and households. Why is this happening? What can be done to tackle this problem?

Give reasons for your answer and include any relevant examples from your own knowledge and experience.

Write at least 250 words.

SPEAKING MODULE

Time: 11–14 minutes

Part 1

Introduction to interview (4–5 minutes): The examiner will begin by introducing himself or herself and checking your identity. She or he will then ask you some questions about yourself based on everyday topics.

Let's talk about fashion.

- Do you follow fashion trends?
- What kinds of fashion trends are popular in your country right now?
- What's your favourite shirt? [Why?]
- What colours do you prefer in your clothes and shoes? [Why?]
- Who is the most fashionable member of your family? [Why?]

Part 2

Individual long turn (3–4 minutes): Candidates' task card instructions:

Task Card

Please read the topic below carefully. You will be asked to talk about it for one to two minutes. You will have one minute to think about what you are going to say. You can make some notes to help you if you wish.

Describe a time you participated in a parade, march or demonstration. You should say:

- What the event was and where it took place
- Why you decided to participate
- What you saw and did in the event

Also, explain how you felt during and after the event.

The examiner may then ask you a couple of brief questions to wrap up this part of the test. Further questions:

- Was there anyone with you at the event? Do you know why they wanted to go?
- Do you normally participate in parades, marches or demonstrations? [Why?]
- Does this event happen every year, or was it a one-time event?

Part 3

Two-way discussion (4–5 minutes): In Part 3, the examiner will ask you further questions related to the topic in Part 2.

Let's talk about parades and events for a moment.

- Do any famous parades or festivals take place in your country?
- Why do people enjoy going to and participating in parades?
- What are the benefits of supporting a local event for a business?
- Do you think it's important for children to take part in parades?

Finally, let's talk about socialising.

- What kind of social activities are popular amongst young people in your country?
- How are these activities different from the ones older generations prefer?
- Why is it easier for some people to socialise than others?
- How would younger people benefit from socialising with older generations?
- How could local councils encourage younger people to socialise with the elderly?
- How has the way people socialise changed since the invention of the Internet?

General Training Reading and Writing Test

GENERAL TRAINING READING MODULE

Section 1   Questions 1–14

*Read the text below and answer **Questions 1–8**.*

LOST & FOUND		
A Small, ginger kitten with no collar reading 'Buttercup' found wandering on Queen Katherine's Street, Kendal, by the river. If this is your cat, please call 07700900174 and be prepared to provide a picture.	**C** My daughter misplaced her favourite teddy on a walk in Arnside last weekend. He's a brown bear with a yellow jumper and blue boots. Please let me know if you have any information by contacting Richard at richysutton@denty.com.	**D** I lost my smartphone last week in the vicinity of Morecambe Bay–it's a blue Franzo 650. I have a lot of precious photos stored there that are irreplaceable, so I'm offering a finder's fee of £200—much more than the value of the phone itself. If found please call 01632 345 432.
B A pair of keys has been handed in to Cumbria Birch Trust's reception. For more information, call 01632 542 631. To claim, you must be able to correctly describe the keyring to us.		**E** Wallet containing items including pensioner's bus card and cash located at the end of the line in Ambleside. To claim, visit the lost property office at the bus depot, Penrith with a photo ID.

Questions 1–5

Match the options above with the information in the sentences below.

*Write the correct letter **A–E** in boxes 1–5 on your answer sheet.*

1   a cash reward offered

2   information being requested by email

3   a lost pet

4   an item that can only be claimed by someone who knows what it looks like

5   an item that must be requested in person

Questions 6–8

Complete the sentences below.

*Choose **NO MORE THAN TWO WORDS AND/OR A NUMBER** from the text for each answer.*

6 A lost .... was last seen wearing a jumper.

7 A mobile phone was found near ....

8 People who want to claim the kitten need to send a .... as proof and call the number.

*Read the text below and answer **Questions 9–14**.*

Shoddy Furniture Falling Apart?
Let SOUTHWARK CARPENTERS help.

Want a walk in wardrobe? Fancy a fitted kitchen? Dreaming of a durable desk? Or just want to replace your creaky floorboards? We custom-build furniture and fittings to work with your house, and your vision. We work with a variety of trade suppliers to build you items out of the finest quality woods at the lowest reasonable price.

To receive a quote for your work, please send us an email or pick up the phone and let us know: (1) the work to be completed; (2) the dimensions of the item/flooring to be created; (3) the material to be used; (4) the timeline for the work to be completed. That gives us enough information to create a custom quote, then you can review and book an in-person discussion with one of our professionals.

Our experienced carpenters and joiners are ready to help your projects come to life. We're fanatical about creating wonderful fittings and furniture with wood. Give us a call and let our knowledgeable staff talk you through your options.

CONTACT US TODAY   020 7946 0345   CALLS ANSWERED 24 HOURS A DAY

Hear what our customers have to say

a selection of our reviews from SureSecure:

★ ★ ★ ★ ★

"George was professional, friendly, and went the extra mile to finish the job on the same day. Thank you." *F Trankle (Kent)*

★ ★ ★ ★ ★

"Will definitely use again and recommend to our friends. Lee did such a fantastic job making our bespoke wardrobe." *J Loren (Basingstoke)*

★ ★ ★ ★ ★

"We got a quote for some work from a different carpenter that seemed quite high. Sarah was able to get the work done for half of our initial quote, and didn't skimp on the quality!" *A Dancy (Sussex)*

Questions 9–13

Do the following statements agree with the information in the above text?

In boxes 9–13 on your answer sheet, write

TRUE	*if the statement agrees with the information*
FALSE	*if the statement contradicts the information*
NOT GIVEN	*if there is no information on this*

9   Southwark Carpenter's work is described as 'shoddy'.

10   The company can lay new flooring.

11   Completing projects within a shorter timeline costs more money.

12   Some projects can be completed within 1 day.

13   Sarah completed her work promptly.

Question 14

*Choose the correct letter, **A**, **B** or **C**.*

Write the correct answer in box 14 on your answer sheet.

14   Which reviewer mentions the low cost of the services provided by Southwark Carpenters?

A   F Trankle

B   J Loren

C   A Dancy

Section 2   Questions 15–28

*Read the text of text below and answer **Questions 15–21**.*

Is Your Workplace Culture Healthy?

Workplace culture starts at the top. As managers, it's your responsibility to maintain a healthy work environment, which, in turn, is the most effective way to keep employee morale and productivity high. This document guides you through four different areas to address, in order to ensure a healthy workplace culture.

Stop, Collaborate and Listen

The more your team members work together, communicate and listen to each other's ideas and concerns, the smoother and more integrated your office will be. Communicating and collaborating also helps employees feel a sense of belonging in their workplace, and group discussions can reduce the risk of gossip. Managers should address changes likely to cause unrest openly and listen to the feedback provided by employees.

Step Away from the Desk

Most areas of business will weather the occasional busy period of work, but you should make sure that none of your employees are working too much. Vacations should not only be encouraged, they should be mandatory, and working late should be an occasional circumstance, not a regular occurrence. Make sure to encourage your employees to take breaks and avoid overworking themselves. Well rested employees produce better-quality work.

Flexible Working

Some weeks, it's simply not possible to avoid working longer hours. In cases where employees are working overtime, ensure that they are taking time off to make up for this at a later date. Similarly, be open to occasionally allowing employees time off during their contractual working hours if they are willing and able to make up the hours at another time.

Encourage Openness

Employees should be voicing their concerns to you, where they can be addressed, rather than to each other, where they will create a breeding ground for negative energy. Make sure to have regular one on one conversations with your direct reports, and encourage them to share their thoughts and feelings with you about work. If they voice complaints, take what lengths you can to address these, and if they offer suggestions, consider implementing them.

If you'd like to learn more about creating a healthy workplace environment, you can access our manager's resources portal for further reading.

Questions 15–20

*Answer the questions below using **NO MORE THAN THREE WORDS** from the text.*

Write the answers in boxes 15–20 on your answer sheet.

15 Who is the intended audience for the passage?

16 How should managers talk to employees about potentially stressful changes?

17 What should be mandatory in order to ensure a good work environment?

18 Other than taking vacations, what might cause employees to be given time off during working hours?

19 What type of communications should managers try to get from employees during one on one conversations?

20 Where can individuals go to read more about the topic addressed in the passage?

Question 21

Choose the alternative which best completes the sentence below. Write the correct answer A, B, C or D in box 21 on your answer sheet.

21 When discussing work-related topics with employees, managers should

A bear in mind that employees may not understand the situation accurately.

B attempt to include suggestions and solutions proposed by employees.

C do their best to convince employees why certain decisions have been reached.

D make sure to only talk to employees individually.

Questions 22–28

*Read the text below and answer **Questions 22–28**.*

The Pomodoro Technique is one of the simplest productivity methods you can implement into your work schedule. Perhaps this is why the technique is so popular; since its creation almost 30 years ago, the technique has gained much popularity in self-improvement and productivity circles. Using the technique can prevent procrastination, help you to keep working at a regular pace, and help you to complete the ever-increasing list of items on your to-do list.

The Pomodoro Technique was created in the 90s by the Italian entrepreneur Francesco Cirillo. As a student, Cirillo found success by breaking his larger projects down into manageable chunks, and then timing himself with his kitchen timer shaped like a tomato. This is where Cirillo got the name for his technique, as pomodoro is Italian for tomato. Cirillo also made sure to take short breaks in between each chunk of work. Cirillo found that timing himself while completing short sections of work helped him to stay focused while he was working, and taking short breaks in between each section of work made it easier for him to keep working throughout the day.

When used consistently over a longer period of time, The Pomodoro Technique can even help to improve your attention span, and increase the rate at which you complete projects. The technique has been used by a wide range of people in a variety of circumstances, particularly those who work in an office, writers trying to finish a novel, and students who need to complete assignments.

The Pomodoro Technique is extremely simple to utilise, and it's also fairly flexible. You can adjust the size of your pomodoros as you see fit, depending on the type of work you need to complete, and the number of tasks you have. Below is an outline of the classic Pomodoro structure that beginners can use to make a start with this technique.

1. Choose a series of short tasks to complete during your pomodoros. If you have only one large task to work on, divide this into small, manageable chunks. Each pomodoro of work will be 25 minutes long, so try to divide work into sections that can be completed in this period. However, when you're just starting out with this technique, don't worry too much about how much time each task will take you to complete, you can adjust the size of your pomodoros as you begin to get used to your pace of work, and you may also find that you speed up the more you practice completing pomodoros.

2. Set a timer for 25 minutes, and work only on your first pomodoro during this time. If any distractions come up during this time, try to address these quickly, by scheduling a time to discuss after your pomodoro is complete. If it's not possible to delay a distraction, you must end your pomodoro early. If you finish your work before the timer goes off, end your pomodoro at this point and move on to the next step. Similarly, if you have not finished working when your pomodoro timer sounds, you must stop working and have a break at this point; you can return to your pomodoro later.

3. Take a 5 minute break, then move onto your next pomodoro. Stand up during this time, and try to move around. You might want to use the bathroom, or make something to drink while having your 5 minute break. The key is to leave your desk or workspace, so that you return once the 5 minutes are over feeling refreshed.

4. After you have completed 4 pomodoro cycles, take a longer break of 20–30 minutes. This is a good time to have something to eat if you're hungry, or move around some more.

After you've had some practice following the basic pomodoro method outlined above, you can begin to make changes. If you find you have more energy to keep working at the end of your pomodoros, or are working with tasks that require more than 25 minutes for one chunk, you can extend the length of each pomodoro. If you find you're competing work too quickly, try to make each chunk of work longer, or complete 2 different 10–15 minute chunks of work as one pomodoro.

Questions 22–26

*Complete each sentence with the correct ending, **A–I**, below.*

*Write the correct letter, **A–I**, in boxes 22–26 on your answer sheet.*

22 The Pomodoro Technique was created

23 Using the technique on a long-term basis

24 A pomodoro should be ended early

25 People using The Pomodoro technique can eat

26 If an individual task is shorter than one pomodoro

A	when an entrepreneur began learning to cook.
B	during the longer break that occurs after completing 4 pomodoros.
C	can help people work at a quicker pace.
D	following even minor disruptions.
E	while completing a pomodoro.
F	combine it with other tasks to create a larger chunk of work.
G	by an Italian student in the 1990s.
H	it is not suitable to be used for The Pomodoro Technique.
I	if the scheduled work is completed before the timer has run out.

Questions 27–28

For **Questions 27–28**, choose **TWO** answers, **A–E**.

Write your answers in boxes 27–28 on your answer sheet.

Which **TWO** of these titles could be used to describe the above text?

A   Work faster and improve your efficiency

B   Using fresh tomatoes in the kitchen

C   How to handle time-sensitive decisions

D   Boost your productivity with this simple method

E   Use this technique to help you pass your college exams

Section 3   Questions 29–40

*Read the text below and answer **Questions 29–40**.*

London Double Decker Buses

If you've ever visited the capital of England, you will know that the brilliantly red London Routemaster buses are a global icon; tourists hop on these buses to take a sightseeing ride as soon as they reach the city. As of today, there are approximately 8,600 of these buses operating across more than 700 routes and stopping at over 19,000 bus stops. Their colour makes them instantly recognisable due to the London Transport paint standards, first implemented at Chiswick Works Laboratory. Each bus is painted following a standard set of guidelines, which require the use of a painted card from the manufacturers, in order to match each bus's colour. This has become known as the Chiswick Colour Standard.

The paint colour of London buses was controlled by Chiswick Works Laboratory from the 1950s until around the 1980s. There was no master colour for the paint being created at this time; instead, the colour was mixed fresh for each bus. As a result, it was possible to detect slight discrepancies between the colours of London buses in the earlier years of their production.

In the 1970s, paint producers started to use white in their mixes to reduce costs and improve coverage. Lead was banned in paints at this time, which meant that buses had a slight pastel sheen compared to earlier vehicles that had a much brighter finish. With modern paint techniques, the colour is now sprayed by a few select firms, including PPG, who named the shade with the code FLT 1123 Bus Red. This differentiates the colour from Post Office Red, which is for mail boxes, and also from the colour of London's equally iconic red telephone boxes. These boxes are now nearly defunct in Britain, due to the rise of the mobile phone. Some boxes outside London have been repurposed for various uses, some as community book sharing points, and others even house defibrillators, which can be used to treat people suffering from cardiac arrest. However, the primary function of red British telephone boxes is to stand in tourist spots such as Buckingham Palace and on the runway of the peninsula of Gibraltar, allowing visitors a photo opportunity.

Bus spotters and enthusiasts can be fanatical about London Transport, with these obsessive hobbyists writing in to find out how they can get hold of authentic Bus Red paint for their models. The London Transport Museum has stated that there are several paint tones available to the public, and have made the list available on request. However, transport buffs on the Routemaster Owners and Operators Forum have uncovered that the Transport for London (TfL) tender documents list the paint as 'ICI London Bus Red P498 FPF 3', although it remains unclear how this code will be deciphered and the colour obtained for public use.

The colour was adopted in the 1900s to make the buses stand out from competitors operating at that time in the capital. The entire bus was hand painted red. However, it is estimated that only around a third of today's buses are actually red. The roof is now painted white to help with heat emissions in the summer, when public transport in London is notoriously sweltering. Adverts on buses take up a growing amount of bus bodywork, as promoters strive to come up with ingenious ideas to cover the space available without obscuring the driver's view. In recent years, TfL has come under fire for allowing zealous religious and political groups to advertise, as well as permitting risqué jokes in ads for movies and plays. Despite the thousands of people that see these ads all over the city, the number of complaints is relatively low: between fifty and two hundred complaints are registered for each investigated poster.

Many more complaints are have been received by TfL about the environmental impact of London's buses. Such complaints have sparked changes to the production of the classic diesel-fuelled bus, with the introduction of new 'green buses', which cut down CO_2 emissions through hybrid engines and particulate filters. Despite the name, these buses will continue to resemble the classic bus in style and colour, while creating cleaner, more environmentally friendly air for city-dwellers to breathe.

Questions 29–32

Choose the correct letter: **A, B, C** *or* **D**.

Write your answers in boxes 29–32 on your answer sheet.

29 According to the passage, which of the following statements is true of Chiswick Works Laboratory?

    A   They painted the first bus in London.

    B   They created a master paint for the London Routemaster buses.

    C   They created the first London bus.

    D   They helped to make the colour of London buses more uniform.

30 Post Office Red …

    A   is used for mail boxes and telephone boxes.

    B   is derived from an earlier shade used on London buses.

    C   is distinct from the red used on London buses.

    D   is also known as FLT 1123 Box Red.

31 London buses began to look more pastel in colour

    A   when a master paint was created.

    B   at the same time as more white was added to the paint.

    C   when painted card was used as a reference.

    D   once lead became more commonly used in paint.

32   Which of the following statements applies to the original London buses?

   A   They used diesel.

   B   They were not painted red.

   C   They were environmentally friendly.

   D   They have all been retired.

Questions 33–37

Do the following statements agree with the claims of the writer in Reading Passage 3?

In boxes 33–37 on your answer sheet, write

   YES   *if the statement agrees with the claims of the writer*

   NO   *if the statement contradicts the claims of the writer*

   NOT GIVEN   *if it is impossible to say what the writer thinks about this*

33   Red buses are not found outside of London.

34   Most British telephone boxes are now used to treat cardiac arrest.

35   Members of the public are permitted to use certain paint tones to create items in a similar shade to London buses.

36   London buses have displayed political advertisements.

37   Recently, some London buses have been painted green.

Questions 38–40

Complete the sentences below.

*Choose **ONE WORD ONLY** from the passage for each answer.*

Write your answers in boxes 38–40 on your answer sheet.

38   Chiswick Works Laboratory .... paint colour for London Routemaster buses until the 1980s.

39   The .... of earlier London buses is not consistent due to the lack of a master paint.

40   Bus enthusiasts want to use the authentic London bus paint colour to paint ....

GENERAL TRAINING WRITING MODULE

Writing Task 1

You should spend about 20 minutes on this task.

> *A student you know is coming to visit the town or city where you live next weekend.*
>
> *Write a letter to the student. In the letter,*
> - *tell the student about some places in your town or city that he/she should visit.*
> - *give instructions about transportation in your city.*
> - *give contact details for the student so he/she can get in touch with you.*

Write at least 150 words.

You do **NOT** need to write any addresses.

Begin your letter as follows:

Dear ...

Writing Task 2

You should spend about 40 minutes on this task.

Write about the following topic:

> *Some people think that homework should be banned from schools while others think that it is an important part of a student's education.*
>
> *Discuss the advantages and disadvantages of homework and give your own opinion.*
>
> *Give reasons for your answer and include any relevant examples from your own knowledge or experience.*

Write at least 250 words.

IELTS Practice Test 2

LISTENING MODULE

🎧 **Practice Test 2, Track 5**

Section 1   Questions 1–10

Questions 1–5

Complete the notes below.

*Write **NO MORE THAN TWO WORDS AND/OR A NUMBER** for each answer.*

Healthy Eating, Healthy Living Workshops

Prices

Single Tickets: £7.50   Family Tickets: **1** ....

Recommended arrival time: **2** ....

Location: St Peter's Church, **3** .... Road.

Car Park situated **4** .... church hall.

Book workshops by phoning the **5** .... on 01539 55146.

Questions 6–10

Complete the table below.

*Write **NO MORE THAN TWO WORDS AND/OR NUMBERS** for each answer.*

Workshop Title	Date	Details
Healthy Eating, Healthy Living	Saturday the 3rd	Eating and planning a **6** ....
7	Saturday the 17th	Learn new **8** ....
9 .... *Shopping*	Saturday the **10**	How, when and where to buy your food.

🎧 **Practice Test 2, Track 6**

Section 2   Questions 11–20

Questions 11–13

*Choose **THREE** staff from the box and write the correct letter **A–D**, next to **Questions 11–13**.*

Staff
A   cleaning and maintenance staff
B   office staff
C   the speaker
D   Mr Cazorla

Groups

11   Barcelona ....

12   Madrid ....

13   Marbella ....

Questions 14–15

Complete the summary below.

*Write **ONE WORD ONLY** for each answer.*

Welcome Pack

The welcome packs include a schedule for the induction day, as well as a camp map detailing the buildings and areas on the site. Information on the people **14** .... for the different parts of the programme is also included. The welcome pack also includes information on the correct safety measures which should be used for all of the **15** .... The supervisors will be responsible for explaining the information in the welcome pack to the staff.

Questions 16–20

Complete the notes below.

*Write **NO MORE THAN THREE WORDS AND/OR A NUMBER** for each answer.*

SCHEDULE
08.30 – Introduction
09.00 – Carla Smith from **16** .... will be explaining employee payment and handing out tax forms.
09.30 – Marcos Cazorla: Director **17** .... will go through the campus and explain the Spanish language centre's mission, and then demonstrate the **18** .... and take you to the assembly points.
10.15 – Coffee Break
10.45 – Video presentation at the Open Cinema, which was created by the **19** .... and will explain safety procedures for the workplace as well as the local area.
11.45 – **20** ....
12.45 – Staff will be sorted into teams and introduced to supervisors.

Practice Test 2, Track 7

Section 3   Questions 21–30

Questions 21–25

*Choose the correct letter, **A, B, C** or **D**.*

Write your answers in boxes 21–25 on your answer sheet.

21 Mark tells Lydia that he feels Professor Whitaker

    A   is able to inspire his class.

    B   never gives fascinating lectures.

    C   is not available as often as he would like.

    D   is under a lot of pressure.

22 Lydia says Dr Pattinson

    A   was her tutor the term before.

    B   is more charismatic than Professor Whitaker.

    C   had a good rapport with her group last year.

    D   misses her.

23 In the lecture, Lydia took

    A   more notes than she thought she had.

    B   fewer notes than she thought she had.

    C   far too many notes.

    D   fewer notes than Mark.

24 Mark wants to

    A   discuss his notes.

    B   listen to what Mindy has to say.

    C   photocopy Lydia's notes.

    D   take some more notes on the lecture.

25 Lydia says

    A   Mark writes too fast.

    B   her notes are all in Spanish.

    C   that going to the lecture wasn't such a good idea.

    D   she used two different languages in her notes.

Questions 26–30

Answer the questions below. Write **NO MORE THAN FOUR WORDS** *for each answer.*

Write your answers in boxes 26–30 on your answer sheet.

26   What will Lydia do with her notes once she's typed them up?

27   What does Lydia think she usually fails to understand?

28   How does Mark feel if he pays too much attention to detail?

29   What's the name of the book they talk about?

30   Mark says that the book is about the limitations of what?

🎧 **Practice Test 2, Track 8**

Section 4   Questions 31–40

Questions 31–36

Complete the sentences below.

Write **NO MORE THAN THREE WORDS** *for each answer.*

31 When learning a new language, one of the most common student complaints is the lack of ....

32 Many students believe they need to improve their ....

33 Teachers are getting ....

34 As a result, these teachers may not be able to plan more .... classes.

35 The new system was presented by a saleswoman from a .... of global materials.

36 The workshop's aim is to .... to evaluate and assess course books.

Questions 37–40

*Choose the correct letter, **A, B** or **C**.*

37 In the first part of the workshop, participants will help each other to

A   evaluate a new course book together.

B   develop a set of standards to assess course books with.

C   assess a set of course book criteria.

38 The speaker may use the information gained from the first part of the workshop to

A   carry out additional research or help more schools and teachers.

B   research the selected criteria further.

C   help schools select the proper teachers.

39 The workshop will also enable teacher to

A   take the material perspectives into account.

B   analyse learner's communicative considerations.

C   look at the resources from the students' point of view.

40 The speaker believes that most teachers

A   choose materials based on all contents of a course pack.

B   choose materials based on contents of textbooks.

C   choose materials based on their language centres.

ACADEMIC READING MODULE

Reading Passage 1   Questions 1–12

*You should spend about 20 minutes on **Questions 1–12**, which are based on Reading Passage 1 below.*

War in the Sunny Alps

Estorick Collection, London, Islington

Finally reopened to the public following a five-month renovation, the Estorick Collection in Islington is celebrating its return with a major exhibition of rarely seen works documenting the role of British forces in Italy during the final years of World War One. A collection of drawings, paintings and photographs from local and official war artists highlights an easily forgotten aspect of Britain's involvement in this terrible conflict which took place almost a hundred years ago.

The collection makes an effort to challenge expectations. There's no mud, or trenches, or blood. There aren't any dead bodies, or bombs, or weapons. Despite the collection's title, though, there isn't any sunshine, either. Poverty, destruction and desolation are consistent themes throughout the exhibition, despite the perhaps ironic efforts of some of the contributors to add an apolitical romanticised aura to the conflict. Shattered churches are covered in pure white snow under the warmth of a friendly sun; disillusioned youngsters smile with apparent innocence; war tanks are surrounded by pretty young ladies carrying colourful flower baskets; heroic troops in beautiful uniforms march into the mountain-peaked horizon. These are just some of the many controversial and perhaps misleading landscapes presented in the collection that might lead one to believe the war never truly happened.

Philip Carson's remarkable drawings and paintings of aerial battles focus on the plastic beauty of one of the ugliest times in human history. The landscapes are breath-taking enough to cause you to consider what fantastic holiday destinations the war bases would have made. Carson first created these pieces while serving as a fighter pilot, which might explain his reputed emotional detachment from the more brutal aspects of the conflict. Such detachment would have been a helpful survival tool when one was both a soldier and an artist in the midst of a war. His work appears to present a version of the war emotionless enough to allow him to accept what was happening at the time. Carson produced images that would make the act of destruction seem less horrific and more factual; simply a moment in human history. Somehow, as an artist if not as a pilot, Carson missed his mark. His top-down approach to the events on land can generally only be found amidst charity fundraising luncheons of those who are willing to help the less fortunate as long as champagne is provided.

The photographer Edward Banks who served on the Western Front, (some say he asked to be transferred there so as not to miss any of the action) makes a Hollywood-inspired contribution to the collection. The photographs he took during his assignment to Italy sensitively represent the daily difficulties faced by frontline troops and dispossessed Italian civilians scratching a living behind Anglo-Italian lines. Banks's scenes work beautifully with the impressive, mountainous landscapes, but unfortunately, some of his portraits take on a strong resemblance to backstage shots from a period soap opera.

Despite the failings of some of the work, the collection does have its merits, and these come largely through the work of Peter Paul Carroll. His work reveals a passionate feel for the stunning views of the Italian Alps, interspersed with sympathetic images of young Italian women working for the British Army Service Corps, unloading railway wagons, cooking for the 'enemy' or washing British Army uniforms. Carroll's work gives a true representation of what life would have been during and shortly after the conflict, without presenting sterile, emotionless images. The dense atmosphere is masterfully conveyed and the expressions of grief and desperation are sensitively portrayed by the artist.

Aside from the fact that the exhibition does not give a sunny vision to the viewer, making the title blatantly misleading, *War in the Sunny Alps* offers very different perspectives on this final apocalyptical stage of the First World War, fought in what was one of the most formidable landscapes of the entire conflict.

Questions 1–6

Do the following statements agree with the writer's opinion in Reading Passage 1?

In boxes 1–6 on your answer sheet, write

YES	*if the statement agrees with the writer's opinion*
NO	*if the statement contradicts the writer's opinion*
NOT GIVEN	*if there is no information about the writer's opinion*

1   The art gallery looks smarter after its five-month renovation.

2   Local artists have forgotten about the late events of World War One.

3   Some of the pieces could be interpreted as ironic.

4   There are some remarkable paintings of several aerial battles.

5   None of the photographs were taken after the sunset.

6   Peter Paul Carroll disliked the local women.

Questions 7–12

*Choose the appropriate letters **A**, **B**, **C** or **D** and write them in the boxes 7–12 on your answer sheet.*

7   According to the writer, Philip Carson

   A   enjoyed fighting in the war.

   B   had a detached personality.

   C   did not express any feelings towards WWI in his work.

   D   enjoyed fundraising events.

8   The writer believes that Edward Banks

    A   took photographs that look as if they were staged.

    B   was a sensitive artist.

    C   was extremely unimaginative in his artistic choices.

    D   was skilled at presenting a realistic image of the events.

9   The writer admires the work of

    A   Philip Carson.

    B   Edward Banks.

    C   Woody Allen.

    D   Peter Paul Carroll.

10   The writer believes that Paul Peter Carroll's work

    A   is largely emotionless in tone.

    B   Presents a realistic image of the events.

    C   has a limited number of merits.

    D   is unsympathetic to the grief and desperation felt by others.

11   The writer concludes that

    A   the exhibition portrays World War One from different angles.

    B   World War One was misleading.

    C   different perspectives are important in art.

    D   the sunshine undoubtedly made the conflict less apocalyptical.

12   The writer describes the scenery of the Alps as

    A   plastic.

    B   apocalyptical.

    C   sunny.

    D   formidable.

Reading Passage 2   Questions 13–26

*You should spend about 20 minutes on **Questions 13–26**, which are based on Reading Passage 2 below.*

A   Though the new 12-sided pound coin is still a charming novelty to most British people on the high street, for policymakers at the Royal Mint and the Bank of England, it may be the solution to a serious problem: counterfeit coin manufacturing.

B   Counterfeit money has been in circulation for almost as long as legitimate currency. During the founding of the American Colonies, shells were often traded as a form of currency. Blue-black shells had a higher worth than the more common white coloured shells. As such, some traders would attempt to paint white shells with blue and black paint in order to illicitly create more valuable currency. During the American Revolutionary War, counterfeit American money was produced tactically by British subjects, with the intention of lowering the value of legitimate American currency by flooding the market with forgeries, and causing an economic disaster.

C   Today, counterfeiters are very rarely motivated by such political aims. Most forgeries are created simply in order to provide the counterfeiters with more disposable income. But whatever the reason for creating counterfeit money is, the significant problems it imposes on the economy remain the same.

D   A study in May 2015 found that 2.55% of pound coins in circulation at that time were fakes, down from an estimate of 3.03% in May 2014. Over the preceding decade, the percentage of fake coins had almost doubled, as counterfeiters began to make use of more advanced technology to produce these illegal items. In total, there are around 30 million fake pound coins in circulation, making it a much more commonly forged item than the £2 coin, which is harder to replicate due to its bimetallic composition. Other commonly forged currencies include the Euro: in the second half of 2016, over 350,000 fake Euro banknotes were removed from circulation by monitors.

E   In 2016, an East London gang were found to have created £16,000 worth of counterfeit money in only a month. The gang created their own counterfeit coin press and used ingots of metal to create one and two pound coins. Though Royal Mint experts claimed the forgeries were very crude copies, which were magnetic and different in size to authentic coins, the counterfeit coins would have been convincing enough to fool unsuspecting cashiers.

F   It is often possible to tell whether a pound coin is fake or not by looking at the edges of the coin to see whether they are rough. If they are rough, this proves that the coin is a fake, as an authentic pound coin should have smooth edges. Another way to check that currency is not counterfeit is to check to see if the designs on each side of the coin are slightly out of alignment with each other. Counterfeit coins are often unable to match the precision and symmetry of an authentic coin.

G   Although the only certain way to detect a forgery is to examine the coin with a specially designed scanner, many less competent counterfeiters leave deficiencies in one or more of the already described areas. There are plenty of urban legends about other ways to tell a fake: for instance, it is commonly believed that a false pound coin will lose its colour if its surface is scraped with a copper 1p or 2p coin. In fact, this will only be the case with the shoddiest, least proficiently produced forgeries.

H   Most commonly, however, people who are given a fake coin simply remain unaware of its status. Sometimes, people discover the truth when they try to use their coin in an automatic vending machine or parking meter, as these devices can be fitted with machines that authenticate coins based on their chemical composition. The Royal Mint encourages anyone who spots a fake coin to take it to their local police station, but since no replacement money can be given for these technically worthless items, it is perhaps unsurprising that few people who detect false coins ever hand them in. It's also been suggested that, if people begin to recognise and hand in fakes in larger numbers, police officers might in fact be displeased, as they would then have to spend much of their time and energy on registering fake coins. Technically, anyone who elects to use a coin that they know to be false is breaking the law, while in practice the authorities will usually only pursue those who are using or manufacturing fake money in bulk, anyone who knowingly uses even one of these coins is officially guilty of a crime.

Questions 13–20

*Reading Passage 2 has eight paragraphs, **A–H**.*

Choose the correct heading for each paragraph from the list of headings below.

*Write the correct number, **i–xi**, in boxes 13–20 on your answer sheet.*

Headings	
i	Identifying forgeries
ii	How to mint money
iii	A modern day example
iv	Modern motivations of counterfeiters
v	Counterfeiting through the ages
vi	Why are so many counterfeits never reported?
vii	How most counterfeits are produced
viii	Misconceptions for spotting forgeries
ix	The punishments given for counterfeiting money
x	An original solution
xi	How much of our money is counterfeit?

13   Paragraph **A**

14   Paragraph **B**

15   Paragraph **C**

16   Paragraph **D**

17   Paragraph **E**

18   Paragraph **F**

19   Paragraph **G**

20   Paragraph **H**

Questions 21–26

Complete the summary below.

Choose ***NO MORE THAN TWO WORDS*** *from the passage for each answer.*

Write your answers in boxes 21–26 on your answer sheet.

Counterfeit money has existed almost as long as **21** .... During the American Revolution, counterfeit money was produced in an attempt to trigger an **22** .... Today, counterfeit money is simply produced in order to allow the counterfeiter to buy more things, though counterfeit money still causes significant damage to the UK economy. **23** .... of pound coins were found to be fake in the UK in 2015. In 2016, a gang in London produced counterfeit money by pressing **24** .... of metal into a homemade coin press. Fake coins will often have rough sides and edges, and the image on each side of the coin will often not line up, whereas they will always be perfectly aligned in legitimate coins. It is an **25** .... that a fake coin can be detected by scraping another coin along the surface of it, as this will only work with the **26** .... counterfeit money in current circulation.

Reading Passage 3   Questions 27–40

*You should spend about 20 minutes on **Questions 27–40**, which are based on Reading Passage 3 below.*

Elizabeth Blackburn's Research on Telomeres and Longevity

A   American scientist Elizabeth Blackburn is known for her ground-breaking research into the field of longevity. In the 1980s, Blackburn and her team began research on telomeres, the caps on our genes that determine our longevity, that become shorter each time our cells divide. While working with graduate student Carol Greider at the University of California, Blackburn discovered an enzyme called telomerase. This enzyme slows down the shortening of telomeres, providing a means of slowing the ageing process.

B   20 years after Blackburn's discovery, Elissa Epel, a postdoctoral student from UCSF asked Blackburn for help with a study she was carrying out, looking into the behaviour and health of mothers of chronically ill children. Epel believed that the wear and tear within cells, which is a key process in ageing, could be affected by the levels of stress experienced. Epel's test asked these women to assess their own stress levels, after which Epel's team would measure the mothers' telomere lengths and telomerase levels.

C   This collaboration marked the first time in Blackburn's career that her experiments focused on the real lives of individuals. Blackburn herself did not think it would be possible to find any meaningful connections between levels of stress and telomerase. Prior to Epel's experiment, genes were seen as the one and only factor of telomere length. The idea that psychological and environmental factors could impact telomere length was extremely controversial.

D   During the experiment, 58 blood samples were collected, with 29 samples from stressed mothers and the other half from a control group. To Blackburn's surprise, the results were extremely suggestive. For all participants, the more stressed the mothers were, the lower their levels of telomerase and consequently, the shorter their telomeres. Results indicated differences of up to a decade of ageing between the most stressed mothers and the least stressed ones. For the first time, there was scientific evidence to support the popular belief that stress accelerates the ageing process.

E   As soon as the paper was published, an explosion of further research was triggered. Many scientists regarded the findings with disbelief, so more evidence to confirm or deny these findings was sought. However, since Epel's initial study into the links between stress and telomere length, many other findings have been published that appear to demonstrate a link between environmental factors and telomere length. Studies have demonstrated that a stress hormone called cortisol can significantly reduce telomerase levels. Studies also show that other health conditions such as diabetes and obesity appear to shorten telomeres.

F The big question now, is whether telomeres work simply as a unit of measurement for the ageing process, or whether they play an active role in age-related health problems. It is known that genetic disorders that affect telomerase generate symptoms of early and accelerated ageing as well as premature organ failure, but linking reductions in telomere length caused by stress to health problems and accelerated ageing is a more complex matter.

G Many believe such a connection to be unlikely due to the naturally broad variation in telomere lengths, but Blackburn is convinced that levels of stress do matter. Currently, in collaboration with the care consortium Kaiser Permanente, Blackburn is measuring the telomeres of over 100,000 people. Blackburn believes that by combining telomere length with data from medical records, she will find additional links between genetic mutations, diseases, telomere length and levels of telomerase in the body. Blackburn has already found that people with longer telomeres live longer, as people with shorten telomeres do not usually surpass the 75-year-old mark. Data shows that the average telomere length is longer at age 75–85 than it is at 65–75 confirms this.

H Blackburn now believes that both a healthy lifestyle and emotional support help, but meditation is the most effective way of keeping levels of telomerase high. This is backed up by one of her studies in which Blackburn sent participants to a meditation retreat. The results were astonishing. People who took a three-month meditation course had 30 per cent more telomerase than a similar group who had not yet started the course. This very same group would then increase their levels by an average of 30 per cent by the completion of the course. It could be said that meditation boosts levels of telomerase, but many are still sceptical of the idea that it might be related to stress.

I Blackburn believes that such scepticism is a product of unfamiliarity with meditation. It is common knowledge that the practice of meditation involves exercises aimed at slow, regular breathing for relaxation. What most people don't know is that meditation, according to Sara Lazar—a Harvard neuroscientist, is even capable of changing brain structure. Studies have also reported a broad range of benefits such as depression relief and lowering of blood pressure. Another study of 239 healthy women found that those who were able to keep high concentration levels for longer periods had significantly longer telomeres than those whose minds wandered often. Blackburn's take on this study is that meditation is indeed a fair topic to study, and that Buddhist and Taoist traditions suggest that more attention should be paid to ancient wisdom and cultures.

J Now, Blackburn and Epel believe it is time to put these studies into practice by inviting governments to pay more attention to telomeres and the social adversities that erode these protective caps. They believe that children are the age group most exposed to damaging behaviours from bullies, abusive parents, rough neighbourhoods, low socio-economic status, and environmental pollution.

Blackburn and Epel are determined to find useful methods for prevention rather than ultimately failing to cure. If action is taken now, the next generations might be protected from stress, which is now, more than ever, a fatal modern disease.

Questions 27–32

*Reading Passage 3 has ten paragraphs, **A–J**.*

Which paragraph contains the following information?

*Write the correct letter, **A–J**, in boxes 27–32 on your answer sheet.*

27 something Dr Blackburn had not previously experienced

28 a method to increase the levels of an enzyme

29 an invitation that would change the focus of Dr Blackburn's career

30 a project Blackburn is currently engaged in

31 an age group at a particular risk

32 an occurrence that started a series of studies

Questions 33–40

Do the following statements agree with the information given in Reading Passage 3?

In boxes 33–40 on your answer sheet, write

TRUE	*if the statement agrees with the information*
FALSE	*if the statement contradicts the information*
NOT GIVEN	*if there is no information on this*

33 Telomerase can slow down the ageing process.

34 In the 2000s, Epel was studying the effects of stress on chronically ill children.

35 Some researchers did not accept the idea of stress-related telomere erosion.

36 Stress can be used as a unit of measurement for the ageing process.

37 Meditation can cause the brain to become larger.

38 Meditation lowers high blood pressure and relieves depression.

39 Blackburn believes religious people live longer.

40 Meditation is an efficient method of stress prevention in children.

ACADEMIC WRITING MODULE

Task 1

You should spend about 20 minutes on this task.

The tables below give information about fossil fuel and electricity use in two different countries.

Summarise the information by selecting and reporting main features, and make comparisons where relevant.

Write at least 150 words.

Fossil Fuel Use (% of total energy)

Country	2013	2015
Sweden	34	31
United Kingdom	88	85

Electricity Consumption per Person (kWh per year)

Country	2013	2015
Sweden	14,934	14,290
United Kingdom	5,701	5,452

Task 2

You should spend about 40 minutes on this task.

Write about the following topic:

Some people find that following a strict routine allows them to feel more in control. Others, however, think that a varied schedule makes life more interesting and less predictable.

Discuss both these views and give your own opinion.

Give reasons for your answers and include any relevant examples from your own knowledge and/or experience.

Write at least 250 words.

SPEAKING MODULE

Time: 11–14 minutes

Part 1

Introduction to interview (4–5 minutes): The examiner will begin by introducing themselves and checking your identity. He or she will then ask you some questions about yourself based on everyday topics.

Let's talk about your family.

- How big is your family?
- How much time do you spend with your immediate family?
- How do you keep in touch with members of your extended family?
- Who do you admire most in your family? [Why?]

Part 2

Individual long turn (3–4 minutes): Candidates task card instructions:

Task Card

Please read the topic below carefully. You will be asked to talk about it for one to two minutes. You will have one minute to think about what you are going to say. You can make some notes to help you if you wish.

Describe a game or sport you enjoy playing. You should say:

- What kind of game or sport it is
- Who you normally play with
- When you first played the game or sport
- When and where you play it now

Also, explain the main reasons why you enjoy doing it.

The examiner may then ask you a couple of brief questions to wrap up this part of the test.

Further questions:

- Do you prefer to play sports yourself or watch other people playing sports? [Why?]
- What is the most popular sport in your country?
- Do you enjoy watching sports on television? [Why?/Why not?]

Part 3

Two way discussion (4–5 minutes): In Part 3, the examiner will ask you further questions related to the topic in Part 2.

Let's talk about sports.

- How has your interest in sports changed since you were a child?
- Are there any popular sports in your country which are not so popular in other countries?
- Do you play or have you ever played any unusual sports?
- Why should young people be encouraged to participate in sports in school?

Finally, let's discuss games.

- What games did you use to play when you were a child?
- How have games changed from the time you were a child? How are they different today?
- How do you think games will change in the future?
- Why do you think people enjoy playing games so much?

General Training Reading and Writing Test

GENERAL TRAINING READING MODULE

Section 1 Questions 1–14

Read the text below and answer Questions 1–7.

AVG Transport

Penalty Fares

Fares for use of AVG buses are £1.50 for any journey. Bus drivers are no longer able to accept payment for travel. You must have a valid transport pass, AVG card or a contactless credit or debit card to pay for your journey.

If you fail to touch your AVG card or contactless credit or debit card to the sensors when you get on the bus, or you do not have a valid transport pass, you may be charged a penalty fare.

Penalty fares are £80. If fees are paid within 21 days, the penalty is reduced to £40.

How to Pay

You may pay the penalty fare online at avgtransport.co.uk.

You may pay by phone by calling the AVG Buses penalty fare notices payment line: 0808 157 0452.

You may mail your payment in the form of a postal order to:

IRCAS
PO Box 212
Petersfield
GU32 9BQ

No personal cheques are accepted.

Appeals

If for any reason you would like to appeal your penalty fare, you must do this within 31 days from the date on the penalty fare notice. You must provide:

- The station where your journey began on that day
- Your phone number and email address
- The reason why you were unable to show the conductor a valid ticket for your journey

If the evidence you provide is accepted, you will not have to pay a penalty fare.

If the evidence you provide is not accepted, you will be advised what to do next.

You will receive an email to notify you of the outcome of your appeal.

Questions 1–7

Read the sentences below.

*Choose **NO MORE THAN THREE WORDS OR A NUMBER** from the text for each answer.*

Write your answers in boxes 1–7 on your answer sheet.

1   Bus drivers cannot .... for any journey.

2   You may be charged a penalty fare if you do not correctly use your AVG card or contactless card when you get on the bus or if you do not have a ....

3   Fines paid within 21 days cost ....

4   If you mail your payment, you must pay via ....

5   In order to challenge your penalty fare, you must provide .... you departed from.

6   The penalty fare is dismissed if the evidence provided is ....

7   An .... will notify you whether your appeal has been successful.

*Read the text below and answer **Questions 8–14**.*

Pregnancy and Parenting Classes
Hampstead Heath Lamaze Centre

Introduction to Lamaze

Have you been hearing your nurse use the term 'Lamaze' but unsure what that means? Come to this introductory one-day course to learn more about this breathing system that women have been using for decades.

Next course: May 4th, 11:00 am

Cost: £50

Lamaze Group Class

Drawing on the strength of the people in your community, this class will help expecting mums and their partners to prepare for a calm, peaceful childbirth. This class also offers opportunities to build the support group you will need after the birth of your baby. Classes are twice a week for six weeks.

Next course: Begins May 6th, 7:30 pm

Cost: £250

Baby and Child CPR

This course gives you the basics of this life-saving procedure you'll need in an emergency. At the end of the course, all attendees receive a certificate. Course delivered by certified paramedic.

Next course: May 18th, 12:00 pm

Cost: £100

Parenting Group Class

What should the temperature be in the house? When should my baby start eating solid food? These questions and many more will be answered in this course focused on skills you'll need as a new parent. Classes are twice a week for four weeks.

Next course: Begins May 21st, 6:00 pm

Cost: £200

Private Classes

Many new parents would prefer to have support in their own home. Our trained nurses visit your home, help you prepare the nursery for your baby or to prepare for childbirth at home. Courses can be booked at the Hampstead Heath Lamaze Centre.

Cost: varies

Questions 8–14

Do the following statements agree with the information given in the text?

In boxes 8–14 on your answer sheet, write

> **TRUE**   *if the statement agrees with the information*
>
> **FALSE**   *if the statement contradicts the information*
>
> **NOT GIVEN**   *if there is no information on this*

8   The Introduction to Lamaze class is not appropriate for women who have used Lamaze before.

9   Partners are unable to attend the Lamaze Group Class.

10   The Lamaze Group Class occurs only after the baby is born.

11   The Baby and Child CPR class is taught by a qualified teacher.

12   The Parenting Group Class occurs before the baby is born.

13   The Parent Group Class meets eight times.

14   The private nurse instructor makes home visits.

Section 2   Questions 15–28

Questions 15–21

*Read the text on the following page and answer **Questions 15–21**.*

*The text on the next page has seven sections, **A–G**.*

Choose the correct heading for each section from the list of headings below.

*Write the correct number, **i–ix**, in boxes 15–21 on your answer sheet.*

List of Headings	
i	Feet Placement
ii	Arm Exercises
iii	Put Your Screen at the Right Height
iv	Take a Break
v	Support Your Back
vi	Eye Strain
vii	Keyboard Placement
viii	Chair Placement
ix	How to Use Your Mouse

15   Section **A**

16   Section **B**

17   Section **C**

18   Section **D**

19   Section **E**

20   Section **F**

21   Section **G**

Desk Posture for Computer Use

Follow the tips below to ensure that you protect your spine and your overall health!

A   To avoid strain on your back, you should change your chair to make sure it is supporting your lumbar spine, or the part of your back above your bottom. Your chair should be touching this part of your back. This might mean tilting your chair back slightly. Your knees should be at a 90-degree angle from your waist. Sit on a pillow or cushion if you find the bottom of your spine hurts at the end of the day.

B   Your feet should be comfortably flat on the floor. You may need to lower your chair if you are not able to put your whole foot on the floor. Your employer should provide a footrest if necessary. Don't cross your legs, as this can restrict the flow of blood to your foot and strain your back and stomach.

C   You should be at a height that allows you to rest your wrists and arms at a 90-degree angle to the floor. Adjust the height of your chair to accommodate your requirements. Your arms should form an L-shape on your chair. Your chair should have a firm but flexible back. Your employer should have adjustable chairs for all staff.

D   Keep your arms bent in an L-shape and ensure that you are able to rest your arms on your desk. Your back should be straight or slightly tilted back, with shoulders squared. Your keyboard should be approximately 4–5 inches away from you and at the height of your ribs. You may ask your employer for a wrist rest for use when you are typing.

E   Continuous use of computers has been shown to cause damage. Shift the position of your computer monitor to ensure there is no glare from sunshine or overhead lights. You can adjust the settings on your monitor to make it more or less bright. If you wear glasses, make sure your monitor is at the correct height, so you do not need to adjust your head or neck to see clearly.

F   You should not need to crane your neck in order to see your monitor clearly. It should be directly in front of you, not to one side or the other, and be at eye-level. You may need a stand to raise your monitor, especially if you are working on a laptop.

G   It is incredibly important to shift your position frequently to avoid strain to your back and eyes. It is better to take more frequent, shorter breaks, than only one or two long breaks as you will be less able to sit in the same position for long periods.

Questions 22–28

*Read the text below and answer **Questions 22–28**.*

Customer Service at InkTech

Managing Customer Complaints

At InkTech, we view customer complaints as an opportunity to support good relationships with our clients and to learn from our mistakes. Never ignore a customer complaint. All complaints should be resolved to the best of our abilities within 72 hours of the complaint being received. Here are some tips about how InkTech expects you to handle a complaint from a customer.

Stay Calm and Listen Carefully

While it may seem obvious, a customer complaint, even when directed at you, is not an attack on you personally. Remain calm and do not try to "win" an "argument" with a customer. It is important to never interrupt to customer; instead, you should listen to the situation the customer describes. Be sure to ask follow-up questions as necessary and take notes! When the customer is finished speaking, make sure you have understood. Say, "What I hear is…" and repeat the customer's concerns. Allow the customer to make any clarifications. Finish by acknowledging the customer's feelings, either of disappointment or frustration. You don't need to take responsibility for the situation that caused the complaint, but you should acknowledge the feelings the situation has caused. By listening carefully and recognizing the customer's feelings, this will help calm an angry customer and make it possible to find a solution.

Offer a Solution

It is important that you don't try to give a solution to a customer's complaint until you have understood it well and the customer has given you the necessary details. This is another reason, aside from how frustrated it makes everyone feel, why you must not interrupt a customer as they make a complaint. When you offer a solution, you agree to provide a service that meets our client's needs. You will be expected to ensure any offer you make to a customer is completed as you have agreed. You must be aware of what you are able to offer the customer as a replacement or for delivery. If you are unsure, follow the procedure outlined in the attached document.

How to Escalate a Complaint

While you are expected to be aware of standard operating procedures, in case of difficulty, do not hesitate to contact the manager on duty when you receive the customer complaint. Ask if you can place the customer on hold, complete your customer notes, then call the manager. Customer notes include the customer's name, location, date of delivery and details of the customer's complaint. These details should be completed in the online system before calling the manager. Then, transfer the customer's phone call to the manager's number. When the manager is done speaking with the client, follow-up with the customer and apologise for the inconvenience before ending the call.

Questions 22–26

*Choose the option that best completes the sentence. Write the correct answer, **A, B, C** or **D**, in boxes 22–26 on your answer sheet.*

22   Customer complaints should be closed

    A   with the fastest solution possible.

    B   within 72 hours.

    C   by the manager.

    D   by the customer service agent.

23   Listening fully to a customer means

    A   the customer service agent can take detailed notes.

    B   the customer service agent takes responsibility for the problem.

    C   the customer will calm down and it will increase the likelihood of finding a solution.

    D   dismissing the customer's feelings.

24   Don't give a solution until

    A   you have understood the situation well.

    B   you have asked the manager on duty.

    C   you know what the customer wants.

    D   you finish the call.

25   When you have offered a solution,

    A   you take responsibility for the problem.

    B   you must make sure the solution is carried out as agreed.

    C   you make a promise to the customer.

    D   you must contact the manager.

26   You should contact the manager if

    A   you are unsure what solution you can offer the customer.

    B   you do not know the standard operating procedures.

    C   the customer is unsure what solution is best.

    D   whenever you are ready to end a call.

Questions 27–28

Complete the flow-chart below.

*Choose **NO MORE THAN THREE WORDS** from the text for each answer.*

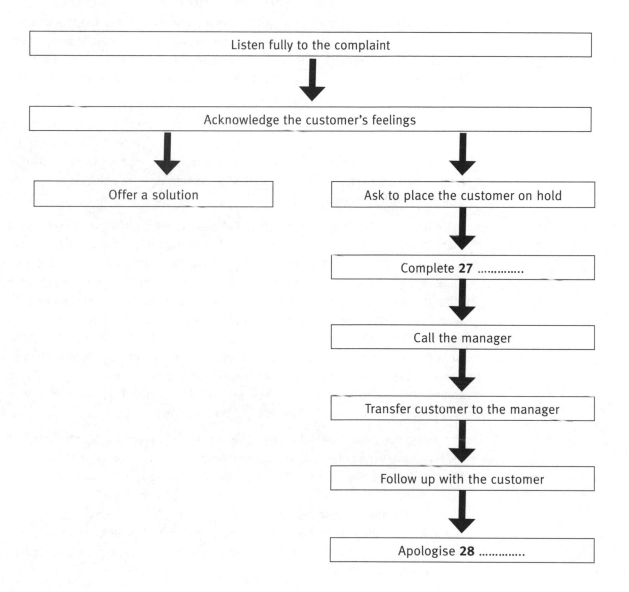

Listen fully to the complaint

Acknowledge the customer's feelings

Offer a solution

Ask to place the customer on hold

Complete **27** ....

Call the manager

Transfer customer to the manager

Follow up with the customer

Apologise **28** ....

Section 3   Questions 29–40

*Read the text below and answer **Questions 29–40**.*

The History of Denim

A   When people mention denim today, they are almost always referring to jeans. It's almost impossible to separate the two, thanks to decades of fashion icons, and the evolution of million-dollar jean brands. However, it may surprise you to know that the material itself was created by accident and was originally a tough textile used for horse blankets and wagon covers.

B   A similar material called dungaree, which predates denim, had been produced in India for hundreds of years. The name dungaree is believed to come from the Indian town Dongri, near Mumbai. In the UK, the term dungaree came to mean a type of bib overalls typically associated with working clothes, however in the U.S. this term refers to thick trousers.

C   In mid-18th century France, in the city of Nîmes, weavers attempted to recreate a material called 'serge', a tough cotton corduroy made in Genoa, Italy. They were unsuccessful, but instead, through experimentation, created a strong cotton material where one thread, called the warp thread, is passed under two or more other threads, called the weft threads. With the warp threads dyed indigo, and the weft threads left white, it gave the material a blue colour on one side, and white on the other. You can see this if you turn your blue jeans inside out. The material these weavers created was called 'Serge de Nîmes', which means 'serge from Nîmes'. This was eventually shortened to 'de Nîmes', then 'denim'. The word 'jeans' also comes from the history of denim. The French word for Genoa, Italy, where the serge fabric the French weavers imitated came from, is Gênes.

D   The indigo dye used in denim is one of the oldest dyes used to colour textiles. The oldest known example was found in South America and was from 6,000 years ago. Most of the leaves used to make indigo dye are from tropical regions and many different plants have been used historically to make the dye. India began to grow plants especially to create indigo dye and the country became a major exporter of the dye. The indigo colour which was used as the dye when denim was invented was incredibly cheap thanks to the busy trade routes that brought the plant leaves the dye is made from into Europe.

E   In the early 1800s, about half a century after denim was invented, a Frenchman called Guimet invented an artificial indigo dye, and in the 1870s a synthetic indigo was produced. Indigo remained a cheap and available dye for cotton products and was commonly used because the dark-blue colour lasted a long time and was colour-fast, meaning it could withstand washing many times without fading.

F   Denim blue jeans are a staple of American clothing thanks to a European immigrant who brought the fabric to workers in the American West. In the 1850s, a German by the name of Loeb Strauss emigrated to North America, where he changed his name to Levi and started a wholesale goods business. In the 1860s in California, gold was found, leading to the Gold Rush which brought people from all over the United States and the world to find their fortune. Levi Strauss followed the Gold Rush to San Francisco, opening a West Coast branch of his business, where he sold clothing, bedding, and bolts of fabric.

G At the same time in Reno, Nevada, another immigrant from Latvia received an order to sew a pair of tough work pants. The tailor, named Jacob W. Davis, filled the order from a woman who asked specifically that the pants for her husband, a woodcutter, be 'as strong as possible'. Davis was known for using tough material to create tents, blankets for horses, and covers for wagons on the railroad. The fabric Davis used came from Levi Strauss's wholesale business.

H The pants Davis made for the woodcutter used copper rivets to enforce the weak points of the seams and pockets. The sturdy design proved popular with working men, such as miners, ranchers and cowboys, and over the next couple of years, over 200 orders came in for the same "blue jeans" as they became known. By 1871, Davis could not make the pants fast enough for every worker who wanted them. Davis realised there was an opportunity due to the demand for his work to apply for a patent to protect his invention. He asked Levi Strauss, who supplied his fabric, to provide the financial backing for the patent, which they were granted in 1873.

I Modern versions of denim include not just the original indigo colour, but all the colours of the rainbow. The indigo colour is still achieved by a dyeing process called indigo dyeing, while other colours are achieved through sulphur dyeing. In some cases, spandex is added to the material to give jeans more stretch, though this shortens how long the denim lasts. 'Green' environmentally friendly manufacturing processes are becoming more popular as this process uses nearly 92% less water and 30% less waste to produce a pair of jeans.

Questions 29–35

*The text has nine paragraphs, **A–I**.*

Which paragraph contains the following information?

*Write the correct letter, **A–I**, in boxes 29–35 on your answer sheet.*

29 early customers of blue jeans

30 modern jean production

31 the creation of synthetic dye

32 where the word 'jeans' comes from

33 the origin of indigo dye

34 the first pair of jeans

35 what brought Levi Strauss to California

Questions 36–40

Do the following statements agree with the information given in the text?

In boxes 36–40 on your answer sheet, write

TRUE	*if the statement agrees with the information*
FALSE	*if the statement contradicts the information*
NOT GIVEN	*if there is no information on this*

36 The term 'dungaree' originated for an Indian material.

37 French weavers duplicated serge from Genoa in the mid-18th century.

38 Indigo was a cheap dye to use due to trade routes.

39 Levi Strauss accepted credit for inventing blue jeans.

40 Green denim production produces no waste.

GENERAL TRAINING WRITING MODULE

Writing Task 1

You should spend about 20 minutes on this task.

Your neighbours have been smoking in their apartment.

Write a letter to the management company. In your letter

- *give details about the problem*
- *explain how you would like the problem to be solved*
- *describe other issues you've been having with the neighbours*

Write at least 150 words.

You do **NOT** need to write any addresses.

Begin your letter as follows:

Dear ...

Writing Task 2

You should spend about 40 minutes on this task.

Write about the following topic:

Some people believe that celebrities should be role models for young people. Other people believe that parents and teachers should be role models for children. Discuss the advantages of both and give your own opinion.

Give reasons for your answer and include any relevant examples from your own knowledge or experience.

Write at least 250 words.

IELTS Practice Test 3

LISTENING MODULE

🎧 **Practice Test 3, Track 9**

Section 1   Questions 1–10

Questions 1–10

Complete the form below.

*Write **NO MORE THAN THREE WORDS AND/OR A NUMBER** for each answer.*

WESTMINSTER EDUCATION SUPPLY POOL AND TEMPING AGENCY
Application Form

Applicant's Name: Betty **1** ....

Email Address: betty1994@memail.co.uk

Candidate is a: ~~Graduate~~ Student ✔

University: **2** .... Subject: Modern Art

Is the candidate interested in studying towards a **3** .... in Education? YES ✔ ~~NO~~

Is the candidate interested in: Primary ✔ ~~Secondary Sixth Form~~?

Candidate's Address: **4** .... Street, London

Postcode: **5** ....

Is the candidate interested in **6** .... ? ~~YES~~ NO ✔

Does the candidate have experience in SEN? ~~YES~~ NO ✔

(If no, suggest fortnightly **7** ....)

Interview Date: **8** ....

Documents to bring:

Passport

A proof **9** ....

University Degree (or Acceptance Letter if still studying)

A completed DBS application

*NB: We will need **10** .... and .... of all documents.*

🎧 **Practice Test 3, Track 10**

Section 2   Questions 11–20

Questions 11–16

Complete the sentences below.

*Write **NO MORE THAN TWO WORDS OR A NUMBER** for each answer.*

11   The Palau Güell is one of the .... works by Gaudí built in Barcelona.

12   Circa .... , Gaudí moved from Reus to Barcelona.

13   The Palau Güell is an excellent representative of Gaudí's ....

14   The Palau Güell needed to be majestic but also .... , because the land available for it was limited.

15   .... and .... stayed in the basement.

16   .... obscured the viewing windows on the guest rooms' walls.

Questions 17–20

Complete the table below.

*Write **NO MORE THAN THREE WORDS** for each answer.*

The Palau Güell - Timeline		
1885 – Güell tasks Gaudí with building a new home for him and his family	**1888** – Inauguration ceremony is scheduled at the same time as the **17** .... Exposition	**1889** – Building is completed
1895 – Chimneys are added on the palace's roof	**1910** – Every member of the Güell family except the **18** .... move out of the palace	**1945** – The palace is sold to the provincial government of Barcelona
1986 – The palace is given **19** .... status by Unesco – renovation plans are made	**1990–1993** – **20** .... assist in rebuilding missing parts of the palace's chimneys	**2004–2011** – The palace remains closed to the public during extended restoration works

🎧 **Practice Test 3, Track 11**

Section 3   Questions 21–30

Questions 21–25

*Write the correct letter, **A, B** or **C** next to questions 21–25.*

You may choose any letter more than once.

> What does Anna tell her friend about each of the following course options?
>
> **A**   She will sign up for it.
>
> **B**   She may or may not sign up for it.
>
> **C**   She won't sign up for it.

21   Studying Television Form and Methods

22   Adaptation Studies

23   An Introduction to Documentary Techniques

24   Writing Comedy

25   Script Analysis

Questions 26–30

*Choose **FIVE** letters A–H.*

Write your answers in boxes 26–30 on your answer sheet.

Which **FIVE** pieces of advice does Clarke give Anna?

A   Use script analysis textbooks for her 1,000-word report.

B   Research visits to studios.

C   Network whenever you have the opportunity.

D   Enquire often about forthcoming business events.

E   Participate in as many screenwriting competitions as possible.

F   Make a list of respectable websites offering internship opportunities.

G   Don't overanalyse the 1,000-word report question.

H   Wait a bit before looking for an internship.

🎧 **Practice Test 3, Track 12**

Section 4   Questions 31–40

Questions 31–33

*Choose the correct letter, **A, B** or **C**.*

31 This lecture follows another which focused on

    A   people's responses to catastrophe.

    B   media responses to terrorist attacks.

    C   people's ability to assess risk.

32 Scientists have found that we are

    A   irrational in most of our actions.

    B   extremely skilled at assessing potential danger.

    C   often more scared by activities which are less likely to kill us.

33 The speaker believes we are not instinctively scared of riding in cars because

    A   they do not look as terrifying as snakes and spiders.

    B   cars are a relatively recent invention.

    C   cars were created by humans.

Questions 34–38

Complete the sentences below.

*Write **NO MORE THAN TWO WORDS** for each answer.*

34 Many years of evolution have provided humans with .... , such as jumping when we are startled.

35 The media coverage of terrifying events causes people to .... the likelihood of being involved in such an event.

36 People are generally more scared by cancer than .... , even though it causes more deaths than any other illness.

37 Many people find the lack of control they experience when flying to be ....

38 Rewarding yourself after exercise by eating more than you usually would removes some of the .... effects of the activity.

Questions 39–40

Answer the questions below.

*Write only **ONE WORD** for each answer.*

39   How often do people die from watching television?

40   How do we tend to see television compared to sports?

ACADEMIC READING MODULE

Reading Passage 1   Questions 1–13

*You should spend about 20 minutes on **Questions 1–13**, which are based on Passage 1 on the following pages.*

Questions 1–8

*Reading Passage 1 has eight paragraphs, **A–H**.*

Choose the correct heading for each paragraph from the list of headings below.

*Write the correct number, **i–xi**, in boxes 1–8 on your answer sheet.*

Headings	
i	Who is affected?
ii	Sleep paralysis defined
iii	Examples of different experiences
iv	Four out of ten know what it's like
v	The silver lining for sufferers
vi	Famous depictions
vii	A contradictory thought
viii	The experience of sleep paralysis
ix	A terrifying exercise
x	Cultural interpretations
xi	Tips to reduce episodes of sleep paralysis

1   Paragraph **A**

2   Paragraph **B**

3   Paragraph **C**

4   Paragraph **D**

5   Paragraph **E**

6   Paragraph **F**

7   Paragraph **G**

8   Paragraph **H**

Waking Up in a Nightmare

A   Imagine the following. It happens out of nowhere: one second you're fast asleep, then, with a snap, you're suddenly wide awake. The room around you is dark, but you can feel a presence lurking in the shadows; somehow, you know it intends to harm you. As it draws closer you try to scream for help, but the words remain stuck in your throat. You try to raise your arms, to reach for the bed covers and drag yourself off the mattress, but your fingers refuse to move. Your heart beats rapidly; you feel like you're choking. Then a few minutes later, out of the blue, it stops. You're back in control of your body and you can finally move again.

B   Many people who suffer from chronic sleep paralysis begin to experience the phenomenon in early childhood, though the disorder can strike at any stage of life. Sufferers may think they are alone in their suffering, but recent studies reveal that this is far from the case. According to a study published by *Sleep Medicine Reviews*, around 8% of the population has suffered through the experience of sleep paralysis at least once in their lives, with that number climbing to nearly 30% for psychiatric patients and, curiously, students (although that might have more to do with the average age of a student rather than a person's inclination towards academia).

C   A separate study conducted by James Cheyne, a psychologist at the University of Waterloo, suggests that the number of those in the general population who experience sleep paralysis at least once is actually closer to 40% with up to 6% experiencing regular incidents of sleep paralysis.

D   So what is sleep paralysis, exactly? To this day, scientists fail to agree on a satisfactory definition, though throughout history there have been a variety of differing hypotheses. Among other things, sleep paralysis has been attributed to demons, ghosts, aliens, or even malevolent female horses riding on sleepers' chests. The Chinese use a name that roughly translates as 'Ghost Depression' for it, while the Turks call it 'The Dark Presser'. In German, the mare who was said to cause it was known as the *Nachtmahr* which, as you may be able to guess, is where the English word 'nightmare' comes from.

E   Sleep paralysis has been heavily documented in art, too: Herman Melville's novel *Moby Dick* is a notable example, as well as the 1781 Henri Fuseli painting, *The Nightmare*, portraying a woman lying on her back with a demon perched atop her and a sprite lurking in the background. More recently, Rodney Ascher's 2015 docudrama *The Nightmare* uses a range of special effects to convey to viewers the often terrifying sensations experienced by those who suffer from sleep paralysis.

F   Though a resounding definition for sleep paralysis is still yet to be found, we do know that sleep paralysis occurs during REM sleep, when our muscles are locked and cannot move. Presumably, this is to prevent us from acting out our dreams and lashing out. In the vast majority of cases, sleep paralysis is completely harmless, though it certainly might not feel that way for the sufferer. Symptoms may vary quite widely: some people are able to open their eyes while others can't, some people sense a foreign presence near them, some experience yet more vivid hallucinations, such as 'a little vampire girl with blood coming out of her mouth', as Brian Sharpless, a clinical psychologist at Washington State University, describes one of his patient's recurring experiences.

G   Surprisingly, sleep paralysis holds the possibility for a pleasant experience, too. Jorge Conesa Sevilla, a psychologist at Northland College, believes sleep paralysis sufferers can be taught over time to remove themselves from their panic-stricken state while retaining the waking levels of awareness they experience during sleep paralysis, which would allow sufferers to turn a sleep paralysis incident into one of 'lucid dreaming', that is, a dream where the dreamer not only is aware that they are dreaming but can also exert some degree of control over the dream and manipulate it to their liking. Lucid dreams allow one to direct and act out impossible fantasies, experience the impossible, and take control of their dreams.

H   For those who are less interested in mastering lucid dreaming, and simply want to stop experiencing sleep paralysis, there are a few things which can be done to lower the chances of an episode of sleep paralysis. Sleep paralysis is associated with irregular sleeping patters and sleep deprivation. As such, making sure to get at least six hours of sleep every night can help, as can regularly going to sleep at the same time. Avoiding large meals or exercise in the evening is also helpful, and so is making sure your sleeping environment is dark, quiet, comfortable, and has a slightly cool temperature. Sleeping on your side is also less likely to trigger a sleep paralysis episode than lying on your back, so this is also often recommended to sufferers. Some sufferers find that simply reminding themselves that the experience, though it may be extremely scary, is not actually capable of causing them harm, helps to calm them when they find themselves experiencing an episode of sleep paralysis.

Questions 9–13

Do the following statements reflect the claims of the writer in Reading Passage 1?

In boxes 9–13 on your answer sheet, write

YES	*if the statement agrees with the claims of the writer*
NO	*if the statement contradicts the claims of the writer*
NOT GIVEN	*if it is impossible to say what the writer thinks about this*

9   There is a link between someone's education and the likelihood of experiencing sleep paralysis.

10   Germans blamed evil female horses for sleep paralysis in the past.

11   The novelist Herman Melville wrote about his experience with sleep paralysis.

12   Sleep paralysis is a potentially dangerous condition.

13   The way you position yourself when you sleep can trigger a sleep paralysis incident.

Reading Passage 2   Questions 14–27

*You should spend about 20 minutes on **Questions 14–27**, which are based on Passage 2 below.*

The Dead Sea, a highly salt-rich lake situated between Jordan and Israel, is dropping by more than 1 metre (3 feet) per year. It is located at the lowest point on the surface of the planet, some 420 m (1,380 ft) below sea level, and is the end point of the River Jordan. It is the saltiest body of water on the planet, up to ten times as salty as the ocean. The falling of the Dead Sea is not only a threat to the tourism industry and local businesses, but also also risks the lives of locals and visitors by the increased risk of the startling and often unpredictable formation of giant sinkholes.

Over the decades, dams built along the River Jordan by surrounding Middle Eastern countries to produce hydroelectric energy and divert water for irrigation have reduced the volume of water that flows into the lake. Essentially, this means that water is being removed from the lake (through both human interference and evaporation) more quickly than it is being replenished through rainfall. This causes a rapid drop in the water level. Large evaporating basins around the lake, used to separate out valuable phosphates, are also contributing to the problem. One major consequence of this drop in surface level is the increasing number of sinkholes appearing along the banks of the lake, particularly on the western side.

After many years of study, scientists now understand the geology of the phenomenon much better. Sinkholes can take thousands of years to form. They are the result of what is known as the karst process, where soluble bedrock (such as limestone or chalk) is dissolved by acidic rainwater. There are two distinct types of sinkhole; cover-collapse, which seem to appear out of nowhere; and cover-subsidence, which can often be identified before they collapse. If the sinkhole is the cover-collapse kind, most of the signs suggesting its formation will be buried underneath a layer of soil or sediment until the last moment. If it's the cover-subsidence kind, the bedrock will become exposed and holes will appear on it, which will then turn into ponds. Either way, a sinkhole can take anything from a few minutes to hours to collapse once the cavity below the surface is big enough. Some areas, such as Florida in the USA, are more prone to sinkholes due to the solubility of the bedrock they've been built on.

The karst process can occur naturally, but most of the sinkholes that occur today are the result of human interference. This is usually due to poor drainage systems combined with heavy rainfall: plenty of the most recently collapsed sinkholes occur near constructions where rainwater is concentrated on a particular patch of land rather than spread across a wider surface, or drained into the sewers properly. However, a sinkhole can also occur during building construction, for example, when digging underground, in order to create a basement in a house, or a large-scale underground metro line commission—as with the sinkhole that swallowed a whole building complex in Guangzhou, China, in January 2013.

The sinkholes occurring in the Dead Sea are formed by the dropping sea level leaving behind layers of salt underground. The salt layers, which are particularly unstable along local geological fault lines in the Jordan Rift Valley, get dissolved by the fresh groundwater that flows in from local aquifers, rocks which water can pass through, as the lake water retreats. As these layers dissolve, they leave behind unstable chasms under the ground. Often, the only sign on the surface that such a chamber is present is a small hole a metre or so wide. The collapse of these chambers is often prompted by earthquakes or periods of heavy rain, but many occur spontaneously and without warning, causing considerable damage to the local area.

When formed, many sinkholes can be up to 100m across and 80m deep, and several occurring close together may collapse into each other, creating huge canyons. The deepest known sinkhole in the world is the Xiaozhai Tienkeng, located in China, which is 662m deep, while one of the widest sinkholes is the Qattara Depression in Egypt, which expands over a surface of between 80km and 121km. The number of sinkholes is increasing year-on-year as the lake surface continues to drop, with as many as 700 appearing in 2016, compared to a few dozen in the 1990s. There are now over 5000 documented sinkholes in the Dead Sea area, some of which have swallowed up local businesses and roads, disrupting tourism and transport. One proposed solution to the crisis is to create a pipeline to draw in salt water from the Red Sea. This would have the dual benefit of halting the drop in water level, as well as refilling the salt chambers, slowing down the rate at which they are dissolved and hence the rate of formation of sinkholes.

How quickly a sinkhole will collapse depends on a variety of reasons, explains Dr Vanessa Banks of the British Geological Survey: 'Different rock types behave in different ways.' This means that some types of ground, such as sandstone, will take longer to disintegrate as they are more consolidated, while others, such as gravel, are easier to wash away. The acidity of the surrounding water is also a determining factor in how quickly a sinkhole will form.

Fortunately, and despite what media coverage might suggest, sinkholes are rarely lethal. The most famous case of a sinkhole-caused fatality is that of Jeff Bush, a 37-year-old man whose bedroom was swallowed by a 6-metre wide sinkhole as he slept—and even in that case, the five other people who were with him in the house managed to escape. This is because most sinkholes tend to be localised. Unfortunately, this is also the reason there's been so little research on how frequently sinkholes occur. At the moment, all we have is a list of karst areas around the world—areas prone to sinkholes—such as The Dead Sea, Mexico, Belize, Croatia, some parts of Italy and huge sections of China. Many experts are now pushing for more research. Given how sinkholes are becoming widespread both in urban and rural settings, perhaps governments will soon be more inclined to listen to these pleas.

Questions 14–19

*Complete each sentence with the correct ending, **A–F**.*

Write your answers in boxes 14–19 on your answer sheet.

14   A cover-subsidence sinkhole

15   The karst process

16   The Guangzhou

17   Dams created for water irrigation

18   The Dead Sea

19   The Qattara Depression

A	is surrounded by unstable underground caverns.
B	is the deepest sinkhole in existence.
C	will appear on the bedrock, which will become easily visible.
D	have caused a drop in the water level of the Dead Sea.
E	is more likely to happen in some places than others.
F	sinkhole was so large that it consumed an entire building complex.
G	collapsed under an underground metro station.
H	measures the size of various sinkholes.
I	is one of the widest sinkholes on Earth.
J	cause water acidity in recent sinkholes.

Questions 20–24

Complete the summary below.

*Choose only **ONE WORD** from the passage for each answer.*

There are two types of sinkholes: cover-collapse and cover-subsidence. Both are the result of the karst process, but the latter Is easier to notice because of the **20** .... that form on the bedrock before the sinkhole collapses. The bedrock's **21** .... is one factor that determines the likelihood of a sinkhole forming in a given area. While sinkholes are a natural phenomenon, the actions of humans when paired with extreme **22** .... can often trigger them. This is because human interference can redirect **23** .... to one particular spot. Thankfully, the effects of most sinkholes are **24** .... , meaning that sinkholes are not as dangerous as we are often led to believe.

Questions 25–27

Answer the questions below with words taken from the passage.

*Write only **ONE WORD** for each answer.*

25   What does rainwater need to be in order for the karst process to take place?

26   What's one example of a deposit that doesn't collapse very quickly?

27   Who does the author hope will listen to the requests for more research?

Reading Passage 3　Questions 28–40

*You should spend about 20 minutes on **Questions 28–40**, which are based on Passage 3 below.*

The Königsberg Bridge Problem

A　During the Middle Ages, the city of Königsberg was an important trading centre and the capital of the German province of East Prussia. Today, however, Königsberg is less famous for its trading history, than for the role it played in the creation of a new field of mathematics: graph theory.

B　Königsberg once lay where the Russian city of Kaliningrad is now, on both banks of the river Pregel (present-day Pregolya). Between the two sides of the city were two large islands, thus dividing the city into four districts—all of which were connected to each other through seven bridges. At some point in history, the citizens of Königsberg came up with a game: was it possible, they said, for someone to travel around the city in a complete circuit using all seven bridges, but crossing each one only once?

C　While for most the question was just a silly riddle, for one prominent mathematician of the time, Carl Gottlieb Ehler, it soon became an obsession. No one could find a way to solve the riddle, but, at the same time, Ehler theorised that one could not be certain there was no solution without solid mathematical proof.

D　Unable to find a solution to his conundrum alone, Ehler turned to Swiss mathematician Leonhard Euler for help. Euler was at first dismissive of the Königsberg Bridge problem, describing it as 'banal' and having 'little relationship to mathematics'. Nevertheless, he too soon found himself tormented by the question. Relenting, he agreed to help his colleague to find a solution. By 1741, Euler had published a paper, *Solutio problematis ad geometriam situs pertinentis*, that not only gave a definitively negative answer to the famous Königsberg Bridge question, but also provided a formula that could be used to solve any similar question in the future.

E　So how did Euler's solution work exactly? As he explained in his paper, one possible way to confirm once and for all whether it was possible to cross all bridges once and end up back where you started would've been to just write down all the possible paths by giving codenames both to the bridges (a, b, c, d, e, f, g) and the land masses they connected (A, B, C, D). Such a tactic, however, would not only be time-consuming and impractical, it would also be impossible for larger-scale problems than the Königsberg one.

F　To simplify things, then, Euler drew a diagram ('network', or 'graph') which represented the four landmasses ('nodes', or 'verteces') and seven bridges ('edges'). Each node could have an even or odd degree, i.e., an even or odd number of edges connected to it. For a graph to function the way the Königsberg Bridge Problem needed it to function, it would need to have either zero or two nodes with an odd degree; any other variation and it would be impossible for anyone to travel through the graph and traverse each edge only once. In the case of Königsberg, all four nodes had an odd degree, as one land mass had five bridges touching it and the remaining ones had three—so it was impossible to travel all seven bridges once in a single round trip. Ehler finally had his answer—and graph theory, or geometry of position as Gottfried Wilhelm Leibniz had earlier called it, was born.

G   As Teo Paoletti of the College of New Jersey explains, graph theory took off almost immediately once Euler's paper was published, with mathematicians such as Augustin Cauchy, Arthur Caley and George Polya working towards discovering "just about everything that is known about large but ordered graphs". It is thanks to graph theory, for example, that we can now tell with certainty which order of moves a knight on a chess board should follow in order to land on each square once and return to his original square. Even today, graph theory is a source of numerous conundrums like the Königsberg one, many of which have yet to receive answers.

H   Unfortunately, the city of Königsberg was not fated to enjoy its fame for very long. Königsberg was one of the many German cities targeted by the RAF during the Second World War, enduring its first attack on the night of 26th August 1944 and a second on the 30th. Following this, the city was also targeted by Soviet troops who arrived in January 1945 and left in April, slaughtering thousands of people and leaving behind them nothing but ruins. Nowadays, very little remains of the original city in Kaliningrad besides a few restored historical buildings such as the Dom or Sackheim Gate. Still, Königsberg remains preserved in the minds of numerous mathematicians who are well aware that without it, graph theory might never have existed.

Questions 28–33

*Reading Passage 3 has eight paragraphs labelled **A–H**. Which paragraph contains the following information?*

NB: *You may use any letter more than once.*

28   an imperfect approach to the Königsberg Bridge problem

29   a similar problem to the Königsberg Bridge problem

30   the original name for graph theory

31   the paper that answered the Königsberg Bridge problem

32   the mathematical term for Königsberg's districts

33   the names of heritage sites in Königsberg

Questions 34–38

Complete the sentence below with words from the passage.

*Write **NO MORE THAN TWO WORDS** for each answer.*

34 Königsberg functioned as a .... during medieval times.

35 Due to the geography of the area, Königsberg consisted of ....

36 Carl Gottlieb Ehler believed .... was needed to confirm that the Königsberg Bridge problem was unsolvable.

37 Leonhard Euler was originally unwilling to assist Ehler because he considered the Königsberg problem ....

38 To solve the problem, Euler created a simplified map of Königsberg which he called a ....

Questions 39–40

*Choose the correct letter, **A, B, C** or **D**.*

39 Euler proved it was impossible to cross each of Königsberg's bridges only once in a round trip because

    A there was an odd number of bridges.

    B there were too many bridges connected to each district.

    C all the bridges had an odd degree.

    D all the land masses had an odd degree.

40 During World War II,

    A the city of Königsberg was destroyed by the Germans.

    B the city of Königsberg was renamed to Kaliningrad.

    C a large number of Königsberg citizens were killed by Russian soldiers.

    D a few damaged historical buildings were renovated.

ACADEMIC WRITING MODULE

Task 1

You should spend about 20 minutes on this task.

> The two maps below show how the island of Petrichor changed from 1987 to 2017.
>
> Summarise the information by selecting and reporting the main features, and make comparisons where relevant.

Write at least 150 words.

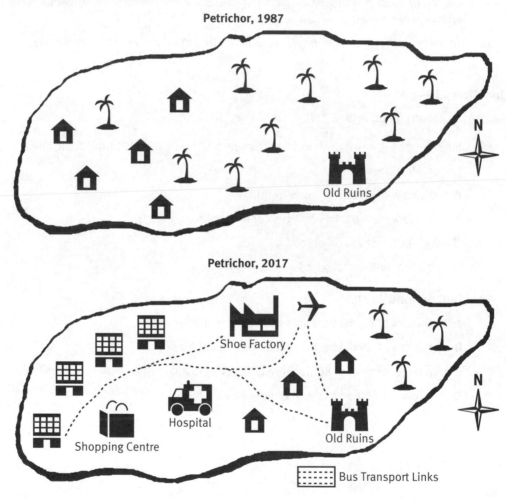

Petrichor, 1987

Old Ruins

Petrichor, 2017

Shoe Factory

Hospital

Shopping Centre

Old Ruins

Bus Transport Links

Task 2

You should spend about 40 minutes on this task.

> We have long imagined the possibility that life exists on other planets. Do you believe that there is life in the universe outside of Earth? What would be the implications of proving that alien life exists?

Give reasons for your answer and include any relevant examples from your own knowledge and experience.

Write at least 250 words.

SPEAKING MODULE

Time: 11–14 minutes

Part 1

Introduction to interview (4–5 minutes): The examiner will begin by introducing himself or herself and checking your identity. She or he will then ask you some questions about yourself based on everyday topics.

Let's talk about names.

- What's your first name? Do you like it? [Why?/Why not?]
- Why did your parents give you that name?
- If you could change your first name, what would you pick? [Why?]
- How do people in your country pick their children's names?
- What are the most popular first names in your country, and why do you think this is?

Part 2

Individual long turn (3–4 minutes): Candidates' task card instructions:

Task Card

Please read the topic below carefully. You will be asked to talk about it for one to two minutes. You will have one minute to think about what you are going to say. You can make some notes to help you if you wish.

Describe a time you met someone you immediately liked. You should say:

- Who that person was
- Where you met and how
- What you liked about them and why

Also, explain whether your opinion of them changed or developed later on, and why.

The examiner may then ask you a couple of brief questions to wrap up this part of the test. Further questions:

- Have you met that person again since that first time?
- How quickly do you normally decide whether you like someone or not?
- Have you ever changed your mind about someone you initially liked?

Part 3

Two-way discussion (4–5 minutes): In Part 3, the examiner will ask you further questions related to the topic in Part 2.

Let's talk about instincts for a moment.

- What are the benefits of listening to your instincts? What are the disadvantages?
- Why do some people trust their instincts more than others?
- What is it that sometimes makes us immediately like or dislike people we meet?
- Are there any situations where you think it's essential to listen to one's instincts?

Finally, let's talk about fortune-telling.

- Is fortune-telling popular in your country? In which forms?
- Why do people go to fortune-tellers?
- Do you think it's possible to predict the future?
- Should fortune-telling be made illegal?
- Are people in your country superstitious? What kind of superstitions do they have?

General Training Reading and Writing Test

GENERAL TRAINING READING MODULE

Section 1   Questions 1–14

*Read the text below and answer **Questions 1–8**.*

TV Licence

You are legally required to have a TV licence if you:

- watch television at the same time as it is being broadcast, on a television, computer or other device.
- watch or download any BBC programing, including BBC iPlayer.

Cost

A TV license costs £154.50 for colour televisions and computer devices (£52 for black and white televisions). These costs are the same for both homes and businesses.

What does a TV licence cover?

A TV licence covers all televisions, computers or other devices used to watch or download content in one property. If you have two televisions in your home, you need only one TV licence.

You do not need a TV licence if you watch non-BBC programing on a catch-up service, i.e., after it has been broadcast for the first time. You do not need a licence to watch DVDs or videos or clips on some websites.

Free or reduced licences

If you are over 75 years old, you may apply for a free TV licence fee. If you have severe hearing or vision impairment you may also been able to apply for a reduced fee. If you live in shared retirement housing, the management organisation for the home should apply for your TV licence for you.

Penalties

The fine for watching or recording live programing, watched at the same time as it is being broadcast, not at a later date, is up to £1,000.

The TV Licencing Agency may perform unannounced home visits to check that you have a valid TV licence.

Declaration of No Need for TV Licence

If you are not watching live programing, BBC or BBC iPlayer, you do not need a TV licence, and you should declare this fact. You can complete the Declaration of No Need for TV Licence online or you may download a copy of the declaration and mail it to the TV Licencing Agency at:

5 Brompton Court
East Finchley
N21 XY12

Questions 1–8

Complete the sentences below.

*Choose **NO MORE THAN THREE WORDS AND/OR A NUMBER** from the text for each answer.*

Write your answer in boxes 1–8 on your answer sheet.

1 You need a TV licence if you watch .... BBC programing or BBC iPlayer.

2 The licencing fees are the same for ....

3 If you have multiple devices or televisions in your home, you need .... TV licence for the entire property.

4 You do not need a TV licence to view clips on some websites or watch ....

5 Individuals with .... problems can apply for a reduced or free TV licence.

6 Fines for watching or recording .... are up to £1,000.

7 Your home may be visited to determine whether you are watching live or BBC programming and you have a .... TV licence.

8 You can .... you do not need a TV licence online or by downloading the form if you do not watch the BBC or BBC iPlayer or live programing.

*Read the text below and answer **Questions 9–14**.*

Park Run

Clothing

Please wear something you feel comfortable running in and that is appropriate for the weather. Remember, there will be young runners with us, so please wear appropriate attire. We will not have warming blankets available, so please wear layered clothing if necessary.

Your Barcode

Unlike other races, you do not need to pin anything to your shirt. You do need to bring your printed barcode, which was emailed to you in your confirmation email when you registered for the race. Some runners who plan to run in more than one Park Run may pay £10 to have their barcode transferred onto a fob that is easy to lace onto your shoe.

Water

We provide water at the finish line of every Park Run, but to reduce the number of plastic bottles we use, we ask runners to bring their own reusable water bottles. There will be stations at the finish line where you can refill your water bottles.

At the Starting Line

If you know that you will complete the 5K race in under 20 minutes, please position yourself closer to the starting line. If you know that it will take you 30 minutes or longer to finish, please place yourself closer to the back. This ensures that there is less crowding as the race begins.

Please remember Park Runs cannot be used to qualify for other events, including the Park City Marathon. Please be respectful of other runners. Any runners behaving aggressively will be disqualified and their finishing time will not be calculated.

At the Finish Line

When you pass the finish line, your time will be recorded, based on the official start of the race. Please do not ask the race volunteers at the finish line for your time as you pass the finish line. Final times will not be given until after the race is completed by all participants.

When you finish the race, follow the marked areas to the finishing area, where you will be given a finishing token. Please hold onto this token and wait in line until each runner has been processed. Give your token to the race volunteer who will update your information to show that you have successfully finished the race. Do not keep your token, otherwise you will be shown as an 'Unknown Runner' in the system and will not receive a final time.

Your Time

Your final time will be emailed to you approximately 3 business days after the race.

Questions 9–14

Do the following statements agree with the information given in the text?

In boxes 9–14 on your answer sheet, write

> **TRUE**   *if the statement agrees with the information*
>
> **FALSE**   *if the statement contradicts the information*
>
> **NOT GIVEN**   *if there is no information on this*

9   You may transfer your barcode onto a tab that you can attach to your clothing.

10   Runners will receive a T-shirt at the end of the race.

11   It is recommended that runners bring their own bottle to the race.

12   Runners will be given their position before the race.

13   Your final time is recorded when you cross the finish line.

14   The online system will be immediately updated with your details after you cross the finish line.

Section 2   Questions 15–28

Questions 15–20

*The text on the following page has six paragraphs, **A–F**.*

Which paragraph contains the following information?

*Write the correct letter, **A–F**, in boxes 15–20 on your answer sheet.*

15   planning and tracking responsibilities

16   starting and leading on new company procedures

17   personal qualities the successful applicant should possess

18   skills and experience required for the role

19   accountancy regulations the post-holder must maintain

20   leading a team

Job Description and Person Specification

Job Title   Senior Accountant

Hours   37 hours per week

Direct reports   Associate Accountants

Job description and key responsibilities

A   To lead and manage the Accountancy Team, ensuring delivery of effective and timely accountancy services to all departments within the organisation. You will be responsible for monitoring performance and motivation among the Accountancy Team, including professional development plans and any training needed.

B   The Senior Accountant will be responsible for ensuring that the organisation follows all legal requirements for accounting, at state and national level, according to the National Association of State Boards of Accountancy (NASBA) and the Public Company Accounting Oversight Board (PCAOB). This includes maintaining proper records and accounts. The post-holder will be expected to ensure the organisation regularly achieves the highest standards relative to these requirements.

C   The post-holder will be expected to update and streamline systems within the Accountancy Team as necessary to meet the above requirements. This will include working with leads of other departments to prepare and deliver updates for rolling out new policies. The Senior Accountant will be responsible for reporting on plans and policy implementation in meetings held every quarter.

D   In addition to quarterly meetings, the Senior Accountant is responsible for all month-end financial procedures. This ensures that the organisation is aware of progress toward annual targets and departments are able to undertake procedures to keep on track toward targets. This should also reflect best practice and the post-holder may manage plans with individual departments.

E   The successful applicant should have five years of experience working in a similar role, ideally in the private sector. The applicant should also be able to demonstrate up-to-date knowledge of financial regulations in the private sector with recommendations for the organisation. The applicant will be expected to provide examples of policies and procedures they put in place in their current or previous role which contributed to increased efficiency and effectiveness.

F   In the interview, the successful applicant will be expected to show interpersonal skills, including strong leadership qualities. The successful application should also be able to demonstrate the ability to manage their time and demands on their time effectively. These qualities will be assessed via the Personal Specifications Criteria, attached in an email inviting applicants to the interview.

Questions 21–28

*Read the text below and answer **Questions 21–28**.*

Leave Allowances and Applying for Leave

A   Every full-time (working 35 hours per week) member of staff is entitled to 25 days of annual leave every year. This does not include the 8 days of national holidays. In you first year of work with the organisation, you will accrue, or earn, your holiday by 2.2 days each month. Therefore, at the end of your first month, you have 2.2 days of leave. However, you are encouraged not to take your annual leave until the end of your 3-month probationary period.

B   Our company works on an April–March calendar for annual leave. After your first year of work, you may take leave before it is accrued. This means that you may take 4 days of annual leave in April. Your total days of annual leave may not equal more than 25 for the entire year.

C   You are expected to take all days of your annual leave within the April-March calendar year. If you are not able to take all of your annual leave, you may carry over five days onto the next calendar year. However, you must use these five days within the first quarter of the new year, which means you must take these days of leave before June 30th.

D   Firstly, before applying for annual leave, check with your line manager. Your line manager will ensure that your leave does not conflict with organisational plans or the annual leave of other members of your team. Your manager will also check your leave allowance to ensure that you have enough days of annual leave available. Managers are encouraged to grant all reasonable leave requests.

E   Once you have informed your manager, log on to MyHR.com and complete the required information. This includes the date you plan to begin your leave, how many days of annual leave you are taking, and the date when you will return to the office. You may also add a note for your manager to remind them the purpose of your leave. Click submit, and wait for the email confirmation after your manager has checked your request and submitted the approval.

F   Ensuring that staff are able to take the annual leave they are entitled to is a priority for all managers and the Human Resources Department. If you feel that your annual leave request has been denied unfairly or you are finding it difficult to organise your work responsibilities, please contact the Human Resources Manager.

Questions 21–22

Complete the sentences below.

*Choose **NO MORE THAN TWO WORDS AND/OR A NUMBER** from the text for each answer.*

Write your answers in boxes 21–22 on your answer sheet.

21   In your first year at the organisation, your annual leave accrual is .... for each month you work at the company.

22   If you carry over five days of annual leave, you must take those days within the .... of the new calendar year, before June 30th.

Questions 23–28

*The text on the previous page has six sections, **A–F**.*

Chose the correct heading for each section from the list of headings below.

*Write the correct number, **i–viii**, in boxes 23–28 on your answer sheet.*

List of Headings	
i	Leave approval
ii	Support for staff
iii	Annual leave calendar
iv	Your leave entitlement
v	Employer contribution
vi	Using the online system
vii	Remaining leave days
viii	Bank holidays

23   Section **A**

24   Section **B**

25   Section **C**

26   Section **D**

27   Section **E**

28   Section **F**

Section 3   Questions 29–40

*Read the text below and answer **Questions 29–40**.*

Fireplaces

In the 1500s, many homes in Britain began to have fireplaces, a special corner of a room where small fires were built for cooking or heating. Before fireplaces were built, fires used to be made on the floor made of bare earth, usually in the middle of the room, with a hole in the ceiling for smoke to escape. In many places in the world, fires like this are still used.

However, British fireplaces of the 1500s had significant hazards and dangers. One common hazard was a dirty chimney. The chimney is the area directly above the fire where smoke and ashes from the fire escape up to reach the outside of the house. Before the invention of the stove, a fireplace was used several times a day for cooking as well as heating. This meant chimneys were often coated in grease from cooking as well as thick soot from wood or coal. During this period of British history, dirty chimneys also caused pollution in the nearby atmosphere such as smog as well as devastating fires from burning ash lingering in the air. Inside the home, a blocked chimney meant that the sparks from the fire were not pulled up into the air, but fell inside the room, causing fires and serious damage.

The Great Fire of London in 1666 destroyed a huge proportion of the city, including 13,200 houses. Some places continued to smolder for months afterwards and it took nearly 50 years to rebuild the city. After the Great Fire, households became acutely aware of the dangers of a dirty chimney, and knew just how easily fire can spread from house to house in a crowded city like London.

Many methods were found for clearing out a blocked chimney. One early method of cleaning chimneys was to tie the legs of a goose together and throw it up into the chimney. The goose would flap its wings and knock the soot down. This led to a saying, 'The blacker the goose the cleaner the flue' (A flue is a passage for smoke and gases from a fire). There is even record of small monkeys being trained for the job, mostly bought from boats at the docks of London.

Another more commonly used method was sending small children down chimneys. The child would go down inside the flue and use their feet to knock down the clumps inside the chimney. The children that were hired to do this came from workhouses, or public buildings where poor people were able to live and receive food in exchange for often difficult, back-breaking work. These children would be hired by tradesmen, called chimney sweeps, who would clean chimneys for a few coins.

By the 1700s, an engineer by the name of Joseph Glass invented a set of chimney cleaning brushes, known as flue cleaners, which were used for many years. This design is the sort seen in the film *Mary Poppins*. The original flue cleaners were made of a long cane made of a substance called Malacca, imported from the Caribbean, and a brush made of whalebone. These brushes were initially used by children working in the chimneys, passed down into the flue once they climbed inside. Many children suffocated or choked to death, some fell, and nearly all contracted lung or respiratory diseases. It wasn't until 1864 that the House of Lords banned the use of Climbing Boys by chimney sweeps in the UK with an Act of Parliament.

This Act led to the introduction of a ball and rope system lowered through the chimney instead of any kind of living being. The weight of the lead or iron ball would push the brush through the chimney. Today, chimney sweeping uses video cameras, inspection tools such as scanners, and special vacuum cleaners to ensure that old houses that still use open fires are safe and fire resistant, and must be checked regularly for birds' nests and clogging in the chimney that could cause sparks to set fire to a building from within its walls.

Nowadays, some people continue to have fireplaces or wood-burning stoves in their homes for heating or because they like the cozy smell and feeling of a fire indoors. However, the old hazards still exist and with better technology, we are now able to understand another danger of burning wood inside the home: lung and respiratory damage. Some wood-burning stoves and fireplaces produce more pollution than a heavy truck or 18 diesel cars. This an cause serious damage to the lungs of the people inside the house as well as others who breathe the air that is released by the chimney.

In places where a fireplace is still used for cooking, the average cooking fire produces approximately 400 cigarettes' worth of smoke per hour. This leads to serious breathing difficulties and cancer. It is also a common cause of death of young children who live in houses where wood is burned for heating and cooking. Children are often expected to gather wood, which is time that they lose on studying or play. Just like Britain in the 1500s, the hazards of indoor fires and fireplaces continue.

Questions 29–34

Complete the summary below.

*Choose **NO MORE THAN THREE WORDS AND/OR A NUMBER** from the text for each answer.*

Write your answers in boxes 29–34 on your answer sheet.

Fireplaces began to be built in British homes in the 1500s, which replaced wood-burning fires built directly onto the bare ground floor. A common danger from fireplaces was a blocked or dirty chimney. The oil and grease from cooking and **29** .... produced from burning wood and coal built up on the side of chimneys and were difficult to clean.

An example of the hazards of blocked chimney and the sparks that can fall into the room instead of up into the air was the Great Fire of London in 1666. The fire destroyed thousands of buildings and showed many people how quickly fires move from **30** .... in a congested urban center.

Different techniques were tried for cleaning out a blocked chimney or **31**............... . Animals such as geese and monkeys were sent into the small spaces to **32** .... the soot, either by flapping their wings or using their small hands and claws.

Unfortunately, poor children were commonly used by **33** .... who hired them to go down chimneys and kick the soot down into the fireplace below. Many children who did this work were killed by it. Modern children are still impacted by the use of fireplaces for cooking and heating as a common chore is to **34** .... and therefore lose time on studying or resting.

Questions 35–40

Do the following statements agree with the information given in the text?

In boxes 35–40 on your answer sheet, write

TRUE	*if the statement agrees with the information*
FALSE	*if the statement contradicts the information*
NOT GIVEN	*if there is no information on this*

35 Open fires were used in Britain for cooking before the invention of the stove.

36 Wood-burning fireplaces were dangerous inside the home but not for other people outside the home.

37 The original flue cleaners were tools that did not require a person or animal to operate them.

38 The 1864 House of Lords Act outlawed the chimney sweep profession.

39 Eco-designed wood-burning fireplaces produce less smoke.

40 Using wood in the home for heating and cooking can lead to death.

GENERAL TRAINING WRITING MODULE

Writing Task 1

You should spend about 20 minutes on this task.

There is building work near your apartment, which has closed an exit from your building.

Write a letter to the building company. In your letter

- *give details about the problem*
- *explain how you would like the problem to be solved*
- *describe other issues you have experienced from the building work*

Write at least 150 words.

You do **NOT** need to write any addresses.

Begin your letter as follows:

Dear ... ,

Writing Task 2

You should spend about 40 minutes on this task.

Write about the following topic:

More and more jobs are becoming part of the informal economy, meaning that they do not receive the same monthly salaries or benefits from the government as typical full-time work. Describe the advantages and disadvantages of this and give your opinion.

Give reasons for your answer and include any relevant examples from your own knowledge or experience.

Write at least 250 words.

IELTS Practice Test 4

LISTENING MODULE

🎧 **Practice Test 4, Track 13**

Section 1   Questions 1–10

Questions 1–10

Complete the notes below.

Write **NO MORE THAN TWO WORDS AND/OR A NUMBER** *for each answer.*

SOFAS FOR SALE	
Large Sofa	Width: 230 cm Depth: **1** .... cm Colour: Black
Medium Sofas	Width: **2** .... cm Depth: 100 cm Colour: **3** ....
Price	Recliner Medium: £250.00 Standard Medium: **4** .... Large: **5** .... Agreed Price: **6** .... for the large sofa and the standard medium sofa

Details of Seller	Name: Mr **7** ....
	Address: Flat 9
	         8 .... Road
	         Town Centre (near **9** ....)
	Time: **10** .... pm

Practice Test 4, Track 14

Section 2   Questions 11–20

Questions 11–14

Answer the questions below.

*Write **NO MORE THAN THREE WORDS** for each answer.*

11 What is Barry Gordon's role at the club?

12 How often are members of the club asked to give a small contribution?

13 What is the registration fee?

14 What time does the reception close?

Questions 15–20

*Choose the correct letter, **A, B** or **C**.*

15 The first thing students need in order to register is their

    A enrolment letter.

    B ID card.

    C driving licence.

16 How does the speaker describe the enrolment procedures?

    A He says they are bureaucratic.

    B He says it is a drama.

    C He says all students need a new card.

17 What does the speaker need for the website?

    A a £5 fee

    B students' badges

    C passport-sized photos

18 What is a requirement to join the group?

    A being an actor

    B experience performing on a stage

    C enthusiasm

19   How does the speaker define the group?

    A   people who want to socialise and have fun

    B   people of all ages who want to become actors

    C   actors who want to move to Los Angeles

20   What is the main objective of the club?

    A   the study of business, arts, law and languages

    B   to help people to understand themselves and others

    C   to help the members achieve recognition

Practice Test 4, Track 15

Section 3   Questions 21–30

Questions 21–22

Complete the table below.

*Write **NO MORE THAN THREE WORDS** for each answer.*

THE MOTHER NATURE SHOW	
Presenter	John Gibbs
Guest 1	Dr Popov – specialist on green technology. Technological solutions to reduce CO_2 **21** ....
Guest 2	Professor Kirsch – **22** .... specialist. The greenhouse effect.

Questions 23–26

Complete the notes below.

Choose your answers from the box below and write them next to questions 23–26.

A	The greenhouse effect
B	Global warming
C	Greenhouse gases

23   .... is caused by the greenhouse effect.

24   .... radiate energy in different directions.

25   .... determine the amount of radiation in the air.

26   .... is a process which happens without human interference and keeps Earth habitable.

Questions 27–30

Complete the diagram below.

*Write **NO MORE THAN TWO WORDS** for each answer.*

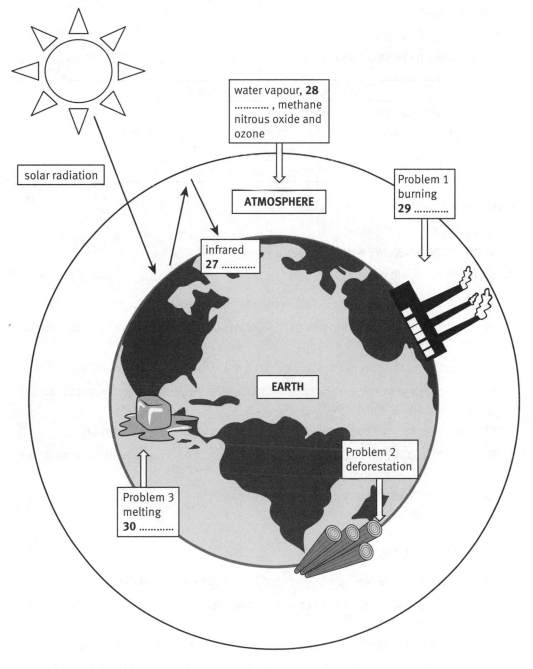

solar radiation

water vapour, **28**
.... , methane
nitrous oxide and
ozone

ATMOSPHERE

Problem 1
burning
29 ....

infrared
27 ....

EARTH

Problem 2
deforestation

Problem 3
melting
30 ....

🎧 **Practice Test 4, Track 16**

Section 4   Questions 31–40

Questions 31–32

Complete the notes below.

*Write **NO MORE THAN THREE WORDS** for each answer.*

Family Structures in the United States	
Main questions to be discussed	What is a family? How and why have **31** .... over time? Why do families matter?
Special thanks to	Professor Garcia and staff at **32** ....

Questions 33–39

Complete the sentences below.

*Write **NO MORE THAN ONE WORD** for each answer.*

According to the speaker:

33 The US Census Bureau's definition of a family is very ....

34 It is no longer .... to use the US Census Bureau's definition to analyse family structures.

35 Western Europeans in the Middle Ages lived with their .... families.

36 The different family structures in Europe during the Middle Ages were caused by varying social and economic ....

37 Marriage for love began to be seen as .... in the mid-18th century.

38 In 19th century America, being a housewife would only have been possible if your husband was particularly ....

39 .... rates increased in the early 1970s.

Question 40

*Choose the correct letter, **A**, **B** or **C**.*

40 Which sentence best summarises the third and final part of the talk?

A The study of different family structures can help us understand who we are as a nation.

B Different family structures are a reflection of different racial groups.

C Children raised by single parents are more emotionally stable in adulthood.

ACADEMIC READING MODULE

Reading Passage 1   Questions 1–15

*You should spend about 20 minutes on **Questions 1–15**, which are based on Reading Passage 1 below.*

One of the most crucial aspects in enabling computer technology to progress is the advances we have seen in data storage. As we continue to finds new ways to store more data on a smaller scale, we are able to create faster, more detailed computers and smart technology, with greater capacities to store more information, whether it's the music and photos stored on a personal laptop, or the plethora of human resource files stored remotely by multinational corporations.

Data storage took off as a result of the invention of magnetic tape. Fritz Pfleumer patented the first brand of such a tape, which fused oxide with paper or film. Sometime after its initial creation, magnetic tape began to be used as a medium through which music and video could be recorded and preserved. Magnetic drums were created in the 1930s, but did not become widely used until the 1950s. These drums were used in early computers to provide a similar function to RAM in modern computers. Magnetic drums stored information in a large metal cylinder which was capable of spinning. This cylinder was coated with a magnetic layer, and multiple read-write heads (which could store and retrieve information) would fire electromagnetic pulses at the cylinder, in order to create binary digits.

Floppy disks as a form of magnetic data storage were first devised in 1967, but weren't available commercially until 1971 with the 8 inch 'Diskette 1'. This was a circular disk with a magnetic surface that was sandwiched between fabric, then encased in a thin plastic cover. The disk, fabric and casing were created with a hole in the middle, allowing a spindle in the disk drive to be inserted in order to spin the disk. Via a hole in the casing at one end, the disk was exposed so that data could be read from it.

The fabric sleeve used in floppy disks performed two functions: to remove any dust that settled on the exposed magnetic disk, and to reduce friction as the disk was spun in the drive. Dust was a serious risk to the information stored on floppy disks, as it could clog up the disk drive over time, leading to the possibility of friction with the plastic shell of the disk, which could easily damage the disk's delicate surface. In fact, the common name 'floppy' arose because these 8 inch disks were very flexible and could easily be bent. There was also the risk of data corruption if the disks were ejected while they were still spinning, not only that, they were highly susceptible to extremes of temperature, moisture and magnetic fields, which meant that disks had to be stored very carefully in order to protect the data from being lost.

This physical structure remained virtually unchanged as floppy disks evolved, shrinking in size and increasing in capacity. The first 8 inch disks could hold 175 kilobytes (kb) of data, with the initial 5¼ inch disks holding 360kb. By the time 3½ inch disks were introduced in 1983, the default capacity of these single-sided disks was again 360kb, although a 720kb double-sided disk was soon released. In 1986, this was then upgraded to a double-sided, high-density format which could hold 1.44 megabytes (Mb) of data, which soon became standard.

With the introduction of the 3½ inch disks, for the first time, the disk had a hard plastic coating which provided greater physical protection. In addition, the aperture through which the disk was read was at this point protected by a spring-loaded metal slider, which would be automatically pushed aside when the disk was inserted into a floppy disk drive. These disks also had a plastic tab in one corner that could be slid to reveal a hole. In this state, the disk would be write-protected and no data could be saved or deleted.

Before the disks could be used for the first time, each had to be formatted, a process where a series of concentric rings (called tracks) and sectors (or, the angular blocks in a track) were created by magnetically aligning the ferromagnetic surface in a specific pattern. For a 1.44Mb 3½ inch disk, this involved creating 80 tracks on each side, each track having 18 sectors, each sector holding 512 bytes of data. By the mid-1990s, large software programs such as operating systems would have to be spread across 10 or more disks.

Following the advent of CD-ROMs in the late 1990s, floppy disks fell out of use. By 2007 only 2% of store purchased computers came with a floppy disk drive. Today, many people are unfamiliar with floppy disks, and would find the amount of storage they provide to be inadequate for their needs. The 1.44Mb floppy, which offered an impressive amount of storage when it was released, would barely be able to store one mp3 song.

Questions 1–7

Do the following statements agree with the information given in Reading Passage 1?

In boxes 1–7 on your answer sheet, write

TRUE	*if the statement agrees with the information*
FALSE	*if the statement contradicts the information*
NOT GIVEN	*if there is no information on this*

1   Improving data storage can make computers run faster.

2   Pfleumer's patented magnetic tape was used to record music.

3   Modern day RAM is used in a similar way to how magnetic tape was once used.

4   Diskette 1 was the name given to the first floppy drive.

5   Commercial floppy disks were created with holes in the middle, which enabled them to spin.

6   The plastic case on the floppy disk was used in order to protect the disk from dust.

7   The fabric used for floppy disks had to be very flexible in order to enable it to be easily bent.

Questions 8–13

Complete the summary below.

*Choose **ONE WORD AND/OR A NUMBER** from Reading Passage 1 for each answer.*

Floppy disks were quite delicate and easily damaged, as well as being **8** .... , hence their name. If floppy disks were ejected before the disk had stopped spinning, there was a high risk of data **9** .... The data stored on the 3½ inch floppy disks was read through an **10** .... in the hard plastic casing, and this was **11** .... by a metal plate when not inserted into a computer. Floppy disks were formatted before use by creating rings on the disks, and blocks within each ring, termed **12** .... The 3½ inch floppy disks had 80 tracks and 18 sectors, allowing it to hold a total of **13** ....

Questions 14–15

*Choose **TWO** letters, **A–E**.*

Which **TWO** of the following would the writer of the passage agree with?

A   Floppy disks have fallen out of use because they are not as sturdy as newer forms of data storage.

B   Modern data storage devices are far superior to floppy disks in terms of storage capacity.

C   Floppy disks are still used today by a small number of professionals.

D   Floppy disks did little to progress the development of data storage.

E   Though floppy disks grew in capacity, their physical structure remained the same throughout their development.

Reading Passage 2   Questions 16–28

*You should spend about 20 minutes on **Questions 16–28**, which are based on Reading Passage 2 below.*

The Colossal Waves

Tsunamis have horrified and fascinated us in recent history. Do we have the knowledge, tools and skills we need to protect ourselves adequately?

Section A

Prior to the catastrophic waves in the Indian Ocean that struck on Boxing Day 2004, killing more than 230,000 people across 14 countries, many of us had never heard the term tsunami. Unfortunately, since then tsunamis have become increasingly familiar to us through news stories, most notably the earthquake and tsunami in Chile, which occurred in February 2010 and the Japanese disaster in March 2011. We are now regularly bombarded with that reminds us of this deadly natural phenomenon.

The infrequency and unpredictability of tsunamis makes them very difficult to study. Although we do know what causes tsunamis, how to measure them and also how to predict when they will reach shores from a specific location at sea, applying this information to real life events in order to protect ourselves is not as easy. Each tsunami has a different size and force, depending on how it was formed, and their formation is difficult to predict. As such, calculating and predicting when a tsunami will strike, which areas will be worst hit when one does, and how much damage they are likely to inflict on areas proves to be an extremely difficult task.

Section B

A common misconception is that all tsunamis are formed by earthquakes. While earthquakes are indeed responsible for about three-quarters of all tsunamis, the caving in of giant icebergs, the eruption of underwater volcanoes, and even meteorites hitting the ocean have all been known to produce giant waves in the past. Professor Gale from Sidney University explains that for an earthquake to cause a tsunami, it would have to be of a magnitude of 6 or above. In addition, shallow earthquakes are more likely to cause tsunamis than earthquakes occurring closer to the Earth's core. According to the professor, "what we know is that the closer to the sea floor an earthquake is, the more likely it is to form a tsunami. Earthquakes generate a large amount of energy and when they are close to the sea floor, this energy has a shorter distance to travel. The main challenge is how to measure the depth of an earthquake."

For example, a magnitude-9 earthquake may not trigger a tsunami, depending on the depth at which it occurs. Both Chile and Japan have suffered earthquakes of magnitude 9 without the further devastating effects of a tsunami. These earthquakes occurred hundreds of kilometres below the earth's surface. On the other hand, the earthquakes in Chile 2010 and Japan 2011 were both shallow and powerful, with depths of just 35 km and 24 km and magnitudes of 8.8 and 9.1 respectively. These sorts of earthquakes are the types that cause the most dangerous tsunamis.

We can measure the size of a tsunami by calculating the difference between the crests, the highest points of the waves. This measurement is called the wavelength. Normal waves typically have wavelengths of around 40 metres. Tsunamis, on the other hand, can have wavelengths as a large as 200 kilometres. That's 500 times bigger than a normal wave. During the tsunami that damaged Japan in 2011, the crests of the waves reached 40 metres above sea level.

Section C

Following the invention of the tsunami tracking system, scientists are able to forecast when and where one could hit the coast. Scientists rely on a series of complex monitoring systems that enable them to track tsunami wave movements. Devices at the bottom of the ocean can measure any increase in pressure and send this information to the electronic buoys on the surface. Data is then passed to satellites and transmitted to monitoring stations on land. "These machines are incredibly precise," Gale says. "Even an extra metre of water on the water column can be automatically detected and reported to the stations."

Even though we are now able to forecast when and where a tsunami will hit, it remains very difficult to predict how the wave will behave once it reaches land. Tsunamis can achieve speeds of up to 850 km/h at sea, but they slow down drastically and somewhat erratically on their approach to shore.

Section D

Tsunamis are hardly ever felt at sea because the height of waves in deep waters is usually no higher than a metre. This is because a tsunami in open sea can be thought of as nothing more than an enormous column of water shifted from a large and sudden displacement of the sea floor. The small wave apparent at sea is like the tip of an iceberg, however, as the column of water goes from the top of the wave all the way down to the sea floor. This column is constantly rising and falling and a massive amount of energy is pushed along from the source. As the water level becomes shallower, the column is squeezed upwards, revealing giant waves as the water approaches land.

The most vulnerable areas are embayments. These areas are particularly prone to tsunamis as enclosed shores can amplify the waves. Conversely, strong cliff lines, and coasts with deep water nearby are the best protected areas. It is also known that coral reefs and mangroves can reduce the wave energy and act as natural barriers.

Questions 16–19

*Reading Passage 2 has four sections, **A, B, C** or **D**.*

Choose the correct heading for each section from the list of headings below.

*Write the correct number, **i–vii**, in boxes 16–19 on your answer sheet.*

List of Headings	
i	Preventing a tsunami
ii	Tsunami terror
iii	Tragedy in Japan
iv	Tracking tsunamis
v	Tsunamis in South Africa
vi	How tsunamis are formed
vii	When tsunamis approach land

16   Section **A**

17   Section **B**

18   Section **C**

19   Section **D**

Questions 20–28

*Complete the sentences below using **NO MORE THAN THREE WORDS** for each answer.*

20   Tsunamis are difficult to study due to their ....

21   .... originate from earthquakes, but about three-quarters do.

22   Tsunamis are more frequently caused by .... earthquakes due to the short distance the generated energy needs to travel.

23   The distance between consecutive waves' crests is known as a ....

24   Tsunamis can now be forecast and followed due to the development of a ....

25   .... receive the information emitted by undersea devices and transmit it to monitoring stations.

26   Tsunamis reduce their speed .... when approaching land.

27   A .... that is constantly rising and falling is the best definition of a tsunami in open sea.

28   The strength of a tsunami can be decreased by .... such as coral reefs and mangroves.

Reading Passage 3   Questions 29–40

*You should spend about 20 minutes on **Questions 29–40**, which are based on Reading Passage 3 below.*

Glass is one of the earliest materials to be created and used by humans. Evidence of man-made glass has been discovered which dates back as far as 4000 BC. In 1500 BC, glass began to form the shape of a hollow container, bringing into being an early kind of glass bottle. Since then, the process of creating glass containers and bottles has been considerably refined, though the essential steps remain familiar.

The main component of glass is sand. Modern glass consists of around 70% sand, and also contains soda ash and limestone. Limestone is used in order to provide chemical stability, and soda ash lowers the melting point of the mixture, which means that glass can be created more efficiently. Other ingredients, such as iron and carbon may also be added in order to provide colour to the glass.

Another important ingredient is recovered glass, which can be obtained from recycling centres. The amount of cullet, as recovered glass is known by glass manufacturers, used can vary considerably, with as much as 40% being used in some areas of glass production. As we become more interested in conservation of materials and recycling, cullet has become increasingly important in glass production, as it lowers the amount of new materials needed to create glass products.

To begin glass production, the raw materials are measured, mixed and stored in batches. These batches are then fed into a glass furnace to be melted in a stage known as the 'hot end' process. The furnaces used can operate at temperatures of over 1500 °C and are fuelled with oil or natural gasses. When the materials are mixed in the furnace, the extreme heat produces a liquid substance called molten glass. This red hot liquid glass can then be moulded into bottles by one of two methods: press and blow and blow and blow.

The method known as press and blow takes place in machines which have between five and twenty sections which carry out the glass bottle forming process simultaneously. They are called individual sections (IS). Each IS machine can produce up to 20 bottles at the same time. At temperatures between 1100 °C and 1200 °C, molten glass reaches a 'plastic' temperature, where it is cooled enough to hold its shape slightly, but still hot enough to be malleable. Once the glass has reached this stage, the press and blow formation can begin. A shearing blade is used to cut and form the glass into cylindrical shapes called gobs. Gravitational force is employed by pouring the gobs from a slight height; the gob falls into blank moulds, cooling further as they fall. The glass is then pressed into the blank mould with the help of a metal plunger. There it assumes the mould's shape and a rounded mass of glass, called a parison, is formed. After this, the parison is transferred to a final mould, and blown to assume the shape of a bottle.

Blow and blow formation also takes place in an IS machine in a similar sequence to the press-and-blow technique. The process of blow and blow differs when the gob reaches the mould. Instead of a metal plunger, compressed air is used to push the gob into the blank mould. The parison is then flipped into a final mould to be blown again to form the interior side of a bottle.

After each of the two processes, the glass bottles have to go through a slow cooling process which ensures that the temperature inside the bottle is kept as similar to the outside temperature as possible. This process is known as annealing and reduces the amount of stain in bottles, which makes them more resistant. In addition to this precaution, bottles also go through a process which makes their inside more chemically-resistant. This process is called internal treatment and involves treating the bottle with a gas mixture of fluorocarbon, usually after its formation, as a second step of annealing.

Once these processes are complete and the bottles have significantly cooled, the bottles are inspected for cracks or pieces of stone that might compromise the quality of the final product. After this final quality check, the bottles are packaged and delivered to various beverage factories, where they are filled up with liquid, sealed, and sent out to supermarkets and shops.

Questions 29–40

Complete the flow-chart below.

*Write **NO MORE THAN THREE WORDS OR A NUMBER** for each answer.*

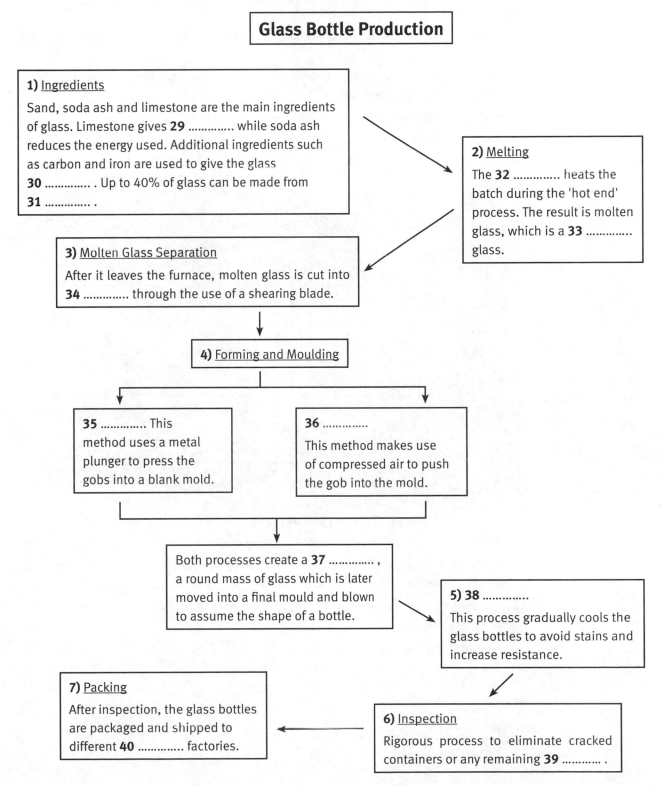

Glass Bottle Production

1) Ingredients

Sand, soda ash and limestone are the main ingredients of glass. Limestone gives **29** .... while soda ash reduces the energy used. Additional ingredients such as carbon and iron are used to give the glass **30** .... Up to 40% of glass can be made from **31** ....

2) Melting

The **32** .... heats the batch during the 'hot end' process. The result is molten glass, which is a **33** .... glass.

3) Molten Glass Separation

After it leaves the furnace, molten glass is cut into **34** .... through the use of a shearing blade.

4) Forming and Moulding

35 .... This method uses a metal plunger to press the gobs into a blank mold.

36 ....

This method makes use of compressed air to push the gob into the mold.

Both processes create a **37** .... , a round mass of glass which is later moved into a final mould and blown to assume the shape of a bottle.

5) 38 ....

This process gradually cools the glass bottles to avoid stains and increase resistance.

7) Packing

After inspection, the glass bottles are packaged and shipped to different **40** .... factories.

6) Inspection

Rigorous process to eliminate cracked containers or any remaining **39** ....

ACADEMIC WRITING MODULE

Writing Task 1

You should spend about 20 minutes on this task.

> *The graph below shows the unemployment rates in the US and Britain between 2008 and 2015.*

> *Summarise the information by selecting and reporting the main features, and make comparisons where relevant.*

Write at least 150 words.

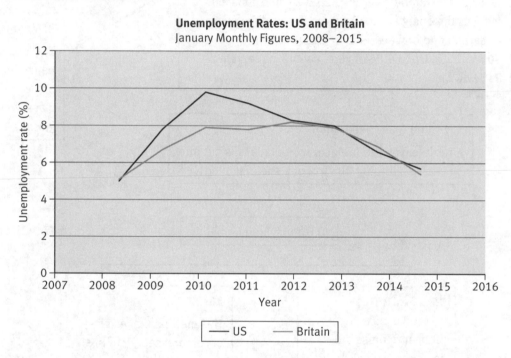

Unemployment Rates: US and Britain
January Monthly Figures, 2008–2015

Writing Task 2

You should spend about 40 minutes on this task.

> *Music is appreciated in every major society and culture of the world today.*

> *Some people believe that music is to be shared. Others, however, believe that music belongs to those who make it and should only be shared with their authorisation.*

Give reasons for your answers and include any relevant examples from your own knowledge or experience.

Write at least 250 words.

SPEAKING MODULE

Time: 11–14 minutes

Part 1

Introduction to interview (4–5 minutes): The examiner will begin by introducing himself or herself and checking your identity. She or he will then ask you some questions about yourself based on everyday topics.

Let's talk about tourism.

- What would you suggest a tourist should do or see in your country? [Why?]
- What is traditional art and music like in your country?
- Do you like or dislike the traditional customs of your country? [Why?/Why not?]
- How has tourism changed in your country in recent years?

Part 2

Individual long turn (3–4 minutes): Candidates' task card instructions:

Task Card

Please read the topic below carefully. You will be asked to talk about it for one to two minutes. You will have one minute to think about what you are going to say. You can make some notes to help you if you wish.

Describe a memorable day in your life. You should say:

- What happened on this day
- When this day was
- Who you were with
- Why this day was so memorable

Also, explain whether you liked or disliked this day, and why.

The examiner may then ask you a couple of brief questions to wrap up this part of the test. Further questions:

- What are the most memorable events of your life?
- Why do you think it is important to remember events like this?
- Do you think negative experiences are easier to remember than positive experiences, or the other way around? Why do you think this is?

Part 3

Two-way discussion (4–5 minutes): In Part 3, the examiner will ask you further questions related to the topic in Part 2.

Let's talk about celebrations for a moment.

- What effect do celebrations have on those involved?
- Why do some people enjoy group celebrations more than others?
- Which are the most important events to celebrate, in your opinion? [Why?]
- How do you think celebrations will change in the future?

Finally, let's talk about school.

- What was your favourite subject at school? [Why?]
- Tell me about your favourite teacher at school and why you liked them.
- How did your experiences at school shape your career goals for the future?

General Training Reading and Writing Test

GENERAL TRAINING READING MODULE

Section 1   Questions 1–14

*Read the text below and answer **Questions 1–6**.*

ULTIMATE FITNESS CENTRE
New Spring Courses

Yoga for Beginners

A foundational course that teaches the basics of yoga, so you can develop a healthy life-long practice. This course teaches fundamental poses, breathing techniques, and some simple anatomy.

Mon, Wed, Fri / 9 am–10:30 am

Location: Studio 1

Cross Training

Get a full body workout and cardiovascular exercise with this high-intensity course taught by our professional training staff.

Mon–Sat / 8 am–9 am, 6 pm–7 pm

Location: Studio 2

Latin Dance

Dance the Rumba, Salsa, Samba and Merengue to lively music for a fun workout in this new group course taught by Latin dance professionals. Beginners and experts welcome!

Thurs, Sat / 2 pm–3:30 pm

Location: Studio 1

Cycling

For people who love to ride, this course delivers a strong cardio workout with low impact. All levels welcome. Spaces and equipment are limited, so please reserve a spot in advance.

Mon–Sun / 6 am–7 am, 5 pm–6 pm

Location: Cycling Studio

Questions 1–6

Do the following statements agree with the information given in the text?

In boxes 1–6 on your answer sheet, write

TRUE	*if the statement agrees with the information*
FALSE	*if the statement contradicts the information*
NOT GIVEN	*if there is no information on this*

1   Yoga for Beginners is only for people who have never done yoga before.

2   Cross Training is taught by experienced fitness trainers.

3   Latin Dance is only for beginners.

4   The Latin Dance class has been held at Ultimate Fitness Centre for many years.

5   Reservations for the Cycling course can be made at the front desk.

6   Ultimate Fitness has only three rooms for group courses.

*Read the text below and answer **Questions 7–14**.*

Office Manager Wanted

Sorgeson LLC is a marketing company specializing in innovative branding and marketing solutions for ecologically responsible businesses. We are looking for a motivated, enthusiastic office manager to join our team.

Responsibilities include:

- Maintain a high standard of organisation in the office
- Answer phones and redirect phone calls to other team members
- Coordinate appointments with external service providers
- Manage travel and excursion scheduling and bookings
- Maintain office supplies (stationery, appliances, etc.)
- Process incoming and outgoing post (sending and receiving)
- Act as the go-to source of service and office information for team members

Successful candidates will possess:

- Strong written and verbal communication skills in English and Spanish, other languages a plus
- Minimum 2 years proven office management experience
- Strong organisational and multi-tasking skills with an attention to detail
- Ability to use computers and adapt quickly to new operating systems
- A positive attitude and willingness to grow with a rapidly expanding company
- Knowledge of current environmental issues is a plus

If you feel you are the right fit for this position, please send a CV and cover letter to us at humanresoures@sorgeson.com. We look forward to hearing from you!

Questions 7–14

Complete the sentences below.

*Choose **NO MORE THAN THREE WORDS AND/OR A NUMBER** from the text for each answer.*

Write your answer in boxes 7–14 on your answer sheet.

7 Sorgeson LLC works with businesses that are ....

8 The office manager must be able to .... a well-organised office.

9 Job duties include making arrangements with ....

10 Office supplies, such as stationery and .... must be maintained.

11 .... will rely on the office manager for information.

12 The office manager should be able to speak and write in ....

13 At least .... of previous experience are required.

14 Strong candidates for the job will also know about ....

Section 2   Questions 15–28

Questions 15–21

*The text on the following page has seven sections, **A–G**.*

Choose the correct heading for each section from the list of headings below.

*Write the correct number, **i–x**, in boxes 15–21 on your answer sheet.*

List of Headings	
i	Working hours for part-time and freelance employees
ii	Overtime policies and procedures
iii	The importance of following the policies
iv	How to submit a request for vacation leave
v	The Galonzo, Inc. philosophy
vi	Full time vs. part time employment
vii	taking time off when sick for all employees
viii	Vacation leave for part-time and freelance employees
ix	Rules and procedures for vacation leave
x	Working hours for full-time employees

15   Section **A**

16   Section **B**

17   Section **C**

18   Section **D**

19   Section **E**

20   Section **F**

21   Section **G**

Working Hours, Vacation and Sick Leave Policies and Procedures

A   At Galonzo Inc., we strive to maintain a working environment that is safe and fair for all employees. Recently, some changes have been made to the working hours, holiday and sick leave policies and procedures at the company in order to ensure that all protocols conform to our company philosophy.

B   It is crucial that all full-time employees at Galonzo, Inc. maintain a forty hours per week schedule. Due to our open-door policy, employees have the freedom to choose when and how they distribute these hours throughout the week. However, employees must not work for more than ten hours on any given day.

C   All part time and freelance employees are eligible for specific exclusions and regulations depending on the terms of their contracts, which are either individual or project-based. Part-time and freelance employees can refer to their individual contracts for the working hour regulations that apply to their specific situations.

D   Occasionally, full-time employees will be requested to work some overtime hours beyond the standard 40 hours per week, for a maximum of 15 overtime hours total per month. In this case, employees will be notified of this request at least 10 business days in advance. Employees will be paid time and a half for every hour they work over 40 hours per week.

E   All full-time employees are entitled to 14 days of vacation leave during their first two years of employment. This period of time increases by one day for every year employees work full-time for Galonzo, Inc. beyond the initial two-year employment period. Employees are required to submit holiday leave requests to the human resources department at least 30 days in advance. Freelance and part-time employees are not entitled to vacation leave.

F   Galonzo, Inc. employees are entitled to paid sick leave. Full-time and part-time employees have the right to self-certify their illness when sick for up to seven consecutive days. After seven consecutive days have passed, employees must obtain a sick note from their doctor to continue to remain on sick leave. Sick days are not factored into freelance contracts. Freelance workers should notify their line manager immediately if sickness may delay or otherwise impact the deliverables specified in their contract.

G   Strict adhesion to these policies and procedures by the company employees and administration will ensure that everyone at Galonzo, Inc. has a productive experience while maintaining their well-being both during and beyond office hours. Please address any concerns and questions to the human resources department.

Questions 22–28

*Read the text below and answer **Questions 22–28**.*

Workplace Discrimination

Discrimination in the workplace takes many forms and can be expressed and interpreted in multiple ways by both employees and employers. The legal, social and psychological consequences of discrimination can be severe. It is important for everyone to have a clear understanding of the different types of discrimination in order to maintain a safe workplace.

Discrimination is not to be confused with prejudice. Prejudice refers to the attitude a person may have about a person or group of people. Someone can be prejudiced against a group of people without discriminating against them.

Unlike prejudice, discrimination involves behaviour. Discrimination in the workplace occurs when an individual is treated unjustly due to a variety of factors. These include but are not limited to race, gender, religious practices, disability, sexual orientation, age and skin colour.

There are various types of discrimination. Direct discrimination is perhaps the most widely publicised variety. Direct discrimination occurs when an individual is treated unfavourably or unfairly by someone else because they have a certain characteristic, like age or skin colour. A more serious form of this is called harassment, which can include jokes, slurs, cyberbullying, or threatening behaviour like physical intimidation or verbal abuse. Direct discrimination can be easy to spot, but it isn't necessarily easy to prove.

Indirect discrimination occurs when rules or requirements that are presented as neutral and universal actually create disadvantages for a certain person or group of people. These can include rules about appearance, such as hairstyles, or height limitations, even scheduling procedures. Indirect discrimination can be harder to spot than direct discrimination, but it is equally important and just as illegal.

Questions 22–23

Complete the sentences below.

*Choose **NO MORE THAN TWO WORDS AND/OR A NUMBER** from the text for each answer.*

Write your answers in boxes 22–23 on your answer sheet.

22 There can be very extreme .... for workplace discrimination.

23 .... is what differentiates discrimination from prejudice.

Questions 24–28

*Look at the list of definitions **A–E**, provided below.*

Match each definition with the sentences below.

*Write the correct letter, **A–E**, in boxes 24–28 on your answer sheet.*

List of Definitions	
A	prejudice
B	harassment
C	discrimination
D	direct discrimination
E	indirect discrimination

24 the feelings someone has about a specific person or group

25 allowing prejudices to influence actions against others, both directly and indirectly

26 verbal and physical threats made by one person towards another

27 treating someone unfairly because of their traits, characteristics, or beliefs

28 upholding policies and rules that cause harm to a person or group

Section 3   Questions 29–40

*Read the text below and answer **Questions 29–40**.*

Gibraltar's Monkeys

A   The British peninsular of Gibraltar hosts one of the largest wild monkey colonies on European mainland. Originating from the Atlas Mountains and the Rif piles of Morocco, approximately three hundred monkeys in five troops occupy the Upper Rock territory of the Gibraltar Nature Reserve, with the most popular of these, Queen's Gate, making daily trips down into the town area. Despite the fact they are tailless Barbary Macaques, the locals refer to them simply as "monos", which is the Spanish word for monkeys. Macaques have become one of the most popular tourist attractions in Gibraltar.

B   The name Barbary relates to the Berbers of Morocco, where the same apes flourish today. The apes are recorded as appearing on the Rock of Gibraltar long before the British occupation in 1704. For example, one hundred years earlier, Alonso Hernández del Portillo, the earliest chronicler of Gibraltar, wrote, "In the mountain, there are monkeys, who may be called the true owners [of the Rock], with possession from time immemorial, always tenacious of the dominion, living for the most part on the eastern side in high and inaccessible chasms."

C   Studying fossils and blood types found in the Gibraltarian monkeys today, it seems that although the monkeys originate in North Africa, they may not all have been stowaways on ships to Gibraltar's port as popularly thought. Instead, DNA links them to being the last survivors of a general European population that spread as far as the UK, driven up the Rock where they could survive uninterrupted away from humans and urbanisation. A more unsavoury reason given for their existence is that the British Army brought them over to breed for shooting practice. Today, thankfully, the monkeys are protected, as they are the biggest tourist attraction in Gibraltar. They are fed fruit, vegetables, and leaves daily, to keep them healthy and in good spirits.

D   Between 1915 and 1991 the British Army and, later, the Gibraltar Regiment were assigned to care for and protect the monkeys. The "Keeper of the Apes" maintained a highly detailed up-to-date record of the monkey population, including births, deaths, dietary habits, even their names, which were often inspired by government and military officials. When UK-based troops withdrew from duty, the Government of Gibraltar assumed responsibility for the monkeys. Currently, the Gibraltar Ornithological and Natural History Society (GONHS) and the Gibraltar Veterinary Clinic care for and monitor the island's monkey population.

E   Caring for Gibraltar's monkey population is a complex process. Macaques are caught regularly in order to monitor their health. Multiple measurements, including their height and weight, are taken and recorded. A small unique number is tattooed onto each monkey, and an identifying microchip is inserted under the skin. This allows the animals to be tracked and identified. The monkeys are all photographed, and their individual characteristics, like scars or marks, are catalogued by the GONHS.

F   Another essential part of maintaining the monkey population is the annual census, which allows the GONHS and the Gibraltar Veterinary Clinic to monitor the reproductive patterns of the monkeys. The data they collect helps with population management and fertility regulation. Due to the improvements here, the Barbary Macaque population in Gibraltar is increasing at a steady rate. This puts pressure on the environment, which must also be carefully monitored.

G   Despite all of the hard work involved in their care and maintenance, the Barbary Macaques remain a beloved feature of Gibraltar. This is reflected in the local culture and in pop culture around the world. The monkeys have been portrayed on Gibraltar's five-pence coin since 1988. They are also feature into a number of novels and films, including a 1987 James Bond film.

H   Over the years, the Queen's Gate troop of monkeys have become used to interacting with tourists. This means that the monkeys are very bold and sociable, and now have inherent pickpocketing skills for jackets, zips, camera bags, and rucksacks, which many tourists find entertaining. However, encouraging the monkeys carries a fine of up to £4,000, and is illegal. Their welfare is important in part because of the local belief that as long as there are monkeys on the Rock, it will remain under British rule. This led Winston Churchill to order their numbers to be replenished during World War II from forest populations in Algeria, when the Rock population had declined to near extinction due to lack of care, a move that today seems somewhat objectionable.

Questions 29–35

*The text on the previous page has eight sections, **A–H**.*

Which paragraph contains the following information?

*Write the correct letter, **A–H**, in boxes 29–35 on your answer sheet.*

29   the Barbary Macaques in local and popular culture

30   authorities in charge of Barbary Macaque care and protection

31   where the Barbary Macaques came from

32   the "monos" of Gibraltar

33   reproduction and its consequences

34   the history of the Barbary Macaques on Gibraltar

35   monitoring and tracking the Barbary Macaques

Questions 36–40

Complete the summary below.

*Choose **NO MORE THAN TWO WORDS AND/OR A NUMBER** from the text for each answer.*

Write your answers in boxes 36–40 on your answer sheet.

The Barbary Macaques of Gibraltar are one of the area's most popular **36** ....
Queen's Gate is one of five **37** .... that occupy Gibraltar, and are considered the
most popular, since they tend to operate in one of the areas most commonly visited by
tourists. The members of Queen's Gate have developed stealthy **38** .... skills, and
have been known to steal food from purses and backpacks.

Encouraging the monkeys to behave badly is **39** .... , and can be punished with
a hefty fine. However, it is not only their popularity with tourists that compels the
government to continue using resources to protect the Barbary Macaques. A local
legend says that **40** .... of Gibraltar will be maintained as long as the monkeys
continue to thrive there.

GENERAL TRAINING WRITING MODULE

Writing Task 1

You should spend about 20 minutes on this task.

> *You have seen an advertisement on a website for a job opening at a bookstore. You decide to apply for the job.*
>
> *Write a letter to the manager of the bookstore. In your letter*
> - *introduce yourself*
> - *describe your skills and experience*
> - *explain why you are interested in the job*

Write at least 150 words.

You do **NOT** need to write any addresses.

Begin your letter as follows:

Dear Sir/Madam,

Writing Task 2

You should spend about 40 minutes on this task.

Write about the following topic:

> *Some people believe that a tax should be added to the cost of unhealthy foods while others think it is unnecessary and unfair.*
>
> *Discuss both perspectives and give your own opinion.*
>
> *Give reasons for your answer and include any relevant examples from your own knowledge or experience.*

Write at least 250 words.

IELTS Practice Test 5

LISTENING MODULE

Practice Test 5, Track 17

Section 1   Questions 1–10

Questions 1–2

Choose the correct letter, A, B or C.

1   How did the caller find out about Cretan Holiday Homes?

    A   She stayed with them before.

    B   It was recommended to her.

    C   She was given a brochure.

2   Why does the caller want to rent houses both in Chania and Rethymno?

    A   Her husband doesn't want to go to Lasithi.

    B   All of her friends have suggested this.

    C   She's worried about travelling times between different regions.

Questions 3–10

Complete the table below.

Write **NO MORE THAN TWO WORDS AND/OR A NUMBER** *for each answer.*

CRETAN HOLIDAY HOMES		
CUSTOMER DETAILS Name: Patty **3** .... Phone Number: **4** .... Dates: *late summer (end of August–beginning of September)*		
Property	Facilities	Price
5 .... apartment by the Old Port	bathroom kitchen **6** .... overlooking the sea air-conditioned bedroom	£60
Maisonette in the Old Town (West)	kitchen bathroom **7** .... currently out of order no cooker	**8** £ ....
9 .... in the Old Town	kitchenette bathroom with jacuzzi living-room **10** .... commanding an excellent view of the city	£75

Section 2   Questions 11–20

Questions 11–14

*Answer the questions in **TWO WORDS ONLY AND/OR A NUMBER**.*

11   What time does the museum close today?

12   Until what time can visitors still enter the museum?

13   Where can visitors find questionnaires?

14   How does the museum guide describe the museum's architecture?

Questions 15–20

Complete the sentences below.

*Write **ONE WORD ONLY** for each answer.*

15   The museum has a big room with headgear from .... in the 1900s.

16   Part of the museum is closed to the public due to a recent ....

17   The .... room is currently being restored.

18   Most of the museum's original hats are kept behind ....

19   .... photography is not allowed in the museum.

20   While entrance to the museum is free, ... are welcome.

🎧 **Practice Test 5, Track 19**

Section 3   Questions 21–30

Question 21

*Choose the correct letter, **A, B** or **C**.*

21 Why did Agnieszka choose to survey people from two countries?

    A It was difficult to find participants from other countries.

    B She considered Poland an adequate representative of Europe.

    C It made it easier to analyse the data.

Question 22

Which graph shows the response rate in Agnieszka's survey?

A

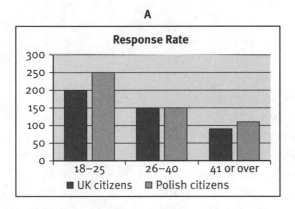

B

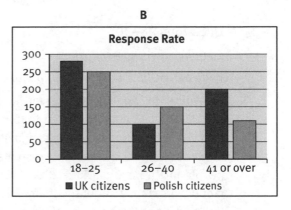

C

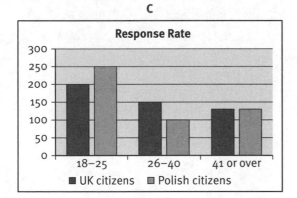

D

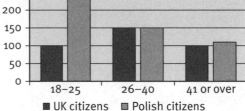

Questions 23–24

*Choose the correct letter, **A**, **B** or **C**.*

23 What percentage of British people surveyed thought immigration had a negative impact?

    A   59

    B   15

    C   23

24 Why didn't Agnieszka divide the 41 and over group into smaller categories?

    A   She neglected to ask people to write their precise age on the form.

    B   There were only negligible differences between the smaller categories.

    C   It didn't occur to her that she could.

Questions 25–30

Complete the summary below.

*Write **NO MORE THAN TWO WORDS** for each answer.*

According to Agnieszka's research, younger people believe that immigrants have **25** .... London and helped to turn it into a **26** .... People in other age groups concurred, but thought some immigrants might find it difficult to get used to **27** .... Unemployment and crime were also mentioned, as well as the impact the arrival of new people might have on **28** .... On the other hand, many people in the 25-40 age group were happy about the many **29** .... that have started due to immigration, as well as the positive effect immigration has had on the economy. Many of the participants in Agnieszka's research shared their **30** .... about immigration, four of which Agnieszka will read out in her presentation.

Section 4 Questions 31–40

Questions 31–40

Complete the table below.

*Write **NO MORE THAN TWO WORDS AND/OR A NUMBER** for each answer.*

LEFT-HANDEDNESS	
General Facts and Misconceptions	Left-handedness has been linked to **31** .... and the devil in the past. Attempts to suppress left-handedness can cause: bad handwriting, poor concentration, shyness, neuroticism, etc. Left-handed people have been a minority for **32** .... or more Contrary to popular belief, most left-handed people are not **33** .... (only about 30% of left-handers are). A common term for a left-handed person is **34** ....
Advantages	Left-handed people are better at **35** .... their (right-handed) opponents' moves in individual sports. Left-handed people get better more quickly when ill because they often train **36** .... of their brain equally. While not necessarily more creative, left-handed people are more adept at **37** ....
Disadvantages	Left-handed people have more issues with driving (except in countries like **38** .... where people drive on the left). Left-handedness has been linked to problems with writing and reading, as well as with social skills and **39** .... Left-handedness has also been linked to **40** .... such as schizophrenia.

ACADEMIC READING MODULE

Reading Passage 1 Questions 1–14

*You should spend about 20 minutes on **Questions 1–14**, which are based on Passage 1 below.*

Recently, nostalgia, or the act of looking wistfully back into our past, has become increasingly common. Our televisions bombard us with period dramas, set in 1950s America, Victorian England, or medieval Europe. Fashions in clothing look insistently backwards to the style of the 70s, the 80s and more recently, the 90s. Superhero movies based on characters created in comic books half a century ago are remembered and reimagined in our most recent films. Politicians make promises to take our country back to the good old days, and authors create novels through which we can relive the climate of our recent past. Strange as though it may seem, our obsession with looking into the past is increasing in persistence in our modern world.

Twenty years ago, if you described symptoms of nostalgia to a doctor, you would have been told that it's unhealthy to focus on the past. Indeed, though little research had been conducted on the neurological origins and effects of nostalgia, psychologists generally agreed that it was a mental disorder. In fact, in 1688, the term nostalgia was initially coined by Swiss medical student Johannes Hofer by combining the Greek words *nostos* (meaning homesickness) with *algos* (meaning pain). Hofer created the term to refer to the often debilitating homesickness Swiss mercenaries endured in foreign battlefields, and the 'disorder' was ascribed as a symptom, by various military physicians, to brain or ear damage caused by the clanging of cowbells. The symptoms of this nostalgia were described as fainting, fever, death—and, of course, a longing for Alpine landscapes.

Thankfully, nowadays we have a slightly better understanding of what nostalgia actually is, and why most of us will experience this phenomenon at some point in our lives. This is largely owing to the work of Constantine Sedikides, a psychology professor who, together with Dr Tim Wildschut, built a research programme at the University of Southampton in the UK in the late 1990s and early 2000s.

One of the first things Sedikides and Wildschut discovered was that the experience of nostalgia is fundamental to human existence and present among all major human civilisations. The researchers compared the effects of nostalgia on people living in 18 different countries from all five continents, and found that regardless of the location, nostalgia generally built empathy and a sense of social connection within society, and helped people who suffered from loneliness and isolation from the community. In an interview, Sedikides described nostalgia as the "perfect internal politician, connecting the past with the present, pointing optimistically to the future."

Sedikides's and Wildschut have since expanded their research of nostalgia into other areas of the phenomenon. They have found that nostalgia can affect the brain in different ways— and it may also be triggered by our environment in ways we might not expect. Bizarrely, we are more likely to become nostalgic in a cold room than a warm one; not only that, but nostalgia can also make us feel as if our environment is warmer than it actually is.

These scientific findings are supported by anecdotal evidence, too: when the findings were published, Wildschut was contacted by a concentration camp survivor who reported that one coping mechanism people used in the camps was remembering the good times of the past in an attempt to alter their perception of the present. 'It was not a solution,' the man said, 'but the temporary change in perception allowed you to persevere just a bit longer.'

Still, not all forms of nostalgia are helpful. In *The Future of Nostalgia*, Svetlana Boym, a novelist and Harvard University professor, divided nostalgia into two distinct types: reflective nostalgia and restorative nostalgia. Reflective nostalgia, according to Boym, focuses on 'longing and loss, the imperfect process of remembrance.' This type of nostalgia accepts that the past is irretrievably gone, giving the experiencer of this type of nostalgia a feeling of empathy and bittersweet consolation. Restorative nostalgia, on the other hand, 'proposes to rebuild the lost home and patch up the memory gaps.' The problem with this form of nostalgia, is that what it strives to produce is a meticulous recreation or resuscitation of the past, and this is, for better or worse, impossible. In addition, restorative nostalgia can manifest in sinister ways, such as with the 'national and nationalist revivals all over the world, which engage in the anti-modern mythmaking of history.' Boym makes reference to the tendency of some to glorify and idolise periods in the past, and to be inspired by this nostalgia to regress to an earlier, but by no means better, way of life.

Nevertheless, most experiences of nostalgia are positive, at least according to Sedikides and Wildschut. Elements of loss and trauma are often present, as can be expected, but these experiences are generally accompanied by feelings of redemption. What's more, in countries where nostalgia is more prevalent, people are more likely to volunteer, be free thinkers, and build strong bonds with their peers—and less likely to value money.

Questions 1–7

Complete the sentences below.

Write **NO MORE THAN TWO WORDS** for each answer.

1   Until recently, nostalgia was considered to be an ………….. habit.

2   The term 'nostalgia' was originally coined to explain the experiences of ………….. .

3   Seventeenth-century physicians believed nostalgia to be the result of injuries caused by ………….. .

4   Thanks to their worldwide research, Sedikides and Wildschut could confirm that nostalgia is a ………….. experience among all human societies.

5   According to Sedikides and Wildschut, a ………….. can prompt a bout of nostalgia.

6   Nostalgia was used as a ………….. in concentration camps.

7   Although nostalgia is usually ………….. , Svetlana Boym believes there are cases when it isn't.

Questions 8–13

Do the following statements agree with the information given in Reading Passage 1?

In boxes 8–13 on your answer sheet, write

> **TRUE**   *if the statement agrees with the information*
>
> **FALSE**   *if the statement contradicts the information*
>
> **NOT GIVEN**   *if there is no information on this*

8 Psychologists' claims that nostalgia is detrimental to one's health were empirically unsubstantiated.

9 There are reported cases of nostalgia from the 1600s that proved fatal.

10 Nostalgia has the ability to affect the way we perceive our environment.

11 Reflective nostalgia can hamper our ability to experience empathy.

12 Svetlana Boym found several nationalists who had experienced restorative nostalgia.

13 Nostalgic people are less likely to behave in an altruistic manner.

Question 14

*Choose the correct letter, **A, B, C** or **D**.*

14 Which is the best title for Reading Passage 1?

    A   The Causes of Nostalgia

    B   The Demerits of Nostalgia

    C   The Forms of Nostalgia

    D   The Power of Nostalgia

Reading Passage 2   Questions 15–28

*You should spend about 20 minutes on **Questions 15–28**, which are based on Passage 2 on the following pages.*

Questions 15–22

*Reading Passage 2 has seven paragraphs, **A–H**.*

Choose the summary of each paragraph from the list of headings below.

*Write the correct number, **i–x**, in boxes 15–22 on your answer sheet.*

	Headings
i	The difficulties involved in applying IP rights to groups rather than individuals
ii	The process used to create Taita Taveta baskets
iii	A brief history of IP, and a new application
iv	A call for change from the author
v	Two new divisions in IP rights
vi	An example of IP usage in South America
vii	A recent development in human rights
viii	The IP protection application process
ix	The results of a recent survey on Intellectual Property
x	What IP is, and how IP rights can help creators

15   Paragraph **A**

16   Paragraph **B**

17   Paragraph **C**

18   Paragraph **D**

19   Paragraph **E**

20   Paragraph **F**

21   Paragraph **G**

22   Paragraph **H**

Basket Weaving and Intellectual Property

More people than ever could benefit from claiming ownership for their intellectual property, but is this right equally accessible?

A   The right to a creator's ownership over the things they create may seem self-evident, but in reality this right has only been a law in recent history with the creation of intellectual property.

B   In its broadest definition, intellectual property (IP) is an ethical system that values human creativity and knowledge. IP refers to creations of the mind, such as inventions, or written and artistic works. In industrialised countries, writers, inventors and other people who create any intellectual goods have access to a legal identity and are able to benefit from IP rights. These benefits will often include recognition for their IP and the ability to earn money from their IP, if others wish to use or buy their IP.

C   Intellectual property has been considered a basic right of all people since the adoption of the Universal Declaration of Human Rights in 1948. The current IP system was developed alongside Western industrialisation and modern technological advances. Under IP law, patents, trademarks and copyright have been used by a wide range of people in a variety of different fields, from major commercial corporations to famous musicians. The use of IP contracts has largely been limited to the developed world; however, in recent years indigenous peoples and local communities in developing countries have demanded the same protection for traditional knowledge systems.

D   Traditional knowledge is developed and passed from generation to generation within a community. This living body of knowledge often contributes to the cultural or spiritual identity of these communities and is still in use. Traditional or cultural knowledge belonging to, say, an entire town or tribe, is not easily applied to current IP legislation, that usually caters to original work by specific individuals or companies.

E   Local communities hope to overcome these difficulties in order to gain two distinct types of IP protection: 'Defensive protection' aims to stop people outside the community from stealing and exploiting traditional knowledge. 'Positive protection' empowers communities to benefit commercially from their traditional knowledge and creations. There is a pressing need to convey the message that IP is both important and achievable for communities in developing countries.

F   In 2012, a focus group of Kenyan entrepreneurs was asked why they had not taken conclusive action towards registering their IP. The results showed that 42% of those polled did not understand IP, 38% said that the process of applying for and receiving the right to own their Intellectual Property was too expensive with no guarantees of return on investment, 14% stated that gaining an IP was not an immediate priority and 6% gave no reason. To combat these views, the World Intellectual Property Organisation (WIPO) hosted a training workshop for basket weavers in Kenya in February 2016. The exclusively female participants came from different basket-weaving groups in Taita Taveta County. Their baskets are laboriously crafted from the hand-twisted fibres of the sisal plant. The method has been passed down through generations of mothers and daughters.

G The process of creating these baskets has been refined over the generations. First, the women peel the sisal leaf with a wooden spatula to extract the fibres, which are then dyed using natural colouring extracted from local plants. They then twist the fibres and weave them into remarkably soft baskets that are resistant to colour fading. As the women weave in spare moments between farm work and housework, it can take anywhere from two weeks to two months to make a single basket. At the workshop, the participants started the process of a branding project focusing on their baskets. The different basket weaving groups came together to form an association, establish an identity and standardise the quality of their baskets. The women learned about the importance of the trademark system and welcomed the idea of having a collective mark to protect and promote their brand. The workshop participants were then able to share what they had learned in subsequent on-site training sessions in two villages.

H Everybody has the right to intellectual property over any knowledge which they have created or inherited, and the access to such a right can be tremendously beneficial to the owner. It is unfortunate that access to IP remains easier for some groups of people than others. The fact that the vast majority of Kenyan entrepreneurs polled either had not heard of IP or found it too expensive, suggests that there needs to be both an increase in awareness and a decrease in cost where IP agreements are concerned.

Questions 23–24

Answer the questions below with words taken from the passage.

Write **NO MORE THAN THREE WORDS** for each answer.

23 What do IP agreements value above all else?

24 As well as allowing creators to earn money, what else can IP agreements provide?

Questions 25–28

Complete the summary below.

Choose **NO MORE THAN TWO WORDS** from the passage for each answer.

The WIPO held an all-female **25** .... for basket weavers, in order to try to encourage more Kenyans to make use of IP rights. The partakers all created their baskets from **26** .... fibres, which are twisted and woven by hand. To make the baskets, the fibres are extracted with a **27** .... These are then dyed and twisted by hand, then woven in a process which can take up to **28** .... to create just one basket, though this is largely due to their lack of spare time.

Reading Passage 3   Questions 29–40

*You should spend about 20 minutes on **Questions 29–40**, which are based on Passage 3 below.*

The Superforecasters

The desire to see the future has defined humanity since the early days of civilisation, from the oracle at Delphi in ancient Greece and the sibyls of the Roman Empire to the siddhi of the Hindu religion. While we've known that predicting the future is impossible since at least the 18th century, psychic mediums and clairvoyants continue to abound today. The term 'superforecasters', or 'supers', might conjure up images of comic book heroes with inexplicable powers of clairvoyance, but there's nothing superhuman about this group of people—except, perhaps, their uncanny ability to predict global events with sometimes frightening accuracy.

The core concept, however, behind being a 'superforecaster' is not reading tea leaves or sensing someone's psychic energy. It's about having a deeper understanding of probability, and the uncertainty that comes attached to future events, especially those of a political nature. Think, for instance, of Britain's invasion of Iraq in 2003: how differently would history have played out had someone persuasively predicted that Iraq did *not*, as the intelligence community believed, possess weapons of mass destruction?

It was this exact question, interestingly, that triggered the establishment of a prediction tournament by the Intelligence Advanced Research Projects Activity (IARPA) in 2011, to determine whether our predictions of how uncertain future events will unfold could be enhanced. The initiative recruited five academic research teams with more than 25,000 forecasters, each tasked with predicting such things as Greece's future in the Eurozone, or Saudi Arabia's attitude towards OPEC production cuts. The leader of one of those research teams, the Good Judgment Project, was Philip Tetlock.

Tetlock, a professor of psychology at the Wharton School of Business who famously made the assertion (following another prediction tournament that ran from 1984 to 2004) that a chimp throwing darts at a board labelled with every possible outcome would predict as many future events correctly as the average political expert. Despite this view, Tetlock's team managed to outperform not only the competing teams, but also intelligence analysts with access to top-secret data. In fact, such was their performance that after two years, IARPA cancelled all its contracts with the other research teams to dedicate all of its resources to the Good Judgment Project's methods.

As it turns out, you need neither be a political connoisseur nor possess a Mensa-calibre IQ to be a good forecaster; all you need is a particular mindset, for which you can be trained. Through his research, Tetlock identified a series of traits common to all superforecasters; first and foremost was open-mindedness, i.e., the ability to cope with uncertainty and the ability to view problems from all sides. Learning how to overcome cognitive bias plays a huge role in open-mindedness: those new to prediction training, Tetlock says, have to be taught how to watch out for confirmation biases which can create false confidence, and 'understand the psychological factors' that could prevent them from seeing patterns in data which actually have no statistical basis. Isaiah Berlin's "The Hedgehog and the Fox" is an appropriate analogy: while most forecasters are hedgehogs, deeply invested in one narrative, superforecasters are foxes, more open to a wider range of experiences and less attached to a specific viewpoint or mental framework.

Another important trait common to superforecasters is self-awareness, and the ability to identify their own mistakes in the methods they use to make predictions. An example of such a possible mistake would be our natural tendency to zoom in rather than out, e.g. focusing on President Assad of Syria when attempting to predict how long he'll stay in power rather than examining past civil wars in the Middle East or the longevity of previous dictators. A superforecaster would be better able to identify when they're zooming in too much than an average forecaster.

Finally, and this is something that applies not only to the superforecasters, but also the organisations they belong to, is tracking. As Tetlock explains, while statistics can be useful, a better way to improve predictions is to 'systematically collect real-time accounts' of the ways in which you make predictions and judgments, all the while "keeping records of assumptions made, data used, experts consulted, external events, and so on." As logic dictates, if one method worked once, it might work again in the future.

Interestingly, the future of the Good Judgment Project itself remains to be seen. While many of the superforecasters are already taking advantage of their special skills to make a profit in fields such as consulting or strategic decision-making in the private sector, the team still hopes that governments will take notice and use their methods to improve the way they make decisions. But that's not all: given proper support, superforecasting might have the ability to change the way all of us go about our daily lives by teaching us how to identify and overcome our cognitive biases. Who knows? Perhaps in the future superforecasters will even put clairvoyants and psychic mediums out of business.

Questions 29–32

*Choose the correct letter, **A, B, C** or **D**.*

29 Britain's involvement in the Iraq war

    A led to the establishment of IARPA.

    B was predicted by superforecasters.

    C was caused by false information provided by intelligence officers.

    D is what caused the IARPA to start its forecasting contest.

30 Philip Tetlock

    A once mocked the prediction rate of political analysts.

    B participated in a prediction competition for twenty years.

    C has set out to dispprove the abilities of superforecasters.

    D asked IARPA for an exclusive contract.

31 One of the most common mistakes amongst prediction beginners is

    A   failing to identify patterns in the data.

    B   allowing their own preconceptions to affect their predictions.

    C   not being able to deal with uncertainty.

    D   having no confidence in their ability to predict accurately.

32 Superforecasters

    A   are content with their earnings in the private sector.

    B   hope their skills will help rid the world of fake clairvoyants.

    C   regularly track how they reached their correct predictions.

    D   desire to have an effect on how governments settle on plans of action.

Questions 33–36

Do the following statements agree with the information given in Reading Passage 3?

In boxes 33–36 on your answer sheet, write

    TRUE   *if the statement agrees with the information*

    FALSE   *if the statement contradicts the information*

    NOT GIVEN   *if there is no information on this*

33 The numbers of clairvoyants and psychics have diminished since the 18th century.

34 IARPA started its prediction tournament in 2011 because it wanted to see if forecasts could be improved.

35 Only a few superforecasters in Tetlock's team have an above-average IQ.

36 The majority of superforecasters have a preference in a particular school of thought.

Questions 37–40

Complete the sentences below.

*Write **ONE WORD ONLY** for each answer.*

37 The author describes the superforecasters' power of prediction as ………….. .

38 Philip Tetlock once likened the prediction skills of political experts to those of a ………….. .

39 ………….. knowledge is not required to become a superforecaster.

40 ………….. how you previously made accurate predictions can help to improve your prediction rate.

ACADEMIC WRITING MODULE

Task 1

You should spend about 20 minutes on this task.

The two tables below show the number of books borrowed per genre each week for two different libraries in 2016.

Summarise the information by selecting and reporting the main features, and make comparisons where relevant.

Write at least 150 words.

North London Library			
	January–April	*May–August*	*September–December*
General Fiction	25	27	34
Literary Fiction	12	10	10
Young Adult Fiction	43	60	58
Thriller/Horror	45	58	60
Science Fiction	5	1	6
Other	20	24	20

South London Library			
	January–April	*May–August*	*September–December*
General Fiction	12	13	30
Literary Fiction	3	3	3
Young Adult Fiction	10	11	12
Thriller/Horror	45	46	41
Science Fiction	15	20	23
Other	28	24	26

Task 2

You should spend about 40 minutes on this task.

Children as young as eight own a mobile phone nowadays. Do the advantages of this outweigh the disadvantages?

Give reasons for your answer and include any relevant examples from your own knowledge and experience.

Write at least 250 words.

SPEAKING MODULE

Time: 11–14 minutes

Part 1

Introduction to interview (4–5 minutes): The examiner will begin by introducing himself or herself and checking your identity. She or he will then ask you some questions about yourself based on everyday topics.

Let's talk about budgeting.

- Are you good at saving money? [Why?/Why not?]
- Do you ever think twice before buying something new? [Why?/Why not?]
- How important is it for you to save money? [Why?]
- How do you budget your money?
- Do you use cash or cards more? [Why?]

Part 2

Individual long turn (3–4 minutes): Candidates' task card instructions:

> **Task Card**
>
> *Please read the topic below carefully. You will be asked to talk about it for one to two minutes. You will have one minute to think about what you are going to say. You can make some notes to help you if you wish.*
>
> Describe a time you tried a new food. You should say:
>
> - What the food was
> - Where you tried it and why
> - Who you were with
>
> Also, explain whether you liked the food or not, and why.

The examiner may then ask you a couple of brief questions to wrap up this part of the test. Further questions:

- Would you recommend that dish to others?
- Do you like trying out new foods?
- Would you describe yourself as a picky eater?

Part 3

Two-way discussion (4–5 minutes): In Part 3, the examiner will ask you further questions related to the topic in Part 2.

Let's talk about cooking for a moment.

- What are the benefits of cooking your own food rather than eating out?
- In your opinion, why do so many people eat out rather than cooking their own meals?
- Do you think fast food should be banned?
- Do you have cooking classes at school in your country? If not, do you think you should?

Finally, let's talk about health.

- What is the healthcare system like in your country?
- Do you think healthcare should be free?
- Why do so many people have unhealthy habits? What can we do to improve this?
- Do you think people with unhealthy habits should be charged more for healthcare?
- Do you think pharmaceutical companies should be allowed to set their own prices, or should this be moderated by the government?

General Training Reading and Writing Test

GENERAL TRAINING READING MODULE

Section 1   Questions 1–14

*Read the text below and answer **Questions 1–7**.*

Group Packages

A   **Pottery Painting Package at Sunnyside Studios**

Unleash your inner artist at our clean and cosy pottery studio. Create your own personalised vases, dishes, keepsakes, and more! Perfect for gifts and making memories. Great for parties, families, couples and individuals. Book a party package now for only £50! Cost includes four blank pottery pieces of your choice, as well as snacks and soft drinks for four people. Reserve your space now and invite some friends!

B   **Hard Core Climbing Gym Private Lessons**

Have you ever wanted to try rock climbing? Looking for a full body workout that's fun and exciting? Join us for private lessons at our state-of-the-art climbing gym! At Hard Core Climbing, our instructors are all highly experienced climbers and trainers, certified by the National Association of Climbing Professionals. They will guide you through the process from start to finish. Book 10 lessons now for the price of 8! Only £160 for 10 lessons! Call or email us now to get started!

C   **Kidland Play Park**

Kids go bananas for our 800 sq. meter play paradise! Our play park includes a giant indoor playground with swings and slides, a ball pit, arcade games, minigolf, an obstacle course, and more! When you buy one of our weekend passes for £40 from now until 30 May, you'll receive a free weekday pass redeemable for the rest of the year. Adult admission is free every day! (Unaccompanied minors not permitted).

D   **Highland Creek Golf Club Special Offer**

Enjoy a round of golf at our world-class 18-hole golf course, ranked 67th in the top 100 golf courses worldwide! Book a day of golf and receive a golf cart and same-day replay at the Highland Creek Golf Club for 25% off! Players of all levels are welcome to spend a day on our world-class green. Enjoy drinks and a meal at our clubhouse before or after your game! (An initial 15-minute golf cart training course is required for all new members.)

E   EZ Photography Courses

Interested in perfecting your outdoor photography techniques, or simply need to know how to take a better selfie? At EZ Photography, our courses cover a wide range of photographic pursuits, including night shoots, product shoots, photojournalism, portrait photography, and more! Receive a free lesson when you sign up for 10 lessons, from now until 15 October. Don't have the right equipment? Don't worry—you can rent some from us at a flat rate of £20 per course. No matter what you need, we've got it. Book now and don't miss out on this special offer!

F   Priority Status

Have you ever walked by those closed-door VIP airport lounges and wondered: what goes on in there? You don't need to be a celebrity in order to experience the comfort and convenience of luxury travel facilities. Priority Status can get you through those doors and into VIP lounges at airports around the world. We offer three types of membership: Silver, Gold, and Platinum. For a limited time, get all the benefits of a Gold Membership for Silver Membership prices! That's 15% off an all access pass to Business Class level lounges at over 50 international airports. Don't wait—this offer is available for a limited time only!

G   Peter Pan the Musical

This classic tale invites you into a world of pixie dust and eternal childhood—now on stage at the Strathmore Playhouse. Featuring a live orchestra and guaranteed to enchant children and grownups alike! Gallery seating available for £15–£30 each, and a limited number of private boxes are also available for only £50. Get your tickets while they last and experience the magic and wonder of Neverland with the whole family!

Questions 1–7

*The text above has seven sections labelled **A**–**G**.*

*For **Questions 1–7** below, match the sections of the text with the information.*

Write your answer in boxes 1–7 on your answer sheet.

1   certified instructors

2   different levels of membership

3   a free pass covering Monday—Friday

4   details about a package offer for four individuals

5   possibilities for equipment rental

6   seating options

7   the necessity for initial training

*Read the text below and answer **Questions 8–14**.*

Gold and Han Eco-Friendly Workplace Policy

At Gold and Han LLC, we strive to maintain an eco-friendly workplace. If we all work together, we can create an environment we can be proud of. In keeping with our company philosophy of cooperation and sustainability, it is essential that all employees commit to helping conserve our environment to the best of our capabilities. In order to do so, all employees should abide by the standards laid out in the Gold and Han Eco-Friendly Workplace Policy:

1   Only use the copier or printer when absolutely necessary. Copying and printing unnecessarily use valuable paper, toner, electricity, and cause wear and tear to equipment. So please only print and copy essential documents and, if you must print, use the double-sided option whenever possible.

2   Please use appropriate recycling bins for all paper, plastic, and other recyclable waste. Paper recycling bins can be found next to all printers and copiers throughout the building. Other recycling bins are located in the break rooms and hallways on each floor. A list of acceptable items that can be recycled is posted on the wall of each break room. Please check this list carefully and remember to rinse out all liquid containers before depositing them in the appropriate bins.

3   "Ghost energy" is a significant drain on resources and money. Equipment that is not in use still consumes energy even when it is not on. In order to minimise the company's use of ghost energy, switched off plugs at the wall when not in use. Consult the attached list of equipment that must always remain plugged in and turned on, even when not in use.

4   Please always turn the lights off when a room or desk is not in use. Although all lightbulbs in the building have been switched to low-energy alternatives, it is essential that we refrain from wasting energy as much as possible by turning all lights off when leaving a room or stepping away from a desk. This also applies to common spaces and hallways.

5   Carpool or bike to work. All employees are encouraged to bike or drive together to work. Combining commutes significantly reduces gas and pollution and saves money as well. Biking to work is an excellent way to get exercise in an eco-friendly way. Employees can ask at reception for a discount voucher at Connelly's Bike Shop on Arthur Ave.

6   Please bring reusable water bottles and food containers to work. Paper and plastic cups at water coolers and in the breakroom will be discontinued throughout the building as of the end of the month. All employees are encouraged to provide their own reusable water bottles and food containers in order to reduce the amount of waste produced on company premises.

Questions 8–14

Do the following statements agree with the information given in the text?

In boxes 8–14 on your answer sheet, write

TRUE	*if the statement agrees with the information*
FALSE	*if the statement contradicts the information*
NOT GIVEN	*if there is no information on this*

8   Copying and printing depletes many different resources.

9   Employees should ask about what to recycle at work.

10   Employees should throw all items in the recycling bins immediately after use.

11   All equipment should be unplugged or turned off at the wall when not in use.

12   The building uses eco-friendly lightbulbs.

13   A carpool signup sheet is available for interested employees.

14   Disposable dishes will no longer be provided by the company.

Section 2   Questions 15–28

Questions 15–21

*The text on the following page has seven sections, **A–G**.*

Choose the correct heading for each section from the list of headings below.

*Write the correct number, **i–x**, in boxes 15–21 on your answer sheet.*

List of Headings	
i	Time specifications
ii	Dress code
iii	Working remotely abroad
iv	Health and safety of remote workers
v	Security and confidentiality
vi	Who can qualify to work remotely
vii	Code of Conduct
viii	Environmental practices for remote workers
ix	Creating a remote workspace
x	The purpose of this document

15   Section **A**

16   Section **B**

17   Section **C**

18   Section **D**

19   Section **E**

20   Section **F**

21   Section **G**

Company Remote Work Policy

A   At MegaCo, our remote work policy provides guidelines for employees who qualify to work from home or from a location outside our offices. It is important that our company and our employees understand this policy, so that everyone can benefit from this arrangement.

B   This policy is relevant for all full-time contracted employees who qualify to work remotely part time. Only employees who have worked for the company full-time for a minimum of 1 year can qualify. Employees must also show documented proof of his or her ability to adhere to deadlines. A history of exceptional employee evaluations is also necessary to qualify for this program. Finally, only employees who do work that can be accomplished off site can submit a remote work request.

C   Qualifying office-based employees will be permitted to work remotely up to 3 days a week or up to, but no more than, 12 days per calendar month. Remote workers cannot accrue overtime pay during the time they are working off site. Days that are not spent working remotely cannot be collected for use at a later time. All employees who participate in remote work must be reachable by phone and email during regular business hours.

D   Employees who work from home are encouraged to maintain a suitable working environment. The following are recommended:

- Choose a quiet working space free from distractions.
- Ensure that your internet connection is consistent and secure.
- Adhere to company policies about break times and attendance.
- Create a space that adheres to health and safety regulations.
- Ensure that you are able to devote your full attention to your duties during office hours.

E   When working from home, employees are free to wear whatever they find comfortable and appropriate. However, occasionally employees will be required to meet clients off site, even on days during which they are working remotely. In this case, employees are required to dress appropriately for a business meeting, just as they would if the meeting was being held in the office. Please refer to the company dress policy for specific details.

F   All correspondence must be handled through the company's secure server. Even when working off site, it is essential that all employees maintain company standards of discretion, data protection, and confidentiality. Please also ensure that your internet connection is password protected. Detailed guidelines can be obtained from the Human Resources Department.

G   All company employees, including both on site and remote workers, are obliged to protect the company from liability by adhering to all environmental, ethical, and safety regulations. These regulations are outlined in the company's code of conduct, which is reviewed and signed by all employees during the onboarding process. These rules apply to employees of the company whether or not they are working in the office. We expect all employees to uphold our company's standards at all times. Any questions about this policy should be addressed to the Human Resources Department.

Questions 22–28

*Read the text below and answer **Questions 22–28**.*

How to Conduct an Annual Employee Performance Review

Annual Employee Reviews are an essential practice that help managers and employees align expectations, analyse challenges, share ideas, and set goals for the future. Successful annual reviews help employees work to their full potential and help ensure that the both managers and employees are satisfied with their progress and able to thrive in the workplace. They also give workers the chance to address human resources concerns. The following article includes suggestions for helping managers ensure that their annual reviews are beneficial for everyone involved.

Ideally, all managers should meet with employees in January. Take this opportunity to share your annual goals and expectations with employees, so they have a concrete idea about how to proceed with their work during the rest of the year. This will also give you a documented account to refer back to when annual reviews occur at the end of the year.

Set goals for employees using the SMART (Specific, Measurable, Achievable, Results-oriented, Time-bound) framework. That way, both you and employees will be able to track their progress in a tangible way that you can also reference during the annual review. Make sure the goals for each individual employee also align with the goals of the company. Provide employees with a list of these goals, so they can refer to them throughout the year.

Annual reviews are successful only when the manager prepares feedback ahead of time. Rather than filling out the employee feedback form during the review itself, it is advisable to spend some time before the meeting considering the employee's performance and compiling your thoughts. Refer to the goals you set with employees at the beginning of the year. Preparing in advance will help you stay on track and avoid forgetting any essential points you may want to make.

A few weeks before annual reviews, ask your employees to write a self-evaluation. This will give them an opportunity to consolidate their thoughts ahead of time, as well as some time to consider their performance throughout the previous year. Ideal evaluation forms include questions that are open-ended. Try to avoid asking yes or no questions, and instead, encourage employees to express their thoughts and feelings about their own work.

Questions 22–28

Complete the sentences below.

*Choose **NO MORE THAN TWO WORDS AND/OR A NUMBER** from the text for each answer.*

Write your answers in boxes 22–28 on your answer sheet.

22   Annual reviews benefit both ....

23   Annual reviews give employees the opportunity to discuss .... issues they may have.

24   In January, managers should meet with employees in order to share with them their .... for the year.

25   Managers should provide employees with a .... of their goals.

26   If managers prepare their reviews .... , they will be more likely to stay focused during meetings with employees.

27   Before annual reviews, employees should complete a .... in order to prepare themselves for the meeting.

28   The best self-evaluation questions are ....

Section 3   Questions 29–40

*Read the text below and answer **Questions 29–40**.*

Pencils

Pencils have been used to make marks on paper since Roman times, when lead rods were used by scribes to write with. These were known at the time as a "peniculus", meaning "little tail". However, a great discovery of pure graphite made in farmers' fields at Borrowdale in 1564, the journey to the modern pencil began. The villagers went graphite crazy, putting graphite in and on everything, including using it to mark their sheep, and even adding it to their beers! When locals tried to use it like a lead pencil, they found that it was too soft, and needed a coating to hold it firm. Before wood, string was used, wrapped around the graphite and unwound as the pencil wore down. As time went on, it was found that wood casing was easier to use.

Graphite pencil "leads" today are not made of lead at all, but a blend of clay and graphite, with a range of pencils grades varying from soft to hard: the more clay used in the mix, the harder the pencil. Today, there are many pencil grades made in the industry, so that craftsmen can achieve a full spectrum of tones. Architects prefer to use harder pencils that produce a firmer line, while some artists prefer to use softer pencils that can be smudged more easily. Although pencil makers use the same scale to grade pencil leads, there is no basic standard. Most makers in Europe assign their pencils with H ("hardness") and B ("blackness") with a number to show how intense the hardness or blackness will be. For example, a 2B will be two times as black as a B. An 2H will be two times as hard/light as an H. Therefore, the HB is the middle of the scale, and produces the most average pencil line.

Pencils in England are usually painted red and black in stripes, or navy blue, while in China, pencils are painted yellow, which is the colour of royalty. This is because China is the biggest producer of graphite in the world, a fact they are very proud of. The Welsh author Roald Dahl wrote all his books using yellow pencils on yellow paper. He would keep six pencils ready and sharpened on his desk each morning. This is probably because his favourite colour was yellow, and he liked to be around yellow things. For example, his garden shed, which was his writing room, had a yellow door, and his armchair was also yellow.

But Roald Dahl isn't the only famous pencil fan. Thomas Edison, the American inventor credited with developing, among other things, sound recording and motion pictures, had his pencils custom made by the Eagle Pencil company. His ideal pencils contained a softer graphite than other models. They were also thicker than the standard sized pencils and only three inches long. Late night talk show host Johnny Carson humorously kept unusable pencils on his desk on the set of the Tonight Show. In order to avoid any accidents on set, these pencils were created with erasers on both sides. The American author Steinbeck preferred to write with pencils and is said to have used over 300 of the writing implements to compose his famous novel *East of Eden*.

There has lately been much discussion in the pencil industry around what kind of wood to use in pencil production. Traditionally, Chinese linden wood has been used, as this is a good solid grain, and can be chopped from forests on the borders with Russia without much regulation, because the environmental laws are more lax. However, given the emphasis on damage caused by the timber industry to the planet, manufacturers are looking to find sustainable materials. Materials such as incense cedar, a tree that grows much quicker, and that does not warp or splinter easily, meaning less waste, could have potential as a replacement. Some recycling plants are currently using pressurised recycled newspaper to create planet-friendly pencils.

Questions 29–35

*Choose the correct letter: **A, B, C** or **D**.*

Write your answers in boxes 29–35 on your answer sheet.

29 The earliest pencils were made of

  A lead

  B wood

  C coal

  D graphite

30 What was the initial problem with graphite?

  A It was too hard.

  B It was too expensive.

  C It was too soft.

  D It was too rare.

31 What is affected by the amount of clay in a pencil?

  A its darkness

  B its hardness

  C its strength

  D its durability

32 Which of the following is a characteristic of pencils produced in China?

  A They are soft.

  B They are used by royalty.

  C They are dark.

  D They are painted yellow.

33 Why did Roald Dahl use yellow pencils?

  A They matched his furniture.

  B They worked well with yellow paper.

  C They made him feel like royalty.

  D His favourite colour was yellow.

34 What was a distinct characteristic of Johnny Carson's pencils?

    A They were a unique size.

    B They were painted a special colour.

    C They could not be used to write with.

    D They were used as toys.

35 Why are pencil manufacturers interested in changing the materials used for making pencils?

    A to make them more environmentally sustainable

    B to make them cheaper

    C to make the environmental laws more lenient

    D to make them quicker to produce

Questions 36–40

Complete the sentences below.

*Choose **NO MORE THAN THREE WORDS AND/OR A NUMBER** from the text for each answer.*

Write your answers in boxes 36–40 on your answer sheet.

36 Alongside its use in pencils, graphite was once included as an ingredient in
....

37 The first casing for pencils were made from ....

38 European pencil manufacturers label pencils based on their ....

39 Chinese linden wood is commonly used by pencil makers because of the permissive .... in some parts of the country.

40 Some manufacturers are producing eco-friendly pencils out of ....

GENERAL TRAINING WRITING MODULE

Writing Task 1

You should spend about 20 minutes on this task.

> *You have returned from a holiday during which there were some serious problems with your accommodation.*
>
> *Write a letter to the hotel manager. In your letter*
>
> - *describe the accommodations you expected*
> - *say what the problems were*
> - *ask the manager to resolve the problem*

Write at least 150 words.

You do **NOT** need to write any addresses.

Begin your letter as follows:

Dear Sir/Madam,

Writing Task 2

You should spend about 40 minutes on this task.

Write about the following topic:

> *Some countries use closed circuit television (CCTV) to monitor public spaces in order to reduce crime. Some people consider this an invasion of privacy.*
>
> *Discuss both perspectives and give your own opinion.*
>
> *Give reasons for your answer and include any relevant examples from your own knowledge or experience.*

Write at least 250 words.

IELTS Practice Test 6

LISTENING MODULE

🎧 **Practice Test 6, Track 21**

Section 1   Questions 1–10

Questions 1–5

Complete the sentences below.

*Write **ONE WORD ONLY AND/OR A NUMBER** for each answer.*

1   The man was initially planning to take the ………….. service from Basingstoke to London Waterloo.

2   His final destination is Streatham ………….. .

3   The man would have to get to London Victoria by ………….. or cab from Waterloo station.

4   The man is planning to go to London on ………….. , 22nd March.

5   The man needs to be in Streatham before ………….. .

Questions 6–10

Complete the notes below.

*Write **NO MORE THAN THREE WORDS AND/OR A NUMBER** for each answer.*

Train Journey London—Ticket Information	
Train 1	
From:	*Basingstoke, 10.43.*
To:	*Clapham Junction, 6 …………. .*
Train 2	
From:	*Clapham Junction, 11.35*
To:	*Streatham, 11.45*
Ticket	Open Return (Can be used any day after 7pm within 60 days from 7 …………..)
Second Class	£ 31.00
Paid by 8 …………	
Name	9 ………….. Sheppard
Number	3320 1010 4665 1224
Expiry Date	October 10 …………..
Security Code	442

🎧 **Practice Test 6, Track 22**

Section 2   Questions 11–20

Questions 11–15

Complete the notes below.

*Write **ONE WORD ONLY AND/OR A NUMBER** for each answer.*

Virtual Tour: Jurassic Coast
Speaker: Paul Martens
Introduction to the Jurassic Coast The Jurassic Coast was the first **11** .... World Heritage site in England. The coast is roughly 96 miles long. The area is renowned for its **12** .... of sedimentary rock that formed up to 185 million years ago (Triassic, Jurassic and Cretaceous periods). Over the millennia, the Jurassic Coast has been: • arid plains, or a desert • a tropical sea where various **13** .... would have lived in the waters • an ancient forest full of unusual birds • a lush **14** .... , which would have been home to an assortment of reptiles and amphibians Landmarks of interest: Durdle Door—a natural **15** .... arch. Provides a great location for snorkeling. Lulworth Cove—the biggest tourist attraction in Dorset.

Questions 16–20

*Choose the correct letter **A, B** or **C**.*

16   25 million years ago

    A   a huge impact killed all the dinosaurs.

    B   folded rocks contributed to a collision of tectonic plates.

    C   mountains were created as a result of two tectonic plates colliding.

17   Durdle Door is unusual because

    A   its layer of limestone stands horizontally out of the sea.

    B   its view of the Alps.

    C   it has vertical layers of limestone.

18   The Jurassic Coast is unusual because of

    A   the quantity of fossils that can be found there.

    B   its vivid landscapes.

    C   the way the rocks are arranged.

19   The number of dinosaurs increased in the

    A   Triassic Desert.

    B   Jurassic Period.

    C   Crustaceous swamp.

20   Professor Rhoades is about to discuss

    A   the flowering plants in the Crustaceous swamps.

    B   hunting for fossils.

    C   the number of fossils on the Jurassic Coast.

🎧 **Practice Test 6, Track 23**

Section 3   Questions 21–30

Questions 21–30

Complete the form below.

*Write **NO MORE THAN TWO WORDS AND/OR A NUMBER** for each answer.*

STUDENT APPLICATION
Applicant: James Southgate
Interviewer: Matthew Forsyth
Relevant Information:
Impressive results in **21** ....
Sent letter with relevant information about the interview process;
Interview:
Discuss **22** .... and experience (45 Minutes)
Group Dynamics
Academic Background:
Degree in **23** .... with Media Studies
Graduated in 2005
Work Experience:
Experience as **24** .... at Wellington University
Taught a variety of subjects: EAL, History of Radio and TV, Writing for **25** ....
Also responsible for running workshops on **26** ....
English Language teacher in Argentina during his **27** ....
Notes:
Ability to thrive under pressure—had to improvise when teaching English language to **28** ....
History was his **29** .... at school.
Very passionate with impressive **30** ....

Practice Test 6, Track 24

Section 4   Questions 31–40

Questions 31–35

Answer the questions below.

*Write **NO MORE THAN THREE WORDS** for each answer.*

31   Other than being a teacher, what is Thomas Rugely's role on the course?

32   What does Thomas describe the first lesson as?

33   How long is the course?

34   What equipment is not considered appropriate for the course?

35   What can students download to improve their typing skills?

Questions 36–40

Complete the notes below.

*Write **NO MORE THAN THREE WORDS AND/OR A NUMBER** for each answer.*

CREATIVE WRITING FOR BEGINNERS	
COURSE INTRODUCTION	
Module 1	Character Development: The **36** .... of creative writing.
Module 2	Plot Development
Module 3	Points of View: working on **37** .... for writing in the first or third person.
Module 4	Description Strategies: Presenting the world of your story and its inhabitants.
Module 5	A revisit of the relationships between your characters.
HALF TERM BREAK	
Module 6	Dialogues: discussing and **38** .... basic techniques involved in writing interesting dialogues.
Module 7	Voices: How to arouse readers' curiosity through compelling voices.
Module 8	Setting: Creating a **39** .... rich in interaction, struggles and conflict.
Module 9	Beginnings: What to reveal and what to hint at.
Module 10	Open Endings: How to give readers a **40** .... without marking a definite end.
EXTENDED ASSIGNMENT	

ACADEMIC READING MODULE

Reading Passage 1   Questions 1–14

*You should spend about 20 minutes on **Questions 1–14**, which are based on Reading Passage 1 below.*

Gritting Britain's Roads

In winter, plunging temperatures combined with a notoriously high chance of rain cause chaos on Britain's roads. When rainwater freezes on the road surface it forms a layer of ice that is extremely treacherous to drive over. The Highway Code warns drivers that in rainy weather, stopping distances are twice the length they would be on dry roads. On ice, this stopping distance becomes ten times greater. Similarly, in heavy snow, most road vehicles struggle to grip adequately, making steering and braking less controlled, causing skidding and leading to many road accidents. In 2003, the 1980 Highways Act was amended to place a legal obligation on local councils to keep their roads clear.

The primary way that ice is prevented from forming on Britain's roads is through the use of what is commonly known as 'salt' or 'grit'. This brownish substance is dispersed along roads and motorways in cold weather by vehicles known as 'salt spreaders' or 'gritters', which are large trucks and lorries equipped with grit dispersing apparatus. Prior to the 1970s, these trucks would have dumped the grit into a pile in the middle of the road, which would then have been spread evenly across the tarmac by men. Now, however, grit trucks distribute the grit evenly on the road through the use of an impeller which is attached to a hydraulic drive.

As its names suggest, the 'grit' or 'salt' used on roads is made up of a mixture of crushed grit and rock salt. It is the rock salt which is the main active ingredient, the grit being there simply to aid traction and tyre grip on the asphalt. The rock salt works by dissolving into road surface water, lowering the freezing point and preventing ice forming. Rock salt can effectively prevent ice from forming at temperatures as low as −5°C, but its effectiveness drops off when temperatures decrease further. Any lower than −10°C and the rock salt has no effect at all. Not only that, the rock salt needs to be crushed by vehicle tyres into smaller particles to allow it to dissolve into the moisture on the road. It is this saline slush which prevents freezing, and stops snow from setting onto the roads.

The UK has two major rock salt mines, one in Cleveland, Country Antrim, and the other in Winsford, Cheshire; although in times of need, rock salt is also imported from the continent. Upwards of 30,000 tonnes of rock salt can be mined from the UK salt mines per week. In total, over 2 million tonnes of salt is used on Britain's roads every year, at a cost of some £150 million. Local councils now stockpile rock salt throughout the year in preparation for the freezing temperatures during the coldest months.

Councils install weather monitoring stations across their region, and also keep an eye on meteorology reports in order to be aware of future drops in temperature. The monitoring must be precise and detailed, because the timing of gritting is crucial. The main aim of gritting is to prevent freezing in order to prevent road accidents. The rock salt itself cannot melt snow or ice after it has formed, so it has to be spread before water freezes or snow falls. This means that if a stretch of road is gritted too early the road will still be dry, and the rock salt will just be blown away by air drafts from passing vehicles. If the road is gritted too late, snow, rain or hail may have already frozen onto the road, creating dangerous driving conditions. As the rock salt itself would still need to be crushed by tyres to allow it to dissolve, salting roads that are already too dangerous to drive on is significantly less effective at not only dissolving the ice already on the road, but also from preventing more ice from forming. Gritting late in the day can also lead to gritting machines getting caught up in rush hour traffic, delaying the vehicles and preventing them reaching all the routes they need to spread grit over. Not only this, the rock salt on the roads needs to be topped up throughout the day as it dilutes, decreasing its effectiveness. A London borough can use up to 85 tonnes of rock salt in a single day over the course of four or more gritting runs.

The US is experiencing a further issue caused by using grit on roads. In the states that typically experience colder weather, large amounts of rock salt are used each year in order to prevent the roads from becoming dangerously icy. Much of this salt is carried into the local environment, eventually finding its way into lakes, streams and rivers. Over the years, the saline (or salt) levels in these waters has increased, and continues to increase. Over all lakes in the US, the concentration of chloride ranges from 0.18 to 240 milligrams per litre. This is still quite low (seawater, for instance, contains around 35 grams of chloride per litre), but levels of salt are certainly rising. Biologists are concerned that if bodies of water continue to become saltier, freshwater fish and amphibians will steadily be replaced by saltwater animals, which could cause havoc to ecosystems.

In the UK, there is less knowledge concerning the effects of grit on our local wildlife. So far, no populations seem to have been directly affected by the increase in salt caused by gritting. Still, gritting remains an imperfect precaution against ice roads, though at the moment, it is the best solution to an impractical issue.

Questions 1–4

Complete the table below with words from the passage.

*Write **NO MORE THAN TWO WORDS** for each answer.*

ATTENTION: ROAD SAFETY

Please familiarise yourself with the following road safety precautions for icy weather:

- Ensure windows and mirrors are adequately defrosted to allow complete visibility before driving.
- Be aware that while driving on ice, normal stopping distances become **1** .... greater.
- In heavy snow, reduced ability to grip creates a lack of control on roads, which can lead to **2** .... , and an increased risk of collision.
- Make sure your roads are safe. local councils have a **3** .... to ensure their roads are free of ice and snow.
- Salt spreaders will prevent ice from forming by **4** .... grit on the roads.

Questions 5–14

Complete the sentences below.

*Choose **NO MORE THAN THREE WORDS** from the passage for each answer.*

5   Crushed grit is used in road salt in order to .... to prevent tyres from skidding.

6   Rock salt is totally ineffective at combating ice at temperatures below ....

7   Rock salt needs to .... in order to be effective. This generally happens when it is driven over by vehicle tyres.

8   When rock salt supplies in the UK are low, ... can provide further supplies.

9   More than .... of rock salt is used each year, costing local councils hundreds of millions.

10   .... can warn councils of impending drops in temperature, alongside the use of weather monitoring stations.

11   If a road is gritted too early, rock salt can be propelled off the road by .... from cars.

12   If a road is gritted after ice has already frozen onto the road, it's defrosting abilities are much ....

13   The amount of .... in America's lakes is rising, though at the moment it does not pose a serious risk to the environment.

14   Though gritting roads is the most common solution to icy roads in the UK, it can be described as an ....

Reading Passage 2   Questions 15–26

*You should spend about 20 minutes on **Questions 15–26**, which are based on Reading Passage 2 below.*

The Development of Photography

The British aristocrat William Henry Fox Talbot is an important figure in the history of photography. He is remembered today for his discovery in 1839 of the negative-positive process, inspired by the camera obscura, an ancient device used for amusement and as a drawing aid by artists.

The name *camera obscura* can be translated from Latin to mean 'dark room'; though this device is not the dark room process some readers may be able to recall as being used in photography production. A *camera obscura* is a device that makes use of a very dark room or object that has a very small hole for the viewer to look through, into a very bright scene. Through this process, objects seen scatter and reform by the law of optics, and appears upside-down to the viewer.

Henry Fox Talbot's desire to create a mechanism to photograph scenes and objects began during a visit to Lake Como in Italy, where he became frustrated with his inaccurate attempts to sketch the scene. Talbot discovered that, while exposing photographic paper to a very short light exposure would not immediately show an image, the image was there nevertheless. Talbot found that this image could be developed into a negative, and then fixed (in order to prevent further development) with the use of chemicals. From here, Talbot found that repeating the process of developing the photograph into a negative would allow him to print numerous positive photographs from the negative sample.

Though today, most people think only of Talbot when considering the birth of photography, what is less well known is that there were a number of photographic processes developed by different people in the first half of the 19th century, each competing with Talbot's. It is now widely accepted that the first photograph was created, not by Talbot, but by a French inventor named Nicéphore Niépce, of the view outside his window in the late 1820s.

Niépce had been developing a new way to copy engravings, but he soon realised the possibilities that light sensitive printing could hold in its own right. Unfortunately he died in 1833, leaving his younger partner Louis Daguerre to continue his work. It was in fact Daguerre, rather than Talbot, who created the first commercially successful form of photography, named the daguerreotype. This method, using a camera to create a unique, one-off image on a thin sheet of metal, caused a storm of publicity in France and made Daguerre into a wealthy celebrity. The daguerreotype was reliable and relatively cheap to produce, and by 1850 it was the most widespread form of photography, found all across the globe.

Talbot, on the other hand, found it much more difficult to profit from his invention in its early years. At first it seemed as though his negative-positive method, also known as the calotype, was superior to Daguerre's, because instead of creating a single image, it produced a paper negative from which unlimited positive copies could be made. But Talbot was unable to bring his own invention up to the technical quality of his main rival—while daguerreotypes never faded, calotype pictures were known to lose their definition very quickly. In 1846, for example, Talbot arranged for over 7,000 of his photographs to be distributed with a popular arts magazine, only for almost every single print to go completely blank, causing huge public embarrassment for Talbot, along with financial difficulties.

However, by the 1870s daguerreotypes had fallen out of favour, as a number of younger inventors refined Talbot's method, making it easier, cheaper and more reliable. As daguerreotypes sank into obscurity, the principles established by Talbot became the standard, making photography a medium uniquely suited to mass distribution, driving its use throughout the 20th century, right up until the digital era.

Questions 15–18

Answer the questions below.

*Write **NO MORE THAN TWO WORDS** from the passage for each answer.*

15   What inspired William Henry Fox Talbot's photographic discovery?

16   How do images appear when observed through a *camera obscura*?

17   Describe William Henry Fox Talbot's illustrations.

18   How many photographs could be produced from a single negative using Talbot's negative-positive process?

Questions 19–26

Complete the summary below.

*Choose **ONE WORD ONLY** from the passage for each answer.*

Write your answers in boxes 19–26 on your answer sheet.

Aside from Talbot's discovery, there were many other **19** .... processes created in the 1800s. Nicéphore Niépce may not be very well known, but it is generally believed that he produced the **20** .... photograph. Niépce had originally been interested in making copies of engravings, which led him to discover the ability to use light sensitive printing. After his death, his work was taken up by his partner, who provided a **21** .... fruitful method of producing photographs prior to Talbot's discovery. Niépce's partner named this method the **22** .... This form of photography was inexpensive to produce, as well as being **23** .... Unfortunately, Talbot's negative-positive process, or **24** .... was not as successful. The quality of photographs produced by Talbot's method was not as good as the rival method, though it was **25** .... in it's ability to produce multiple copies from one negative. Eventually, helped along by the improvements made by other inventors in the field, Talbot's method became the **26** .... in the development of photographs, on which has only recently fallen out of usage.

Reading Passage 3   Questions 27–40

*You should spend about 20 minutes on **Questions 27–40**, which are based on Reading Passage 3 below.*

The Everlasting Storm

Lake Maracaibo and its lightning

The area in north-west Venezuela where the Catatumbo river meets Lake Maracaibo is not simply noteworthy for its natural beauty, but also for one of nature's most spectacular phenomena: the Beacon of Maracaibo.

Lake Maracaibo has the highest incidence rate of lightning strikes on Earth. The area where the Catatumbo river meets the lake attracts an average of 28 lightning strikes per minute, which is about 1.2 million lightning flashes in a year. 'The Never-Ending Storm of Catatumbo', as the lighting in the area is sometimes called, was once used by explorers in the Caribbean as a reference point to help them navigate during the night, due to frequency of the lightning. The area has recently been declared by NASA to be the lightning capital of the world, and has even earned a place in the 2005 edition of the Guinness Book of World Records for the highest concentration of lightning, with an average of 250 lightning bolts per square metre each year.

A study conducted by the National Oceanic and Atmosphereic Administration calculates that the odds of being struck by lightning once in your lifetime for people living in the United States are 1 in 12,000. In the areas surrounding Lake Maracaibo, 1 to 3 people are struck by lightning every year.

How exactly is this phenomenon produced? For hundreds of years, travellers have been captivated by these incredible light shows from 'Maracaibo's Lighthouse', which can last as long as 10 hours through a period of, on average, 297 days each year. Indigenous tribes once believed that the lightning storms were triggered by encounters between fireflies and ancestral evil spirits that were believed to have inhabited the area—the lights produced by the lightning showed the efforts of a fight between good and evil. Such tales are still popular today, commonly fed by the low, seemingly absent thunder which accompanies the lightning and the spectacular colours produced in the sky by the illuminating effects of the lightning.

In addition to the numerous indigenous folk tales, however, many modern theories have also attempted to explain the reason behind the everlasting storm. One of the most popular of these is that vast uranium deposits present in the bedrock surrounding the lake are responsible for attracting the lightning. Another popular idea is that the large number of oil fields in the region release methane in the atmosphere increasing the conductivity of the air above the lake. There is also the theory that humidity plays an important role in the lightning activity since the longest hiatus between events happened during Venezuela's severe drought in 2010.

However, Dr Cybil from Caracas University has asserted that none of these theories are correct. To counter them, she has put forth a theory of her own to explain the large amount of lightning present in the area. In her view: 'The area is surrounded by the Andes with its high mountains trapping the warm winds coming from the Caribbean Sea. When this hot moist air meets with the cooler air from the Andes, it is forced upwards. This is when large amounts of vapour begin to condense, forming clouds that discharge electricity in the form of lightning bolts. The old tales of fireflies fighting ancient evil spirits is a much appreciated aspect of the local folklore, but they're just stories.'

The myth of silent lightning storms in Lake Maracaibo is also easily discredited by scientists and some of the local sceptics. Dr Cybil explains that people believe the storms are silent due to the sluggish speed of sound compared to the speed of light. The scientist says that the lightning storms do not happen near the shore of South America's largest lake, but about 40–70 miles far from the observers, and this is why thunder cannot be heard: 'It is practically impossible to hear thunder if you are 15 miles or more from the spot where lightning is striking.'

The flashes appear in a wide variety of colours ranging from blues and purples to reds and oranges. Dr Cybil attributes the colour change to the presence of dust particles: 'As white light passes through varying amounts of dust particles and moisture, it gets absorbed or diffracted making it appear as different colours.'

Though the colourful lightning shows are not caused by magical battles between fireflies and mythical sprites, the Maracaibo lightning storms remain one of the most remarkable, natural phenomenon on the planet.

Questions 27–36

Do the following statements agree with information given in Reading Passage 3?

In boxes 27–36 on your answer sheet, write

TRUE	*if the statement agrees with the information*
FALSE	*if the statement contradicts the information*
NOT GIVEN	*if there is no information on this*

27   Lake Maracaibo is situated on the north coast of Venezuela.

28   More than one million lightning bolts strike the area every year.

29   Venezuelans are proud of their inclusion in the 2005 edition of Guinness World Book of Records.

30   The odds of being struck by lightning in the areas surrounding Lake Maracaibo are 1 in 3.

31   Many people find the lightning storms fascinating.

32   The disproved stories of native people remain prevalent.

33   The number of storms in 2010 was below average.

34   Dr Cybil believes that the varying temperatures in the surrounding atmosphere impact the amount of lightning produced around Lake Maracaibo.

35   The lightning storms occur close to the edge of Lake Maracaibo.

36   Some believe that dust particles are responsible for the high number of lightning flashes in the area.

Questions 37–40

Complete the sentences below.

*Choose **NO MORE THAN TWO WORDS** from the passage for each answer.*

37   Every .... Lake Maracaibo gets hit by about 28 lightning bolts.

38   A scientist from .... believes that topography and wind patterns are the main causes of the phenomenon.

39   Thunder is very unlikely to be heard from distances above ....

40   A process of .... diffraction makes lighting flashes appear in different colours.

ACADEMIC WRITING MODULE

Writing Task 1

You should spend about 20 minutes on this task.

The table below contains information on meat consumption in four different countries in 2015.

Summarise the information by reporting some of the main features, and making comparisons where relevant.

Write at least 150 words.

Meat consumption in kilograms per capita, 2015

Country	Beef	Pork	Poultry	Lamb
South Korea	9.6	28.4	14.2	0.2
Paraguay	25.6	21	6	1.3
South Africa	10.7	3.4	30.6	3.1
Turkey	8.3	0	16.5	4.1

Writing Task 2

You should spend about 40 minutes on this task.

Write about the following topic:

It is generally believed that talent is something you are born with. Some say it might even be genetic. However, there are those who claim that talent is a combination of exposure to a good teacher and practice.

Discuss both these views and give your own opinion.

Give reasons for your answers and include any relevant examples from your own experience.

Write at least 250 words.

SPEAKING MODULE

Part 1

Introduction to the interview (4–5 minutes): The examiner will begin by introducing himself or herself and checking your identity. She or he will then ask you some questions about yourself based on everyday topics.

Let's talk about commuting in your country.

- How do you usually travel to work/school? [Why?]
- Have you always travelled to work/school in the same way?
- Do you like travelling to work/school this way? [Why/Why not?]
- Would you like to change the way you travel to work/school in the future? [How and why?]

Part 2

Individual long turn (3–4 minutes): Candidates' task card instructions:

Task Card

Please read the topic below carefully. You will be asked to talk about it for one to two minutes. You will have one minute to make some notes and think about what you are going to say. You can make some notes if you wish.

Describe a competition or contest that you took part in. You should say:

- What kind of event it was
- Where it was and how you found out about it
- What exactly you had to do to win
- What winner received
- How you did

Also, explain the main reasons why you chose to participate.

Part 3

Two-way discussion (4–5 minutes): In Part 3, the examiner will ask you further questions related to the topic in Part 2.

Let's talk about competition at work.

- Do you think it is a good thing that some companies give prizes or bonuses to employees who do well at work? [Why/Why not?]
- Would you say that a competitive work environment can become too aggressive at times?
- What about the job market? Do you think it has become more or less competitive?

Finally, let's discuss competition in schools.

- How do you feel about teachers using competitions to motivate students in class?
- Do you think that schools should encourage children to compete against each other? [Why/Why not?]
- There's also a lot of competition among parents. How do you think that might affect children?

General Training Reading and Writing Test

GENERAL TRAINING READING MODULE

Section 1   Questions 1–14

*Read the texts below and answer **Questions 1–6**.*

A. Receive free pack of luxury cartridge envelopes with every purchase of stamps.

Coupon cannot be used in conjunction with any other offer. No more than 1 pack of C5 envelopes per purchase.

B. SAVE 1/3 ON OWN BRAND DAIRY

Savings can be applied to up to 5 dairy items at checkout. Coupon covers all Wassen ranges with the exception of essentials. Valid until 01/01/20.

C. SPEND £10 at Tommy's when you refer a friend

£10 gift voucher redeemable online only, following your friend's first purchase. Visit www.tommys.com for terms and conditions.

D. £5 off when you spend £20 in store or online!

To use in store, simply hand coupon to cashier. To use online, use code SHOP20 at checkout.

E. Buy 2 get 1 free on FreeMilk chocolate products.

In store only. Offer is limited to 250g bars of chocolate and indulgence range. Expires 22/11/19.

Questions 1–6

Match the options above with the information in the sentences below.

*Write the correct letter, **A–E**, in boxes 1–6 on your answer sheet. You can use each letter more than once.*

1   This coupon can be applied to more than one item.

2   This coupon expires in November.

3   Using this coupon provides a free edible item.

4   This coupon must be used alone.

5   This coupon can be used via the website or in the shop.

6   This coupon is activated when others spend money.

*Read the text below and answer **Questions 7–14**.*

Operating Instructions for Your Droodle French Door Fridge Freezer

Changing the Water Filter

The 'water filter indicator' light will notify you when it is time to change your water filter. The light can be located inside the left door of your fridge, directly behind the ice dispenser. When the light is a constant red colour, you will need to change your water filter. To help you prepare to change your filter, the water filter indicator light will begin by flashing periodically. For best results, change your water filter at the earliest opportunity, to ensure a constant supply of fresh, clean, filtered water.

Follow the steps below to change your water filter.

1. Locate water filter replacement. On purchase of this fridge, you were supplied with 4 water filter cartridges, which should last you a total of 2 years. Once all cartridges have been used, you can purchase more from www.droodleappliances.com/ filtration, or a registered Droodle supplier. Make sure to check the model number of your fridge to purchase an appropriate filter, as some fridges require different filters. DO NOT attempt to replace the water filter with a generic water filter. Using anything other than an official Droodle water filter will void your warranty.

2. Be aware that each water filter will last around 6 months. You may find it helpful to label your water filter with a date 6 months in the future, to help you to remember when you will need to change your water filter.

3. Locate the existing water filter, this can be found directly beneath the ice generator at the top right of your freezer. Remove the existing filter by snapping off the lid of the filter canister, then lift the existing filter out of the canister.

4. Discard the used filter, and remove the plastic film on the bottom of your new filter (if your new filter is not covered, DO NOT USE and contact your supplier for a replacement). Place the new filter in the canister, making sure the arrows on the sides of the filter are pointing upright. Snap the lid back onto the canister to lock it into position.

5. Close the door of the freezer, and press and hold the ice and water buttons for 10 seconds, to reset the filter schedule.

6. Fill and discard two to five large glassfuls of water, as many as needed until the water runs clear.

If you experience any issues with your water filter replacement, you can contact our service team at helpdesk@droodle.com.

Questions 7–11

Complete the sentences below.

*Choose **NO MORE THAN TWO WORDS AND/OR A NUMBER** from the text for each answer.*

7 Customers will need to buy new water filters .... after buying their fridge.

8 Using a .... filter will void the warranty on the fridge.

9 Put a date .... in advance on your replacement filter, to help you to remember when to remove it.

10 You should contact the supplier if your water filter is missing its ....

11 .... will help you to place the water filter into the canister the right way around.

Questions 12–14

*Complete each sentence with the correct ending, **A–E**, below.*

*Write the correct letter, **A–E**, in boxes 12–14 on your answer sheet.*

12 Snap the lid open

13 Press the buttons on the front of the fridge

14 Once the filter is changed, do not drink the water

A	to take the old canister out.
B	until the water runs clear.
C	to restart the programme for the new filter.
D	before taking the old canister out of the fridge.
E	to make sure the filter has expired.

Section 2   Questions 15–28

*Read the text of text below and answer **Questions 15–21**.*

DRD Compassionate Leave Policy

Introduction

DRD recognises that life-threatening illness and death of a loved one can have an emotional and logistical impact on an employee's ability to work. Employees have a right to be provided with adequate time to grieve and make arrangements in the event of serious illness and/or death of loved ones. Our policy was created with the interests of employees and our companies in mind, and is fully compliant with UK laws and regulations.

Policy for Compassionate Leave

Full-time employees are entitled to take up to 3 days of paid leave (more than the minimum legal requirement) following the death of an immediate family member (this is defined as a parent, grandparent, child or significant other). Leave for death or illness of other family members and close friends may be granted upon consideration. This leave should provide adequate time to make funeral arrangements and have time to grieve. Occasionally, employees may be entitled to longer periods of leave. Any compassionate leave provided after the first 3 days will be unpaid.

Employees must notify the company of compassionate leave as early as possible. Employees must also inform the company of the duration, or expected duration, of compassionate leave to be taken.

Compassionate leave can also be taken in the event of life-threatening illness of a dependant. Dependants include: parents, grandparents, children, spouses and those who depend on you for their primary care.

To formally request compassionate leave, you must email your line manager or supervisor and copy in a member of the HR team.

Questions 15–19

Do the following statements agree with the information in the above text?

In boxes 1–5 on your answer sheet, write

TRUE	*if the statement agrees with the information*
FALSE	*if the statement contradicts the information*
NOT GIVEN	*if there is no information on this*

15 The company allows employees paid leave in the event of the death of a close family member.

16 Compassionate leave can be granted for the death of a brother.

17 Employees dealing with the death of a spouse are permitted to take 5 days of leave.

18   Employees who need to plan a funeral for a deceased family member are permitted to take paid leave for longer than 3 days.

19   A parent who is receiving medical treatment at a hospital overseas is classed as a dependant.

Questions 20–21

*Choose the correct letter, **A**, **B**, **C** or **D**.*

Write the correct letter in boxes 20–21 on your answer sheet.

20   The document outlines

    A   how to grieve the death of a loved one.

    B   the laws in a country about compassionate leave.

    C   the process for requesting annual leave in advance for a holiday.

    D   the policy on compassionate leave within a company.

21   The writer suggests that the fourth day of compassionate leave

    A   is not likely to be granted.

    B   will not be paid.

    C   is the maximum amount of time that can be requested after a death.

    D   will result in the loss of annual holiday leave.

*Read the text below and answer **Questions 22–28**.*

Edmonds and Partners Eye Care Scheme for Employees

Our law firm is happy to announce our new eye care policy, which entitles some of our employees to free eyewear and tests.

All employees who use a Computer Monitor Screen (CMS) for 5 hours or more per day are entitled to a free eye test and/or sight test by an optician. Based on the results of this eye test, Edmonds and Partners will also contribute to lenses or spectacles for CMS users, to correct vision and eye issues apparent when using CMSs.

Edmonds and Partners will contribute the value of the basic appliance for lenses or spectacles. If employees would like to purchase a more costly appliance, they will need to pay the additional cost incurred. If eye problems persist with CMS using employees, Edmonds and Partners are willing to consider reasonable requests for further eye tests.

Edmonds and partners will contribute the following amounts for eye care:

- Up to £25* per eye test
- Up to £75* per spectacles or lenses purchased

To be eligible for the above scheme, employees must first complete the Eye Care Scheme Form, and have it signed by both a partner of this firm and an optician. To claim money back after your eye test or purchase of spectacles, please complete an invoice and submit to the finance team with approval from your line manager.

---

* If the total cost is lower than this amount, employees will be compensated for the total fee.

Questions 22–25

Complete the summary below.

*Choose **ONE WORD AND/OR A NUMBER** from the passage for each answer.*

Write your answers in boxes 22–25 on your answer sheet.

Eye Care Scheme

Employees must fill out a **22** .... , which should be signed by a senior member of staff and an optician.

Employees can then book an eye test. The firm will pay up to **23** .... to cover this cost.

If the eye test shows that employees require spectacles to be worn while using a computer screen, employees can also claim a contribution towards the glasses from the firm. If the glasses cost more than the maximum contribution, they will need to pay all **24** .... amounts.

To receive compensation for eye care and spectacles, employees must finally send an **25** .... to the finance department.

Questions 26–28

Look at the following statements (Questions 26–28) and the groups of individuals below.

*Match each statement with the correct group, **A, B** or **C**.*

*Write the correct letter, **A, B** or **C**, in boxes 26–28 on your answer sheet.*

26   These individuals may receive more than one eye test for free.

27   These individuals will determine whether lenses are required.

28   These individuals will pay the total cost of a £15 eye test.

A	employees
B	employers
C	opticians

Section 3   Questions 29–40

*Read the text below and answer **Questions 29–40**.*

Paparazzi

A   The term *paparazzi* was reportedly coined by the Italian film director Federico Fellini as an onomatopoeic reference to the sound of a camera shutter operating. In Italian, the word means 'those who pap.' The paparazzi are traditionally understood to have arisen in Rome in the late fifties; they were originally itinerant photographers who would sell images to tourists. However, as Rome, and especially the cafes of the famous Via Veneto, became a hangout for globally famous Hollywood celebrities in the summer of 1958, these photographers realised they could earn much more money by photographing the stars and selling these images to the international press.

B   Paparazzi are not artists, the pictures they take are not intended to be evocative or beautiful, but simply to document where a famous person is, who they are with, and what they are doing, wearing or eating. As such, paparazzi are classified as a form of journalists. Historically, females have been more commonly targeted, both as the subject of and the audience for paparazzi images.

C   Though the actual term first arose in the post-war era, many identify photographer Erich Salomon, active in the twenties and thirties, as the first paparazzo. Salomon became a famous figure in high society and in the media for his secret photography of legally or politically sensitive events. Salomon seemed an unlikely figure to become a photographer, having first picked up a camera in the late twenties at the age of forty-one. He experimented with hiding a camera in his bowler hat, with a small hole cut out for the lens, and succeeded in snapping a photograph of a police killer on trial in Berlin. Thus began a journalistic career in which Salomon managed to photograph, among other things, the signing of the Kellogg-Briand Pact, an huge international treaty. He also became one of the only individuals to capture images inside the US Supreme Court.

D   Technological advances have historically enabled paparazzi. Salomon was able to carry out his work in the twenties because of the recent development of smaller cameras and sensitive film, while the paparazzi of the fifties took advantage of powerful electric flashes and telephoto lenses to get their shots from unwitting subjects. In more recent decades, powerful telephoto lenses have led to scandals in which celebrities and royalty are photographed without their consent from over a kilometre away. The price of such photos is reported to have reached up to a million pounds.

E   These days, nearly everyone carries a pretty good quality camera around in their pockets, in the form of their smartphone. The rise in handheld phone and camera technology means that even the general public can 'pap' celebrities. Some individuals have even managed to make money from their amateur photographs, by selling images of celebrities to newspapers and gossip magazines for a small fee.

F In a more sinister development, some British newspapers and publications came under fire in recent years for using phone hacking technology to extract personal images from famous and important people's phones, and publishing these images to the public. Unlike the photographs obtained by the paparazzi, such phone-hacking actions are illegal, and the journalists who resort to such methods face imprisonment.

G Today many newspapers, in response to complaints by unwilling photographic subjects, have largely rejected the use of paparazzi photographs. At the same time, a number of celebrities have successfully resorted to court orders to ban paparazzi from gathering outside their homes, and been awarded damages in response to particularly egregious invasions of their privacy. Perhaps these moves are a sign that the age of the paparazzo is finally coming to an end. With the rise of social media platforms being used by celebrities to share their personal lives with fans directly, celebrities have been given a greater control over what to share and what to keep private in their lives. However, it is likely that as long as the public appetite for salacious photographs of celebrities continues, paparazzi, along with other methods which expose the private lives of those in the public eye, will continue to exist.

Questions 29–35

*The text has seven paragraphs, **A–G**.*

Which paragraph contains the following information?

*Write the correct letter, **A–G**, in boxes 29–35 on your answer sheet.*

29 how non professionals can make money as a paparazzi

30 the origin of the term *paparazzi*

31 lengthening the distance at which paparazzi photos can be taken

32 a distinction between art and journalism

33 how famous people gained more control over their privacy

34 a description of the first paparazzo

35 illegal methods used to obtain photographs

Questions 36–40

*Complete the summary using the list of words, **A–H**, below.*

*Write the correct letter, **A–H**, in boxes 36–40 below.*

The name paparazzi is **36** .... in origin, as it sounds like the noise that was once made when taking a photograph. Although paparazzi originally photographed the scenery and architecture in Rome, they began to photograph famous people, as the cafés in the city centre became a common **37** .... for these people. Paparazzi found that selling their photographs to the **38** .... rather than the public to be much more lucrative.

As paparazzi have grown in number, so has the disapproval of the celebrities they photograph. In recent years, many celebrities have won **39** .... from paparazzi invading their privacy. Despite this, it is unlikely that the **40** ....for paparazzi photographs will be eliminated, as the rich and famous will always hold a fascination for people.

A	press	**B**	appetite
C	Greek	**D**	onomatopoeic
E	celebrities	**F**	damages
G	hangout	**H**	hunger

GENERAL TRAINING WRITING MODULE

Writing Task 1

You should spend about 20 minutes on this task.

You have just been offered a job at a different company than the one you currently work at.

Write a letter your current boss. In your letter

- *explain that you have been offered another job*
- *give your reasons for accepting this role*
- *say how much longer you will continue to work at the company for*

Write at least 150 words.

You do **NOT** need to write any addresses.

Begin your letter as follows:

Dear ... ,

Writing Task 2

You should spend about 40 minutes on this task.

Write about the following topic:

Some people believe it is wrong to eat animal products, while others believe that it is natural.

Discuss both perspectives and give your own opinion.

Give reasons for your answer and include any relevant examples from your own knowledge or experience.

Write at least 250 words.

Listening
Scripts

Practice Test 1, Section 1 (Track 1)

EMPLOYEE: Swing With Us, this is Martin speaking, how may I help?

CUSTOMER: Hi! I was given one of your brochures this morning and I'm calling to enquire about the classes you're planning to start in my area?

EMPLOYEE: Great, what would you like to know?

CUSTOMER: Well, I'd like to know a little bit about the timetables, the pricing, that sort of thing. I'm planning to take classes myself and I know my daughter and my son are interested, too.

EMPLOYEE: Right. Do you mind if I just take down your details first?

CUSTOMER: No, not at all. My name is Jane Schmilton, spelled S–C–H–M–I–L–T–O–N.

EMPLOYEE: Perfect. And could I get a phone number as well?

CUSTOMER: Would you like the landline or my mobile?

EMPLOYEE: Whatever you prefer. It's just a formality.

EMPLOYEE: Right, I'll give you my mobile, then. It's 0780 976 2942.

EMPLOYEE: Thank you. And could you tell me which school you're interested in attending?

CUSTOMER: Well, I live between Swiss Cottage and Finchley Road, and I see you've got two schools nearby, the Swiss Cottage one and one in Regent's Park. I think I'd prefer the second one because it's closer to my work.

EMPLOYEE: Right. Just to let you know, the classes in Regent's Park don't start until next month, whereas the classes in Swiss Cottage start next week.

CUSTOMER: Oh, right. Not Regent's Park, then. In that case, I'd rather start as soon as possible.

EMPLOYEE: Swiss Cottage, then. All right. We've got two courses starting next week, one for beginners on the 14th of February and one for intermediate level students on the 16th.

CUSTOMER: Ah, I've taken some classes before, but my children never have. Could you tell me a little bit more about both?

EMPLOYEE: Of course. So, all our classes are continuous enrolment, meaning that we don't actually have terms or anything like that: anyone can sign up any time they want. We do follow a programme of ten weeks for the beginners' class and eight for the intermediate, and when that's finished we start all over again from the beginning. We also have an advanced class which is starting in two weeks in your area, so when you finish the intermediate course you can move on to that if you feel ready for it.

CUSTOMER: Excellent. And how often are classes?

EMPLOYEE: Well, normally they're twice a week but these courses are for busy individuals so they're only <u>once a week</u>, for two hours each session.

CUSTOMER: Right. That's fine, I wouldn't be able to commit to more anyway, and my children have got some after school events this term as well, so that works out.

EMPLOYEE: Great.

CUSTOMER: And what about the prices?

EMPLOYEE: Well, these differ depending on how many lessons you book. As I said, we don't run terms so students pay by the class, but we do offer bulk discounts. Each individual lesson costs £10, but if you book the full ten weeks for your children, you'll only need to pay <u>£90</u>. Or, if you prefer, you could book five weeks instead and that will come to £45. The second time you book five weeks, however, the discount might not be available anymore so you might have to pay for the full amount.

CUSTOMER: Right. And is there a discount for the intermediate course?

EMPLOYEE: Yeah, it's pretty similar, so if you book five weeks it's the same as the beginners, but if you go for the full eight weeks it's going to be £70. Same for the advanced class.

CUSTOMER: Great. I think I'll go for that for myself, then. But I'm going to go just for the five weeks on the beginners course for my two children because I'm worried they might change their minds and I don't want to waste the money or the classes, you know?

EMPLOYEE: Yes, of course.

CUSTOMER: Just a few more questions.

EMPLOYEE: Go on.

CUSTOMER: Well, two questions. First of all, do I need to find my own dancing partner?

EMPLOYEE: Oh, no. We encourage students to bring a partner if they have one, but it's no problem if you don't. You don't need to worry about it, <u>having one is definitely not necessary</u>.

CUSTOMER: Phew! I tried to convince my husband once…

EMPLOYEE: Of course, I understand. And what was your second question?

CUSTOMER: Ah yes. What about equipment?

EMPLOYEE:	People like to dress up in 1920s style clothing when they come to class and that's absolutely fine—in fact, it makes the lesson more fun! However, we recommend that you don't wear shoes with high heels or anything like that. In general, we recommend wearing trainers, or anything that's <u>comfortable</u>, really. That's the most important thing. You can buy shoes at our shop as well, and we can order any pairs you like, too.
CUSTOMER:	Great. Nothing else then?
EMPLOYEE:	Just yourself and plenty of enthusiasm!
CUSTOMER:	Ha, I have heaps of that. Thank you very much. So, how do I book?
EMPLOYEE:	Well, you've got three options really. You can either leave us a deposit over the phone, or you could pop by and do the same—or you could go on our website and book as many weeks as you'd like. <u>The only thing with the website is that we charge the full amount rather than deposits there</u>.
CUSTOMER:	Right. I think I'll pop by after work, then. Thank you.
EMPLOYEE:	Thank you so much for calling. If you have any other questions, don't hesitate…

Practice Test 1, Section 2 (Track 2)

Good morning, everyone! Welcome to Lincoln Hall. My name is Jessica Kendall and I'm a student here at Woodgrange College. I'm also the administrative supervisor here at Lincoln Hall. As you probably already know, most of Woodgrange College's buildings serve both as lecture halls and accommodation, and Lincoln Hall is no exception. In your welcome pack, you will have found a map of the college, together with a map of Lincoln Hall, but just in case, let me quickly run you through the structure of the building.

As you can see, Lincoln Hall has five floors: Lower Ground, Ground Floor and floors One, Two and Three. We're on the Ground Floor at the moment, and behind us is the main entrance. If you have a look at your maps, you'll find that down the hall, past the stairs on the left-hand side, there are three consecutive lecture halls.

Here at Woodgrange College, we take pride in naming halls after notable alumni, which is why each of these halls has both a code name and a long name. The first hall, for example, is named after Andrew Green, a Woodgrange alum who got his PhD at the age of 24 and is now teaching at Yale in America—and the final hall, which is <u>right across the ground floor's toilets</u>, is named after Jessica Cage, who studied Creative Writing here and now works for a major UK network as a TV series creator. Sandwiched between these two halls is the only hall in the college reserved for Engineering students, which is why it's commonly referred to as the <u>engine room</u>.

If you turn to your right, you'll find a corridor which leads to two rooms: the café and the <u>dining hall</u>. There have been plans to knock down the café, which is the smaller of the two, and build a restaurant—but none of this has been implemented yet. Do go to the café and try the organic blueberry muffins: they're excellent.

Moving on down the hall, you'll see there are three more rooms opposite the lecture halls. The biggest one is our fourth and final lecture hall on this floor, which was originally known as the James Brown Hall, but which was recently renamed to <u>Sophie Brown</u>. Next, you'll find a small study room, which can be booked in advance by residents here through the college's website, and then, right before the corridor that leads to the garden area, there's a <u>private room for all faiths and religions</u> which is available at all times.

The garden area is where most of our students like to hang out, especially around the cloisters. Please be advised that you are not allowed to drink alcohol there, and that there should be no chatting or music in the garden after 10 pm, as <u>eight studio rooms are located in the easternmost and northernmost sides of the garden area</u>. You're welcome to have your lunch around the fountain, however.

And now that we've finished our tour of the hall, let's take a moment to discuss some of the most frequently asked questions by new students here at Woodgrange College. You might remember from your induction yesterday that there are all sorts of options and opportunities available for you not just to meet new people and socialise, but also to acquire practical skills which might prove useful to you later on in your careers.

A vast range of societies operate within Woodgrange College, such as the Creative Arts Society, the Reading Book Club Society, and even the Knitting Society. Most of these societies are independently organised by students, but they do report to the Student Union and are regulated by the College. There will be a society fair later this week and you'll have a chance to browse and sign up for the ones you'd like to join. You'll find a sign–up sheet in most tents, on which you'll need to write your email address. You'll then be emailed a link <u>which will direct you to a webpage where you'll need to fill in your details and pay a small joining fee.</u>

The student union can also assist you with identifying volunteering opportunities in the area. This is especially useful to those of you in quite competitive fields, such as marketing and media, or those who would like to work in the public sector, such as in criminal justice. We do get excellent feedback from students who have used our volunteering placement service, and there are some great opportunities out there for you. Just last month, for example, we began cooperating with a local business which is looking for students in the <u>PR sector</u>.

Another thing we do, and Lincoln Hall is particularly renowned for this, is organise and host many different socialising activities. During Welcome Week we have a cheese and wine night in the garden, and on our first weekend of each new school year, we organise a pub crawl around campus. <u>Every two weeks we have language exchange meet–ups</u> in the dining hall, and every three weeks we organise a trip to a neighbouring town or place of interest nearby like Bath or Stonehenge, for instance.

Of course, I'd be remiss if I didn't mention that we also have a lot of buildings on campus just a short walking distance from Lincoln Hall, that you're also likely to find useful. There's the supermarket, for example, which you'll find if you follow the stone path right in front of the entrance, and near that, the cinema, which also has a café on the ground floor. We used to have a theatre next to it, but this has been turned into a hall for Drama students—and the theatre has been rebuilt further down the street. This is also where you'll find a bank—especially useful for those of you who've come from abroad and need to open an account. <u>We've been petitioning the college for a football field, so I'll keep you updated on the developments</u> of that in my monthly emails. I may also ask you to get involved in future petitions, but they are by no means obligatory. Now, let's walk this way, where we'll find…

Practice Test 1, Section 3 (Track 3)

TUTOR: Hello, you two. Please have a seat.

NADIYA: Thank you.

IAN: Thanks.

TUTOR: So, have you got your presentation ready for next week?

NADIYA: Yes. We've prepared the slides and everything, and we've got the handouts with us if you'd like to have a look.

TUTOR: Of course, I'll have a look and email my comments to you later. Meanwhile, would you like to talk me through what you've prepared? Nadiya, why don't you go first?

NADIYA: Okay. So Ian and I decided to join two very different online communities and see how much information we could gather about the people in them and their relationships with each other.

TUTOR: So you joined a movie forum, right?

NADIYA: Yeah, more specifically one dedicated to a 1980s cult classic called <u>Fright Night</u>.

TUTOR: And you, Ian?

IAN: Well, I tried a few different sites before I found the right one. At first I thought about finding another forum on the same film just to see the different types of people the two forums would attract, but then Nadiya and I decided it'd be better to find something quite different. So, then I looked for a forum on metal music, but I couldn't find any recently active ones with a similarly sized community, <u>so I went for one on jazz</u>, instead.

TUTOR:	Right. So how many regular members were there on your forum, Nadiya?
NADIYA:	From my research I discovered there were 62 members registered to the forum, but only about 25 of those posted more than once a day, which is what Ian and I decided to define as 'regular' member.
IAN:	Mine had much more regular members, more than 40 <u>out of 75</u>.
TUTOR:	Great. And how many moderators were there?
NADIYA:	Four that I could see on the Friday Night forum.
IAN:	At first I thought there were four in mine as well, but it turned out that one of them had recently stopped being a moderator and returned to being just a member, so <u>it was just three after all</u>.

TUTOR:	Okay, so let's hear about the results of your research. Nadiya? What kind of personal relationships did you discover amongst the members?
NADIYA:	It was quite interesting, actually. It was like a real-world community, with close friendships, rivalries, and even romantic relationships developing between the members. Most of the members had been visiting the forum for months, some for years, but <u>they were very welcoming</u> from the beginning, they made me feel right at home.
TUTOR:	And what about you, Ian?
IAN:	The people in my forum were a bit more reluctant when I joined, but I suppose I discovered more or less the same things as Nadiya. The most amazing instance was two forum members who lived across the world from each other. One was in Norway and the other was in Chile, and the Chilean guy flew to Norway to meet the Norwegian girl, and then vice versa. Not just that, but during that first trip they <u>started dating</u> and the Norwegian girl now lives with the guy in Santiago.
TUTOR:	Crikey. And what about friendships?
IAN:	It was a very close-knit community, and they always talked of organising a big event for everyone to fly in and meet each other, but I don't think they were serious about it. They did talk through the <u>logistics</u> of it quite often, though.
TUTOR:	Nadiya?

NADIYA: Well, plenty of other people had flown to meet each other in my forum as well, but as Ian said, no group event had been organised. What I did find quite fascinating, however, was that instead of a group meeting, one of the moderators of the forum had bought this purple diary which they'd dubbed 'The Traveller', and this was snail-mailed from country to country and member to member, with each member writing a few pages in it, drawing, attaching photographs, that sort of thing. In the end this was returned to the original moderator, who scanned it into a pdf and circulated it in the forum.

TUTOR: Very interesting, indeed. Did you manage to have a look at that diary?

NADIYA: I did, but I haven't included it in my notes due to privacy. People were sharing really intimate stuff.

TUTOR: Fascinating. So, overall, what was your impression?

IAN: I was amazed, because I'd never expected that level of friendship between people who had never met in person. To fly to another country to meet someone you don't know, and for that person to host you as well. It just seems remarkable.

NADIYA: I agree. I think it speaks volumes about how communications technology has changed the way humans interact. I mean, we've had concepts such as pen pals for a long time, but it simply cannot compare with the way the internet has transformed the ways we communicate, and the opportunities it's given us to meet and speak to people all over the globe.

TUTOR: And what about the two forums? Did you notice any differences?

IAN: The people were quite different, I think—which is to be expected considering the very different forum topics we picked. But fundamentally they were also very similar, in terms of their goals.

NADIYA: I think the only big difference we noted was that trolls were much more likely to frequent my forum rather than Ian's. He did get the occasional ones dissing the music people posted about as geeky, but there was nothing malevolent. Mine were often quite aggressive.

TUTOR: Right. So how do you plan to present these findings to the rest of your class?

IAN: Well, we were thinking of starting with…

Practice Test 1, Section 4 (Track 4)

I know most of you are wondering why we need to spend an entire lesson on something as seemingly rare as accommodating a disabled employee—and the truth is that this is not what students typically expect when they begin studying towards a business degree. Nonetheless, it is pivotal to know your rights and your responsibilities as a future employer, should you find yourself in such a situation. If you want to employ a disabled person, you need to make sure you provide them with a suitable environment. And, you should also be aware of the changes you would need to make in order to support an existing employee who becomes disabled whilst working at your company.

So let's start with the basics, shall we? Here in the UK we have a law called the Equality Act, which covers a variety of situations, including disabilities. What this law dictates is that you, as an employer, must make reasonable adjustments in order to make sure that your disabled member of staff can carry out their duties and responsibilities without any avoidable hindrances, and to make their job as accessible as possible.

I can see a few of you scratching your heads over there at the back. Don't worry, you're not the only ones confused. Whenever I give this lecture, not just to business students like yourselves; but even to employers, or people who have been business professionals for years or even decades, I always receive the same question: what does reasonable mean?

Reasonable, according to the government, is divided into three different categories, starting with changing the way things are done. What that means, practically speaking, is that if you had some established practices in your company that are now creating discrimination against your disabled member of staff, then you would need to change them. Think, for example, of parking. Maybe you have a policy of allocating parking spots far away from your building's entrance in order to make space for visitors at the front. You won't need to allow every employee a parking spot closer to the building, but if your disabled member of staff is in a wheelchair, for instance, you would need to change theirs, so that it was close the the entrance of the building.

Moving on to the second category, which is changing the physical features within a workspace. I think that's pretty self-explanatory but, just in case, what it means is that you might have to make actual, physical changes to the building, adding ramps where needed, for example, or making your doors automatic.

And finally, let me describe what providing extra aids and services means. Imagine, for example, that one of your employees lost much of their hearing ability and were forced to use hearing aids. As an employer, it would be your responsibility to provide them with a portable induction loop. Similarly, imagine that one of your employees, who previously stocked all the top shelves with documents, is now confined to a wheelchair. In this case, providing extra aids would be required, and you would also have to <u>delegate</u> any duties which the disabled staff member could not carry out to a different member of staff.

Let's leave the law to one side for a moment. You're all business students—future business leaders, so you should already know that rules and regulations for employees are made generally, but must be applied specifically to your individual members of staff. What I mean by that is that the law is <u>purposefully unclear,</u> because what's reasonable for me might not be reasonable for someone else. As such, your first action once you've been informed that one of your employees is now disabled should be to talk to them and ask them specifically, what they, as an individual, would need to have changed in order to function as efficiently as possible in their work life. You'll be surprised at the requests they'll have and how simple they might be. Believe it or not, according to research, the most popular request by disabled employees is <u>work flexibility</u>.

Thankfully, there are a host of government initiatives available to help you to accommodate disabled employees, the most notable being Access to Work—which will not only provide assistance to you but will also help you financially, depending on the size of your business. Most medium-sized companies don't need to contribute more than <u>20%</u> to the total cost above a £500 threshold.

Before you implement any changes, these are the things you should take into account: are your adjustments going to be <u>effective</u>? Is it going to be <u>practical</u> to implement them, or are they going to be extremely difficult or even impossible? What kind of costs are we talking about, and what resources do you have available to you? These are the things your actions will be judged on should your employee decide you haven't done enough and resolve to take you to court—although, of course, providing you make the time to listen to your employee's needs, this is quite unlikely to happen.

You all look like you need waking up, so let's do a quick exercise. Turn to the person next to you and decide who will be the employer and who will be the employee. We're going to…

Practice Test 2, Section 1 (Track 5)

WOMAN: Good afternoon, Belvoir Sports Centre. How can I help?

MAN: Hi. Good afternoon. I'm calling about the workshop on healthy eating. I'm really interested and I'd like a little more information, please.

WOMAN: Do you mean the Healthy Eating, Healthy Living workshops?

MAN: Yes. My wife mentioned them—I believe it they teach you how to get a more balanced diet. What to eat and when and so forth.

WOMAN: Yes, that's the main idea. Well, first of all, as you may have already seen, they run every Saturday morning.

MAN:	Fine. Is it open to all ages? My 15-year-old daughter is interested in attending, too.
WOMAN:	That shouldn't be a problem. Any age from twelve upwards is welcome, though we do ask that under sixteens' be accompanied by an adult.
MAN:	Not a problem. The whole family will be coming, I guess. What about cost?
WOMAN:	Well, I think you'll find the fees very reasonable. It's £7.50 per person, but you could get a family ticket, two adults and two children, for only £20. I suppose your daughter could bring a friend along with her.
MAN:	That's very reasonable indeed. And are they held in the sports centre?
WOMAN:	Not anymore. We've got a lot of people interested, so we've decided to hold them in the church hall. It's nearby. Just make sure you arrive 15 minutes before it starts.
MAN:	Absolutely. 10.30, is it?
WOMAN:	Yes, so we'd advise you to get there at about 10.15, if possible.
MAN:	Not a problem at all. Could you give me the full address?
WOMAN:	Yes, it's St. Peter's Church.
MAN:	Right.
WOMAN:	And that's on Streatham High Road.
MAN:	Could you spell that please?
WOMAN:	Of course. It's S-T-R-E-A-T-H-A-M High Road.
MAN:	Excellent; thanks.
WOMAN:	I do need to tell you that there are some road works in the area, so at the moment you may need to leave a bit earlier.
MAN:	Okay, can do. And just one more question. Is parking available nearby?
WOMAN:	On a Saturday morning there are plenty of spaces on the road. There's also a car park just opposite the church hall, so you shouldn't have trouble finding a spot nearby.
MAN:	Do I have to book in advance?
WOMAN:	Yes, and you actually need to book by calling our events department.
MAN:	Oh, I'm so sorry, should I have called them instead of the main sports centre number?

WOMAN:	No, that's absolutely fine. It's just that I can't do the booking from here. I'll give you their direct number. It's 01539 55146.
MAN:	Great. Thank you.
WOMAN:	That's alright. Just be aware that demand is very high, so if you are interested you should call them today if possible.
MAN:	Will do.

WOMAN:	Lovely. Is there anything else I can help you with?
MAN:	Actually, my wife said this would be the first of a series of workshops. What are the other workshops about and when are they being held?
WOMAN:	Yes. This is the first of a series of three workshops. They will be held on Saturday mornings, starting on the 3rd. You already know what the first one is… 'Healthy Eating, Healthy Living'. <u>It focuses on having a balanced diet and eating the right foods at the right time</u>.
MAN:	Yep.
WOMAN:	The second is about cooking tips and recipes if I'm not mistaken… just let me have a look.
MAN:	No problem.
WOMAN:	Yes. The one on the 17th is called <u>'Smart Cooking'</u>. You'll get to learn some healthy recipes and everyday <u>cooking strategies</u>. And the third one is… <u>'Conscious Food Shopp</u>ing', it will discuss how, when and where to buy your food'.
MAN:	That'll be the 24th, won't it?
WOMAN:	Actually, no. The workshops happen every other week, so the last one will be on the <u>31st</u>.
MAN:	Got it. So what I'll do is call the events centre straightaway and book all three of them. They certainly all sound very interesting.
WOMAN:	And they are. I will be attending the first two myself. Unfortunately, I couldn't get the day off work for the last one.
MAN:	Sorry about that. Anyway, thank you ever so much for all your help.
WOMAN:	You're more than welcome, sir. Thanks very much for ringing.
MAN:	I suppose I'll see you on the 3rd then. Bye.
WOMAN:	Yes, see you soon. Bye.

Practice Test 2, Section 2 (Track 6)

Good morning and welcome everybody. I am Marisa Suarez and I am the staff manager here at Spanish Village. We are expecting this year's Spanish camp to attract over 300 students from the ages of 7 to 17, ladies and gentlemen, and you are among 35 extra staff recruited to help look after them. Now, to help things run smoothly we have divided you into three teams, Barcelona, Madrid and Marbella. So first I'll explain how the teams are divided up and then we'll be handing out colour-coded T-shirts with the names of your groups so we can identify you more easily.

First of all, those who will be looking after the extracurricular activities and handling all sports events … you will be in the red team, which is… let's see… Barcelona. Now, we've also put the office staff in the Barcelona group since they'll be offering support in some of the outdoor events such as the Spanish market and our games competitions, or 'juegos locos', as some of our staff like to call them.

Those of you involved in distributing our daily materials and installing equipment in the classrooms will be on the white team, which is Madrid I think… yes, that's correct. And we also put those of you who will be working in the kitchen and the cafes around the camp in the white team, so you'll be getting a white T-shirt as well.

Now, most of our academic staff have been put in the Marbella group and will be getting a purple T-shirt. When I say most of our staff, I am excluding the junior assistant teachers who will be joining the red group because of their involvement in the afternoon activities. The rest of the academic staff… teachers and coordinators, myself included, will be in the purple group.

Those of you responsible for cleaning and maintenance will join the white team where you will be given guidance on directing the traffic in the car parks on the first and final days of each camping programme. We had a couple of complaints about confusion in the car parks last summer, so we just want to make sure that drop-offs and pick-ups run more smoothly this year.

Now, we'll all be working in different areas of the campsite this summer, and this is the main reason we're putting people with different skill sets on each team, so that you can all have each other's backs in case of… touch wood… an emergency, or something like that.

Right, now that everyone knows which teams they belong to, we'll get on with the orientation and training program. First, I'll quickly run through our schedule for today, which you should have inside the welcome pack in front of you. That should give you a general idea of what else is in store for you today. You'll also find in your welcome pack a map of the camp, the names and photos of those responsible for each area of the programme, some basic personal safety procedures for all the adventure activities and, well, your supervisors will take you through the whole thing once you join your groups.

Anyway, back to the timetable. This introduction finishes at 9.00 and then you'll be hearing from <u>Carla Smith who works in the accounts department</u>. She's the one who looks after all temporary staff, and the person to see if you have any problems regarding your wages. Carla will be explaining when and how will you get them, and she will also be handing out your tax forms. I would just like to stress that all tax forms must be completed and returned before the end of the second week, so that your pay can be processed in time.

Following Carla's talk, at 9.30, <u>you will hear from Marcos Cazorla, our Director of Operations,</u> and he will be going over the map of the campsite with you, which will help you understand where and when everything will take place this summer. He will also explain our philosophy and mission as a Spanish language centre, and ask any questions you might have. He'll guide you through the <u>security arrangements</u> and show you the assembly points. Then, at 10.15 there will be a coffee break in the staff canteen, which is located down by the duck pond.

After the break we'll be watching a video presentation, so instead of coming back here, I would like you all to go to the open cinema. Mr Cazorla will have discussed the map of the site with you, so I'm more than certain you'll have no problems finding the open cinema. In case you do, you can always find me in the staff canteen and I'll walk with you to the location. The video was made by the <u>local police</u> and addresses important safety issues in the workplace, and the local area, as some of you might want to explore its bars, clubs and restaurants in your free time.

We'll finish off the morning with a <u>lunch break</u> in the staff canteen, which should give everyone a chance to meet and get to know each other. And yes, we'll be serving you authentic Spanish food so no roast beef or any other British delicacies. After lunch you'll be divided up into your teams to meet your supervisors. If all goes according to plan we'll be finished by 6 o'clock. It's a very long day today, so I won't delay you any longer. Let me hand the floor over to our next speaker…

Practice Test 2, Section 3 (Track 7)

WOMAN:	Mark, don't you think Professor Whitaker is an excellent tutor? I find his lectures fascinating.
MAN:	He's brilliant, Lydia. He's just one of those people. <u>He could talk about the telephone directory and get us all excited about it.</u>
WOMAN:	And he's so demanding, but in a positive way, I mean. He just knows how to get the best out of our tutorial group without putting us under pressure. It's tough, but I'm learning so much.
MAN:	I couldn't agree more.
WOMAN:	We've been so lucky. <u>Last year, Dr Pattinson was excellent as well. He was so charismatic and had such a good rapport with everyone in our group.</u> I miss him.

MAN:	Me too. Anyway, did you take lots of notes in the lecture?
WOMAN:	<u>Yes, I did. In fact, I didn't notice I had taken that many notes till I ran out of paper.</u> Had to borrow some from Mindy, so look at this. My last page is tutti-frutti pink.
MAN:	That sounds just like Mindy. Well, I'm actually glad you've taken so many notes. I was so busy listening to what was being discussed that I hardly wrote anything down. <u>Do you mind if I photocopy yours?</u>
WOMAN:	That might not be such a good idea. Half my notes are in Spanish… when I write too fast I always end up writing in Spanglish.
MAN:	Spanglish?
WOMAN:	<u>Half English, half Spanish.</u> Spanglish… like the film?
MAN:	No idea what you're talking about. But I think I can manage. After all, I took Spanish for two terms in Year 7.

MAN:	Let's have a look… Wow! You're so organised… It looks as if you've typed it up on a computer. Are you always so neat?
WOMAN:	Yep.
MAN:	And there's not much in Spanish… It's all in English here and…. OK, looks like it's all Spanglish from here on… Let me see… Mmm, not so sure I learned that much Spanish back in Year 7.
WOMAN:	*(laughs)* Sorry about that. Don't you keep careful notes? It's important.
MAN:	I used to. Well, it depends on the lecture I guess. It's just that if I'm genuinely interested I just want to enjoy it, you know? Soak it in. But I don't think I'll forget Professor Whitaker's lecture today. Maybe some of the details will fade, but I'm pretty sure—
WOMAN:	Don't worry, I always type up my notes after the lecture, so <u>I can email you a copy when I've finished.</u> Actually, I know you've got an excellent memory, so why don't you fill in anything I might have missed and then send it back to me? I was so busy taking notes that I might have focused too much on the details and missed the broader concept. I'd be interested to hear what you have to say about my notes.
MAN:	Perfect. I'd love to do that.
WOMAN:	Great. I'm such a detail person. I need to have everything written down before I can actually put my brain to work and get the concepts clear in my head. In the end, <u>I usually miss out on the bigger picture.</u>

MAN:	I'd say that's a strong quality. And I don't think you ever struggle to understand the point of our tutorials. You're one of the smartest people I know.
WOMAN:	I'm not saying I don't understand things… It's just that I usually take longer than most in our tutorial group.
MAN:	I'm the complete opposite. And that's a problem. If I start paying attention to details I just clutter up my mind and get <u>ridiculously frustrated</u>. So what I do now is just sit back and enjoy what they have to say… and try to take in as much as I can, obviously.
WOMAN:	Which is a lot I bet. Shall we go to the library? I want to borrow that book Professor Whitaker mentioned.
MAN:	Which one? He mentioned several.
WOMAN:	The one by the Russian man. What was his name?
MAN:	Dostoyevsky. He was discussing the book *Notes from the Underground*. Pretty heavy reading, though. You really want to read it?
WOMAN:	Absolutely. Professor Whitaker was really passionate about it, he made it sound very interesting. So I guess I just want to find out what it's all about.
MAN:	It's seriously depressing.
WOMAN:	So you've read it? Did you understand what Whitaker meant when he talked about the book signifying a turning point in Dostoyevsky's writing? How it's all about his disillusionment by the oppression of corruption within society—
MAN:	And how he goes on to withdraw from society into the underground? Don't get me wrong, it's a fascinating book. It's a dark and politically charged novel, but gets quite full-on. The main point I got from it, is that the more intelligent you are, the less capable you are of ever being resolute and certain. Intellect does not allow you to rise above evolution or "the anthill" of society… it merely constrains you to a life of inner torment, indecision and the realisation of <u>the limitations of being human</u>.
WOMAN:	Wow. Not an uplifting read for you, I take it.
MAN:	I told you it was depressing.
WOMAN:	Yes, maybe I should have a think about whether I'm fully psychologically prepared before I pick that one up. Shall we go get something to eat in the meantime?
MAN:	Pizza?
WOMAN:	You read my mind.

Practice Test 2, Section 4 (Track 8)

'I don't want to study grammar and do boring exercises. I want to learn to speak the language, so that I can actually talk to people in real life.'

This is what one of my students told me during our tutorials last year. It wasn't the first time I'd heard a student voice their frustrations with their lack of practical progress in learning how to speak a different language, and I am sure it will not be the last. It's one of the most common observations we get at our language centre during our opening classes. When we ask new students about their expectations and needs, most claim they need the most help with their speaking skills, so every term we have to reassure learners that they will speak a lot in class.

Another thing I've noticed over the past two or three years, is that teachers are unfortunately becoming increasingly busy. Particularly in a big city like this, where the cost of living is so high, and English language teachers are in such high demand, many teachers end up working extremely long days, with very full classes. Essentially, we have students who feel that they need more communicative lessons and then on the other side busier teachers who do not always have the time to prepare more interactive and detailed lessons. Often, these teachers end up—whether willingly or not— delivering textbook derived lessons.

This is a significant issue, and we need to work towards a solution. Last year, I met a sales consultant from one of the leading publishers of global materials, and during her annual summer visit, she sold me on a new system, one which we will be rolling out today.

This new course focuses on communication, and will help our students to speak more without the added effort of looking for supplementary materials and sacrificing hours to rigorous lesson planning. It's all in here.

Imagine how good it would be if all of us teachers, including myself, could actually meet students' language learning expectations without needing to look for support materials from a variety other sources. How great would it be if the books themselves offered students opportunities to communicate? And how much better if we could offer teachers the required tools to promote communication in class? The main aim of this workshop is to enable teachers to evaluate course books and assess them from a communicative perspective. I believe that this can be invaluable for our professional development, especially for those of us who are only just getting started as language teachers.

During the first part of this workshop, we're going to share our respective classroom issues, and help each other develop a set of criteria for course book evaluation. I believe that we can really benefit from this development and revision. We will be looking into principles of learning and teaching communication, which can help us understand our students better and encourage our own development as teachers. Also, the investigation process and criteria analysis should give us a chance to broaden our strategies and methods of selecting course books from a more communicative perspective. <u>I may choose to take these criteria and use them for further research or as a professional project to help schools and fellow teachers</u> identify and design materials that address learners' perceived or desired communicative needs.

Secondly, it is important to mention that this workshop will help us think about both language teaching and learning. Does the course pack offer what most learners seem to ask for when enrolling at a language course? Does the same course pack give teachers the required tools to deliver communicative content? It will be extremely important for us <u>to be able to analyse materials from a learner's perspective</u> and take their communicative perceptions into consideration.

Finally, another essential aspect of this workshop is that it will highlight the importance of analysing the whole course pack instead of just the textbooks. My experience has made me aware that <u>most teachers, including myself, usually make their course pack selections based solely on the contents of the textbook</u>. Other materials such as resource packs, teaching procedures, websites and CD-ROMs can be taken for granted, or even unexplored in many cases. It is not uncommon to find a teacher who is not entirely familiar with the course packs they have been using.

As for the schools or language centres you work for, I believe they can benefit a great deal from your experience in this workshop. Establishing a set of criteria for future course pack selection procedures can be intriguing, and hopefully, you'll leave the building today with a number of new strategies and procedures to allow you to do this…

Practice Test 3, Section 1 (Track 9)

GREG:	Hi, am I speaking to Betty?
BETTY:	Yes, this is her.
GREG:	Hi, Betty, my name is Greg and I'm calling from Westminster Education Supply Pool and Temping Agency. We received your email yesterday regarding our job ad looking for primary school teaching assistants. Do you have a minute to talk?
BETTY:	Oh, hi! Yes, sure.
GREG:	Great. First of all, let me just check I have your details right. Is your last name <u>Andrews</u>?
BETTY:	Yes, that's correct.
GREG:	And your email address is betty1994@memail.co.uk?
BETTY:	Yes.
GREG:	Excellent. So, can you tell me a bit about yourself, Betty? First of all, are you still studying at university or have you graduated?

BETTY:	I'm in my final year at the <u>University of Westminster</u>, where I'm doing a Bachelor's in Modern Art.
GREG:	And you're looking for a position to start in September?
BETTY:	Actually, it would be better if it started in October, if that's possible?
GREG:	Most schools in the area look for people who can start in September, but there might be a few who might be able to work around a later start. Let me make a note of it. OK, so why don't you start by telling me why you're interested in working in a school?
BETTY:	Well, I've been thinking about my options with the degree I'm doing, and all of my teachers and lecturers have always said that I'm a very patient and communicative person and that I'm particularly good at explaining things, and my thesis tutor actually recommended looking into becoming a teacher. So I did some research and I was told that the best way to become a teacher is to start as a TA, so my plan is to work as a teaching assistant for a year, and then I'd like to apply for a <u>postgraduate certificate</u> in education.
GREG:	Right. And is there a specific reason why you'd prefer to work in a primary rather than a secondary school?
BETTY:	Yeah, the thing is that while I really enjoy learning about history at university, I don't think I'd like to just teach one subject when I become a teacher. I'd much rather teach a few different subjects to have a bit of variety, you know, and I'm also more interested in teaching children than teenagers, so primary just sounds like the best option for me.
GREG:	So, I see that at the moment you're living in Southwark. Do you know by any chance if you're going to be staying there after you graduate?
BETTY:	Yeah, I'm living with a couple of friends and we've got a contract until the end of next year, so I can't see myself moving anytime soon.
GREG:	Great. Could I have the full address, please?
BETTY:	It's <u>12 Meymott</u> Street.
GREG:	Could you spell the street for me please?
BETTY:	Yes, it's M-E-Y-M-O-T-T.
GREG:	Thank you. And the postcode?
BETTY:	That's <u>SE1 8NZ</u>.

GREG:	Is that M as in Mike?
BETTY:	No, N as in November.
GREG:	Great, thank you. So the good news is that we've got a few different schools near your area, so it all depends on what you'd prefer and your qualifications. First of all, you are interested in full-time, right?
BETTY:	Yes.
GREG:	And would you be open to any <u>evening work</u>?
BETTY:	I'm afraid I've got classes in the evenings because I'm tutoring two students and I'm also studying Chinese, so I wouldn't be available.
GREG:	Right. No problem. And do you have any experience with SEN?
BETTY:	I'm sorry, what's that?
GREG:	Special Educational Needs.
BETTY:	Oh. I'm afraid not.
GREG:	No worries, we run a <u>workshop every other weekend</u> on SEN which you might find useful and which will definitely improve your chances of getting a position in one of our schools.
BETTY:	Yeah, why not?
GREG:	Great, I'll discuss this in detail with you when we meet. So, what I would like to do next is arrange a date for you to come to our offices so we can have a more in-depth chat about your options and how we can help you. How does that sound?
BETTY:	Yeah, that sounds great.
GREG:	Would you be able to come this Friday, the 17th of February at 11 am?
BETTY:	Yes, I think so.
GREG:	Perfect, 17th of February, 11 am it is.
BETTY:	Oh, I'm sorry, I just remembered. I've got a class on Friday mornings. Could we do it a bit later, after 1 pm?
GREG:	Hmm, that doesn't work for me. How about the <u>21st of February</u>, same time?
BETTY:	Yes, that works for me.
GREG:	All right, next Tuesday then.
BETTY:	Yeah.
GREG:	Perfect. Just to speed up the process of signing you up, it would be great if you could bring some documents with you. I'll email you a list, so you don't need to write anything down.

BETTY:	OK.
GREG:	So we would need to see your passport, as well as a recent bank statement or any other <u>proof of address</u>, for example a letter from the doctor or the government. Normally we'd also ask for your university degree, but since you haven't graduated yet we'd just need to see your acceptance letter.
BETTY:	OK, cool.
GREG:	I'm also going to email you an application, this is for the Disclosure and Barring Service that you need in order to work in a school, and if you could print it off and bring it along completed, that would be great. Oh, and please bring both the <u>originals</u> and <u>photocopies</u> of all your documents if possible.
BETTY:	Yeah, OK.
GREG:	Great, so we'll see you on Tuesday then.
BETTY:	Thanks so much! See you soon!

Practice Test 3, Section 2 (Track 10)

Welcome back. You're listening to Salt FM and this is Silas Harker with Worldwide History. This week we've been looking at different famous and fascinating buildings from around the world and exploring their history, and tonight we'll be talking about the Palau Güell, or Güell Palace, in Barcelona, Spain.

The Palau Güell is an Antoni Gaudí building, <u>one of twelve in Barcelona</u> and one of his earlier works. Gaudí, for those of you who don't know, was a 19th-century Spanish architect and a unique representative of the Art Nouveau movement in Spain. He was born in Reus in 1852, and <u>lived in Barcelona from around 1870</u> until his death in 1926. Gaudí's most famous building, of course, is the Sagrada Família, also located in Barcelona—but <u>the Palau Güell is just as brilliant an example of his modernist vision</u>.

The story of the Palau Güell starts in 1885, when Gaudí was tasked with designing a palace in the city by Eusebi Güell, a wealthy count and textile industrialist. The palace needed to serve not only as the count's home but also as a suitable venue for expositions and events. While the Palau was to look majestic and impressive, there was little space for it to do so, with a basic surface of 18x22 metres, or 59x72 feet. <u>It was therefore imperative, as you can imagine, that the palace was functional</u>. Gaudí certainly delivered—adding, of course, his own distinctive touch.

There were two large front entrance doors for guests to enter and exit by horse-drawn carriage. There was a carriage hall in the back, with spiral ramps for the horses which led directly to the basement and <u>the stables</u>. <u>The basement was also where servants slept</u>.

The ground floor was designed to be the building's centerpiece, with a library for Güell, administration rooms and working rooms. The main entertaining room was also on the ground floor, and it had a domed, high ceiling where lanterns were hung at night to produce the impression of a starry sky—so you can picture how impressive it must've looked when guests entered the palace.

Guests would have been hosted in the receiving room, on the first floor. Quite interestingly, the receiving room had small viewing windows on the walls, <u>hidden by intricate woodwork</u>. Those were added to the structure so that Güell and his family could sneak a look at their guests from the floor above before greeting them—and perhaps adjusting their attire if necessary.

There was one more floor, or rather an attic, over the family's private rooms on the second floor, and this was where the house personnel resided and where the kitchen, the washing rooms and the food locker could be found.

The Palau Güell truly is an astonishing building. In true Gaudí fashion, it has a stunning entrance, with eye-catching chimneys and wrought-iron works. Inside, the ceiling is decorated with precious stones and the roofs are covered with beautiful wood. The whole palace is an elaborate construction combining the finest materials from pottery to stone and glass.

The inauguration ceremony for the Palau Güell took place in 1888, which coincided with the <u>Universal Exposition</u> being held in Barcelona. Though the building itself would not be fully complete until the following year, and the chimneys on the roof wouldn't be added until as late as 1895.

As its name suggests, the Palau Güell originally belonged to the Güell family, who lived there from 1888. The count and his family stayed there until 1910, when they moved to a mansion inside the enclosure of the Park Güell, another Gaudí project Eusebi Güell had commissioned, this time in the high part of Barcelona. <u>The count's daughter, Mercé Güell, remained at the palace until 1945</u>, when it was sold to the provincial government of Barcelona under the condition that it would be used for cultural purposes and its spirit, so to speak, would be respected and preserved.

In 1969, the Spanish government declared the Palau Güell a historical-artistic monument, and in 1986, exactly 100 years after Gaudí started to design it, it was <u>listed as a World Heritage Site by Unesco</u>. The same year, the Barcelona Provincial Council established a restoration protocol for the building, following an in-depth analysis of the palace's history and its artistic and sociological background. Restoration started with the chimneys in the early 1990s, most of which had sustained irreversible damage to their covering. <u>The coverings had to be rebuilt with the help of several Catalan artists</u>, who admittedly did an impressive job. By 1993, renovation work had begun on the inside of the palace and in 2004, the Palau Güell closed to the public, not to be reopened until May 2011, when restoration was complete and all the structural issues in the stonework had been solved.

Today, the Palau Güell hosts exhibitions and collections, as well as concerts, performances and poetry readings. It can be hired for cultural and educational activities, and it continues to receive thousands of visitors every year. So if you find yourselves in Barcelona, do make sure to pay the palace a visit. As is true of all of Gaudí's brilliant work throughout the city—you won't be disappointed.

Practice Test 3, Section 3 (Track 11)

ANNA:	Hi, Clarke! I haven't seen you for ages, how have you been?
CLARKE:	I'm good, how are you? You're starting your course next month, aren't you?
ANNA:	Yeah, I've been preparing like crazy. I've still got so many questions and it's so difficult to find answers online or in the brochures.
CLARKE:	Oh, well, I'm sure I can answer some of your questions. I remember I had a hard time finding information as well when I started last year.
ANNA:	Could you?
CLARKE:	Of course, what do you want to know?
ANNA:	Well, the thing I'm having the biggest trouble with is selecting my electives. There are just so many options.
CLARKE:	Sure.
ANNA:	So the first elective is Studying Television Forms and Methods. What does that even mean?
CLARKE:	Oh, I took that class. It's basically just having a look at how television programmes are planned and filmed. It examines things from a few different perspectives like directing and screenwriting, which is why it's open to different BA programmes.
ANNA:	Oh. I think I'd prefer something more structured.
CLARKE:	It's a good opportunity to network with director students, and you'll need them later on for your dissertation project.
ANNA:	<u>All right, I'll have a think about it then</u>. So, the next one is Adaptation Studies. Does that have to do with film adaptations?
CLARKE:	Yeah. I didn't do that because you have to read a lot of novels throughout the course and it's quite time-consuming.
ANNA:	Oh, I don't mind that.
CLARKE:	Well, you should give it a go then. I've heard the lecturer is brilliant.

ANNA:	<u>Right. That's one down, then.</u> Then we've got … An Introduction to Documentary Techniques.
CLARKE:	Well, are you thinking of going into documentaries when you graduate?
ANNA:	Not really, but I thought it might be useful to have another option available if screenwriting doesn't pan out.
CLARKE:	To be honest, I wouldn't bother. It's not particularly useful unless you take more modules on documentaries later on and you'll be giving up other modules more closely related to what you want to do.
ANNA:	Hmm… Maybe you're right. <u>Let's cross that off, then.</u> OK, how about Writing Comedy?
CLARKE:	Oh, that's a really good one. The lecturer's so funny and he's been writing comedy for about 30 years.
ANNA:	Yeah, but I'm more interested in writing drama.
CLARKE:	It doesn't just focus on how to write a comedy per se. It's all about the comical element in scripts, which might come in handy even in a dramatic story.
ANNA:	You think?
CLARKE:	Definitely.
ANNA:	<u>All right, I'll put it down as a provisional yes and come back to it.</u>
CLARKE:	Any other modules?
ANNA:	One more: "Script Analysis".
CLARKE:	OK, so in this one you read parts of scripts and watch the relevant movie sections to examine how the script translates to the screen and what role each word in it plays. It's really good because you also have to write your own scripts and analyse them in class.
ANNA:	Hmm. <u>Let's jot that down on the list, then.</u> Great.

CLARKE:	So, is there anything else you're having trouble with?
ANNA:	Well, for one of the compulsory modules I was asked to pick one of my favourite films and find the script online and read it, and then I needed to write a 1,000 word report about it—but the problem is he didn't tell me what the report was supposed to include. I've tried emailing him, but he hasn't replied.
CLARKE:	Is that Dr Duffrey?
ANNA:	Yeah, Introduction to Film Screenwriting.

CLARKE:	Yeah, I remember that. He likes to do that with new students—he's not telling you what to write on purpose, just to see what you'll do with an open question like that. Some students just go to the library and get whatever they can find on script analysis for the report, but I wouldn't recommend that.
ANNA:	So what should I write?
CLARKE:	What it is you like about the movie, and what your impression is of the script. <u>Don't think too much about it, just put your thoughts down</u>. That's all he wants.
ANNA:	OK. And there's another thing: everyone's been telling me to get started early with some internship or something if I want to get a job after I graduate, and that I should look into screenwriting competitions—but the problem is, I don't know where to look. I mean, I've made a list of websites I found, but how do I know which ones are reputable?
CLARKE:	<u>Oh, I wouldn't worry about that yet. After the first semester they'll give you a list of places to look for internships.</u> One of the good things about the course is they're pretty hands-on after you graduate—they don't just dump you with a diploma and that's it. I found my job through a contact I made in one of the school's business events, where they'd invited big TV network and film studio directors and established screenwriters.
ANNA:	Oh, that's great.
CLARKE:	<u>Yeah, just make sure you ask your tutor regularly about these</u> because invitations are only free for the first 100 to sign up and everyone else after that has to pay an entrance fee. Plus, there are usually only about 250 tickets or so.
ANNA:	OK, I'll make a note of that, thanks.
CLARKE:	<u>Oh, and don't forget to look into studio days.</u> They do those every month and usually you get to meet people and talk to them about their productions—but they're severely underpublicised so you need to be alert and book your place immediately. I know a guy who got to work on his favourite TV series after meeting one of the producers in one of those visits and pitching him an idea for an episode, so you never know. Just talk to everyone you meet there and come prepared to tell them about your ideas. <u>In fact, talk to anyone you meet who's working in the field.</u>

Practice Test 3, Section 4 (Track 12)

From the moment we wake up, our mobile phones, TVs, newspapers and radios bombard us with negative information. There are stressful developments in global news, terrorist attacks, airplane crashes, war and cancer.

Perhaps it is unsurprising, therefore, that the average person fears these extreme, and in reality extremely rare, potential threats more than the more often occurring, and yet more mundane risks to our life. In our last session we looked at the way people react when they're suddenly thrust into the middle of disaster; in this lesson, we'll look at how skilled we are at actually identifying danger in our daily lives.

So, are humans good at assessing risk? Short answer: no. Scientists have known for a very long time that we are pretty rubbish at assessing danger. We fear things that have a very slim chance of killing us and unflinchingly embrace high risk activities. There are several reasons for this.

The first, is that many of our irrational fears derive from centuries of evolution. This is why people might be deathly afraid of, say, spiders or snakes. For our ancestors, spiders and snakes posed a serious threat, and so, over many generations of death and injury, we came to regard these animals with fear. The same cannot be said for threats that are more recent, such as car accidents. Give it a few centuries and who knows? Perhaps one day we'll have as many people suffering from amaxophobia, the fear of riding in a car, as those currently terrified of spiders.

But this is not the only way evolution affects us. In order to survive, we've had to develop instinctive reactions to fear that so when something scary happens, we don't need to waste precious time evaluating the danger before we flee. That's why people jump when someone suddenly lunges at them, even if it's a friend playing a prank. The problem with this in our modern, relatively safe world, is that fear strengthens memory, which means that disasters such as terrorist attacks or airplane crashes stay with us long after they're over—and even if we didn't experience them directly, the constant media coverage makes us feel as if we were there. As a result, we overestimate how likely they are to happen to us, while underestimating other, far more common risks such as heart disease or car accidents.

Speaking of heart disease, did you know that 73,000 people die from heart related issues per year in the UK alone? Heart disease is perceived by many scientists to be the leading cause of death around the world, followed by pulmonary disease and lung cancer. Yet far more people fear cancer than they do heart disease, and the reason for this is a sinister one: whereas cancer can strike anyone anywhere, heart disease is the direct result of years upon years of wrong lifestyle choices, and as humans we're ill-equipped to deal with disaster that takes time to build up, even if it's actually easier to do something about it.

Going back to airplane crashes, what do you think it is that makes people so scared to fly? I'm scared of flying: I know it's irrational, I know that accidents are extremely rare and I know the statistics suggest the risk decreases each year, but I'm still scared of flying. For me, and most others scared of flying, the underlying issue is quite basic: it's the lack of control we can't hack. Humans are calmer when they can control a situation. When you're behind the wheel in your car, it's you who decides where to go and how fast, and it's you who will have to react if something goes wrong. You might be terrible at reacting, but you'll be in control. In an airplane, you relinquish control to the pilot and the crew—and this is <u>incredibly frightening</u> for many of us.

Two more things: think of the last time you exercised. How did that make you feel? Did you get a sense of accomplishment when you were done? Of course you did! Exercise releases endorphins, it makes us feel happy, and we also feel proud after completing exercise, especially if it was really difficult. Now ask yourself this: What did you do after you'd finished exercising? Perhaps you spent the rest of the day being virtuous and restrained, for many people this apparently comes with ease. Or perhaps you're like me, and you proceed to cancel out the <u>beneficial effects</u> of exercise by eating more—a bar of chocolate you wouldn't normally allow yourself, of an extra helping of dinner, for instance.

I call this the balancing out effect. Many humans tend to offset a good thing with a bad thing—we tend to think we deserve it, or in the case of risk, that we're safe. This is why studies suggest that people take more risks when they wear their seatbelt in their cars, and why car accidents in snowy conditions actually happen to drivers of four-wheel-drive vehicles more often than not. We have a tendency to substitute one risk with another, and this tends to cancel the safety precautions out, or even sometimes tip the scales towards more danger for us.

This tendency to balance things out leads me to the final reason I'll be mentioning today, which is the balance of benefits and risks. If I asked you to pick between your children playing sports, or watching TV, what would you pick? Most parents, if not all, would obviously pick the former. Yet in 2006 alone, there were 13 reported cases of death amongst teens due to football-related injuries—but there has <u>never</u>, as far as I am aware, been a reported case of death caused by simply watching television. So why do we prefer sports? Because of the benefits the activity can offer. Sports are not just fun: they teach us to be sociable and work in a team, they make us physically fit and give us experience and knowledge we can use in our future careers. Watching television doesn't offer any of that and, even though the risk attached to it is smaller, because the benefits we see are also smaller, on the whole we regard it as <u>worse</u> for us than sports. In other words, we are willing to ignore the threat of danger if we believe there to be something we can gain from it.

Let's look at a case study which I hope will illustrate some of the main points here….

Practice Test 4, Section 1 (Track 13)

MAN:	Hello?
WOMAN:	Hi! I'm ringing about your advertisement on sell-your-stuff-dot-com. The sofas? Can you tell me if they're still available?
MAN:	We've sold the small ones, but we've still got three available.
WOMAN:	Right, Okay. Can you tell me a bit more about them?
MAN:	Of course. What is it that you want to know?
WOMAN:	Actually, I'm looking for something to put in the reception of my new office, so, well, I'm not too worried about the colour since we might be changing the covers, but the size is quite important.
MAN:	No problem. Just give me a second; I've got the details written down somewhere. Yes, so the big one is 230 by 100 cm, and the medium ones… just a second… the medium ones are both exactly the same size. They're 178 by 100 cm.
WOMAN:	Excellent. The medium ones should fit perfectly. As I think I've mentioned already, I'm probably going to end up replacing the cover, but is there anything about the frame that I should know about? Are they in good condition?
MAN:	Yeah. Mint, actually. Both the cushions and the frame, so I wouldn't worry about the cover. And as you have probably seen in the photos, they're black, and black goes with anything.
WOMAN:	Yes, I suppose it does. So, are they both the same price as well?
MAN:	No, one of them is a recliner, so that's a bit more expensive as a result. It's £250.00. We paid £900.00 for it just a couple of years ago, so it's very good value. The other one is the same model but not a recliner. It's a bit cheaper: that one's £170.00. They're both in perfectly good condition and they're very both comfortable and sturdy… I'm sure they'd be an excellent addition to your new office.
WOMAN:	That's good to know. Let's see, what else did I want to ask? Would you say they're both three-seaters?
MAN:	I'd say three people can sit on it comfortably. If that makes it a three-seater, then sure.
WOMAN:	Okay. Oh, can you hang on one moment, please?
MAN:	No worries.
WOMAN:	*(within)* Yes, darling?…. Okay… if you want… okay… I will… *(to MAN)* Sorry about that.
MAN:	No problem.

WOMAN:	My husband just told me we might be able to fit the big one in the corner. There's this little cabinet that he wants to get rid of, so we might be able to fit the big one there once it's gone. You said it was 240 by 100 cm, right?
MAN:	No, actually it's 230 by 100 cm.
WOMAN:	So it would definitely fit there then. Is this one a recliner as well?
MAN:	Not this one, no. It's just a standard sofa.
WOMAN:	Oh, but it costs £500, that's much more expensive than the other ones.
MAN:	That's true, but that's because it's vintage. It was my grandfather's, and if I'm not mistaken he bought it sometime in the 40s. We had it refurbished only last year and spent nearly £300. We'd love to keep it but it would cost a small fortune to ship it to Canada so that's why we're selling it. I suppose it has sentimental value to me.
WOMAN:	I see… It does have a classic look to it, but it's a bit more than what I wanted to pay.
MAN:	Are you taking one of the medium ones as well? I'm sure we can sort something out…
WOMAN:	Ok. Let's say I take the big one and the medium one as well. Not the recliner, the regular one. Would you be able to do a discount on that?
MAN:	So, the big one is £500.00 and the medium one… how much did I say it was?
WOMAN:	£170.
MAN:	That's right. So that would be £670.00 in total. You know what? We're in a bit of a hurry here and you seem to be a very nice woman.
WOMAN:	Thank you.
MAN:	So if you take the big one, I'll just throw the medium one in for a total of £550.00. How does that sound?
WOMAN:	That's very generous of you, thank you! I say we have a deal.
MAN:	Brilliant!
WOMAN:	So, is it all right if I come round and check them out this evening, then if everything looks good I can take them away with me there and then?
MAN:	Of course. But may I ask, how do you intend to take them home this evening? They're quite big.

WOMAN:	My husband and I run a transport business, so we'll just take one of our vans or a small truck. If I'm happy with them we'll definitely take them with us this evening.
MAN:	Fantastic.
WOMAN:	So if you could just give me the details of where you live.
MAN:	Sure, <u>I'm Mr Thornton</u>.
WOMAN:	<u>T-H-O-R-N-T-O-N</u>?
MAN:	That's right, <u>and the address is Flat 9 38 Dean Park Road</u>, that's in the town centre, <u>close to the police station</u>.
WOMAN:	OK… so I'll be coming from Muscliff, can you give me an idea of where you are?
MAN:	Yes, do you know Madeira Road? The police station?
WOMAN:	Yes.
MAN:	<u>Well you take that road, and you go on, past the police station, till you get to a roundabout, take the first exit, then Dean Park Road is the second road to the left.</u>
WOMAN:	So past the police station, first exit at the roundabout, first left?
MAN:	Second left. And I'm at the end of the road. The last building on your left. You can't miss it.
WOMAN:	Got it. So I can be there around at about 8.00 pm, if that's not too late?
MAN:	Can we make it 8.15?
WOMAN:	No problem. Oh, and my name's Amanda… Amanda Blake.
MAN:	Right. I'll see you then, Amanda. Goodbye.
WOMAN:	Goodbye.

Practice Test 4, Section 2 (Track 14)

I'd like to thank you all for coming here today. Sorry about the lack of seating, those of you coming in now, if you could just stand by the far wall for today, I'll make sure we have enough chairs for all of you next week. My name is Barry Gordon and <u>I'm the founder and president of the Drama Club</u> here at Dora Jacobs University. It's just great to see that there are so many people wanting to find out more about our little club. You know, many doubted that this project would ever take off and today it looks as though we're one of the most popular student clubs in the entire university. I'm immensely proud to be part of it, and I hope you'll all begin to feel the same way in a couple of weeks' time.

I'd like to start by talking about joining and membership. All current students are welcome to become members of the Drama Club, and the best part is, it's completely free. Well, almost, as <u>we do ask for a small contribution every term</u>, but it's entirely voluntary. You will never ever be asked to pay a fee to take part in any of our activities. Having said that, <u>you do have to pay an initial £5 charge when you register with us</u>, but that's only to cover the costs of your membership card and welcome pack. You see, everything has to be done outside campus since we are not allowed to use any equipment from the university. So we do have to ask for that initial enrolment fee, just to cover our costs. If you are interested in joining our group, and I'm sure you all will be at the end of this evening, <u>you'll need to come to reception between 1 and 5 pm</u>, Monday to Friday.

When you go to the offices to register, there are four things that you must remember to bring with you. <u>The first thing you'll need is your student card.</u> Without your university student card we cannot register you as a member of the Drama Club. I know many of you don't use your student cards and might not even know where they are, so unfortunately, if that's the case, you'll have to go to the main reception and ask for a new card. <u>I know it's bureaucratic</u>, and I also know there's a system where we could easily check if you're a student or not, but I'm not the one who makes the rules, and rules have to be followed so I apologise in advance for that. Secondly, <u>you must bring a passport-sized photograph, of yourself obviously, when you come to register.</u> We'll need this for your badge and also for the amazing photographs we post on our website. Yes, we will post your photos on our page so make sure you look as good as you all look tonight. The third thing you already know, but I have to tell you again… it's in the script and a good actor always follows the script! Anyway, the third thing is the £5 fee. <u>Last but by no means least, the most important thing you absolutely must remember to bring along with you: enthusiasm, passion, and love for the theatre</u>. Without these qualities, I can't see a reason why anyone would be interested in joining our group. You'd be better off in the computer club, or with… what do you call them? With all the costumes? Anyway, it doesn't matter. What matters is that now you know what the requirements are.

So, now all that's been covered, let's talk about the Drama Club itself. Perhaps you're wondering what exactly it is that we do here. Are we a group of actors who want to get famous, make a fortune, marry models and move to Los Angeles? The answer is, surprisingly or not, no. <u>We are a diverse group of varying people, who want to socialise, meet other students, and above all, have fun</u>. That's why we're here. By joining the group, you will not necessarily be asked to perform on a stage. This is something you can do if you want to, and we will of course offer you help and guidance, but it's not compulsory and it never will be. You'll soon realise that most of your time here will be spent on relaxation exercises, storytelling, improvisation and group work, as well as many other transferrable skills that you will take with you for the rest of your lives. Learning such skills will make a positive difference in whatever it is that you decide to do in your future. Business, arts, law, languages… you name it. It doesn't matter what you're studying for your degree, we're more than likely to have something for you. This is what we do here, we help people understand people better, and we help you understand yourself better, that's the main goal of this Drama Club. But obviously, if you want to be famous and move to Hollywood you're more than welcome here. We wouldn't mind the recognition… maybe get some sponsors… who knows?

Anyway, let me show you our facilities. If you would just follow me I can show you….

Practice Test 4, Section 3 (Track 15)

MAN: Good morning and welcome back to Mother Nature Radio Show. I am your host, John Gibbs, and I have got a great show for you, today. Those of you who caught the first half have already heard Dr Popov's fascinating insights on the technological advances which can help us to prevent CO$_2$ emissions, and we've had some really great call-ins and messages about that already. Keep then coming! Now, my guest is Professor Kirsch, a global warming specialist who is here to explain to us how the greenhouse effect works and how it is responsible for the soaring temperatures experienced not only here in Australia, but all over the world this year. Professor Kirsch, welcome. I have to say it's an honour to have you as a guest on our show.

WOMAN: In all honesty, the pleasure is most definitely mine. I'm an avid listener to the show and I must admit I was terribly excited and not a little nervous, when your team contacted me. It's a real honour to actually be on the show myself, particularly in the same week as the eminent Dr Popov.

MAN: It's always good to know that important people in the field, like yourself, enjoy our show. It must mean we're doing something right. Anyway, welcome once again and let's start trying to tackle these big questions: What is the greenhouse effect and how is it connected to global warming?

WOMAN: Well, for those listeners less familiar with the phenomenon, the greenhouse effect is the process by which radiation within our planet's atmosphere warms the planet's surface to a temperature above what it would be without the surrounding atmosphere. Simply put, greenhouse gases in the atmosphere radiate energy in all directions. Some of this radiation is directed towards the surface, warming it. The amount of radiation will directly depend on the amount of greenhouse gases that the atmosphere contains. Without the greenhouse effect, the average temperature would be about minus 18°C, rather than the present average of 15°C. But the most important thing to understand is that the greenhouse effect is not actually caused by any human action or interference, it's a natural process which makes the Earth habitable. Without it, temperatures would be too cold for most life forms to survive.

MAN: Okay, that makes sense. So why is it then that people blame the greenhouse effect for global warming? If you do an internet search on 'the greenhouse effect', you get all these images of polluted cities, smog, and people wearing masks. So how exactly has a natural process that is supposed to make our planet habitable become such a vilified monster?

WOMAN: The answer is very simple—*we* are the monsters, not the greenhouse effect. Again, I'll explain. On Earth, the atmosphere is primarily warmed by absorption of infrared thermal radiation from the surface, which is heated by solar radiation from the sun. Greenhouse gases in the atmosphere radiate this energy, some of which is directed to the surface and lower atmosphere. The mechanism that produces this difference between the actual surface temperature and the effective temperature is due to the atmosphere and it is known as the greenhouse effect, which as we have already seen, is critical to supporting life. The primary greenhouse gases in Earth's atmosphere are water vapour, carbon dioxide, methane, nitrous oxide, and ozone. Yes John, carbon dioxide. Now the problem, or 'the monster' as you put it is this: Human activities such as the burning of fossil fuels and the clearing of forests have intensified the natural greenhouse effect, and that is what causes global warming. By raising the amount of carbon dioxide in the atmosphere, we are raising the amount of energy which is radiated by the atmosphere.

MAN: So basically what you're saying is, that the more carbon dioxide we pump into atmosphere, the more energy it radiates, and the hotter the earth gets…

WOMAN: … and the further the ice caps in the Arctic melt. Yes. It's a scary thought, but as Dr Popov said earlier, we already know the steps we need to be taking to slow this process. Greener technology can drastically reduce our carbon footprint. However, it will take the collaboration of the entire world. Everybody needs to commit to protecting our planet.

MAN:	Well, as difficult as that will be, it's something of a relief to know that we still have a chance at preserving our current atmospheric conditions.
WOMAN:	A fairly good chance, I would say. We just have to do the right thing, and for you listeners, the right thing starts at home with more efficient appliances and lights, greener energy providers, and so on. We'll start to see improvement when individuals make the effort to live greener lives.
MAN:	Absolutely. It's been an immense pleasure to have you here Professor Kirsch, thank you for that brief explanation.
WOMAN:	My pleasure.
MAN:	We're going to have a short break now, then we're going to go to the phones and answer some of your questions…

Practice Test 4, Section 4 (Track 16)

Clan, tribe, family. Whatever you call it, it's the most ancient and basic building block of society. Our family, to a large extent, defines who we are. When we were children it was our family that shaped us into the people we are now. We get our values from our family; we learn how to live with others through our family. We learn humour, intellect, sports, the fundamentals of life through our family interactions.

I'd like to thank you all for joining me, for this discussion about families. This morning I'll be outlining how family structure has changed in the US over the last one hundred years. Today's topic will be of particular interest to those of you who want to understand the 'hows' and 'whys' of the societies we live in around the world today. In this talk, I'll introduce the three main issues we'll be discussing throughout the day. The first, is answering the question 'what exactly is a family?' Then, we'll ask ourselves how and why families have changed over time. And finally, we'll discuss why this matters. What the significance of different family structures is, and what those differences and developments can tell us about the world.

Before I start, I would like to thank Professor Garcia and New Mexico University for all the support they have provided during the past eighteen months. I would not have been able to carry out this important research if it weren't for their know-how and willingness to make this a successful project, a project that can help us understand many of the socio-economic problems we face today. So thank you Professor Garcia and all the staff at New Mexico University for making today possible.

So, let us begin by analysing what a family consists of. Suppose an alien came to you and asked you the following question: 'What is a family?'

How would you answer that? <u>According to the US Census Bureau, a family is "a group of two or more people who reside together and who are related by birth, marriage, or adoption". It is a very straightforward definition</u> that most of us would agree with on the face of it, but if we take a closer look and think about the world around us, we may decide it needs to be adjusted. Where do married couples who live in different places fit in? What about divorced parents? And the aunts and uncles of the world who look after their nieces and nephews while their parents are at work? Grandparents, stepparents, half brothers and sisters… even godparents. Where do they all fit in? Are they not family? <u>I believe that using the US Census Bureau's definition of family is no longer an appropriate way to examine a family</u>. In many ancient civilizations, all of the people who contributed in some way to the upkeep of the household and the wellbeing of the individual members of the house were considered family. I believe this is a much clearer definition of family, and it's the definition I'll be using when I use the term 'family' throughout this discussion.

The first question we aimed to answer with this research project was how families changed over time and why. What is the "true" family structure? <u>In Western Europe, the nuclear or immediate family, which consists of biological parents residing together with their children, was the norm in the Middle Ages.</u> However, at that same time, Eastern Europeans had two or three generations living together as one family in the same household. These are two parts of the same continent that had extremely different concepts or ideas of what a family structure should be. It can easily be said, and proved with all the data you will see later on, that <u>this is due to different socio-economic realities.</u> Things are not so different here in the US. The United States has also seen numerous types of family structures throughout its brief history. The typical family forms we see today in the US, are actually the result of an evolutionary process that began with the changes in marriage nearly 300 years ago.

For many in the western world, it was not until the mid-18th century that the idea of free choice and marriage for love become a realistic option. Even then, it was certainly not the rule, but merely a notion that was beginning to be considered socially acceptable. Before this point, marriage had not typically been based on love. During the Stone Age, people got married to improve the economic situation of their clans or tribes. In the Middle Ages, marriage was used as an economic and political tool to satisfy the needs or desires of a particular extended family. Over time, marriage evolved into a union based on love. Many other economic and cultural developments in western society would also mold the structure of the American family. The 19th century unquestioningly upheld the idea of men as breadwinners and women as housewives. But how many families could achieve that? With very few jobs paying high wages that could actually support a single-earner family, this ideal was often seen as something that belonged only to the wealthy. And as a consequence, it turned into a goal or an ideal for the struggling lower classes, something to be achieved. Then suddenly, World War II was over, the economy grew and the American dream was born. Couples married young, remained married, had a lot of kids. For the most part, the husband would provide and the wife would look after the house and the children. However, in many countries, during the War, while men had joined the army and fought overseas, women at home had stepped up and starting working in their absence. When the war was over and the men returned, many women decided that they would continue to work, and would contribute to the family in a more financial, rather than homemaking sense.

From the early 70s onwards the divorce rate began to increase, as a result, the number of single parents became higher than ever, and people in their early twenties decided not to marry as young as their parents had. They weren't ready to settle down, they wanted to enjoy their lives a bit more before the big commitment. A large contributing factor to this was women's increasing access to education, birth control, and paid work.

This overview should give you an idea of the ways in which the family unit has adapted to economic and political changes in the American society. And we don't expect the changes to stop anytime soon.

Let's address the final question for this introduction: why does it all matter? Why do these changes matter? Why do families matter? The answer is quite simple, family structures matter because they help us understand who we are as a nation. Different family forms are a reflection of different groups of people. Not all societies worldwide participate in each family type. The same can be said about socio-economic factors. Each type of family structure... married with kids, single parents, divorced parents. New research suggests that children raised by only one of their parents are more likely to become a single parent themselves, may also have greater difficulty finding financial and emotional stability in adulthood. Some people say that the eyes are the window to the soul, well, I say that family structures are the window to a society. It can show us who we are, where we come from and where we're going.

Practice Test 5, Section 1 (Track 17)

EMILY: Cretan Holiday Homes, this is Emily speaking, how may I help?

PATTY: Hi! Well, I'm planning a holiday to Crete this summer and a friend of mine who stayed with you last year recommended you. He stayed with his family at one of your seaside properties in Chania and said the house was excellent, so I was wondering if I could ask a few questions about the houses you're advertising on your brochure?

EMILY: Of course! Just give me a second to get a form. OK. So, first of all, have you decided on the dates you'll be travelling to Crete, yet?

PATTY: We're still working on that! It's quite a big island and my husband and I were thinking of starting with Chania, then moving on to

Rethymno for a few days and just using a rental car to get to Heraklion and Lasithi. I don't know if that makes much sense, you probably know better than I do.

EMILY: Well, most of our clients choose a similar route—although they usually prefer to make one home their base and use the car to go everywhere else.

PATTY: Yeah, I thought of that, but the problem is, is that Chania is on the westernmost side of the island and I'm assuming the distances will be big so it'll take a while to get all the way to Lasithi from there, but my husband and I really want to stay there for a bit—all of our friends who've been there have really sold us on the idea!

EMILY: It's true, Chania is an extremely beautiful region—and you're right, the distances are definitely big. Thankfully, we do have properties in both Chania and in Rethymno. Do you have any specific properties in mind?

PATTY: Yeah, I've got a few here.

EMILY: Excellent, so let me just quickly take down your details and then we can have a look at the properties, how does that sound?

PATTY: Sure.

EMILY: So, do you mind giving me your name?

PATTY: Sure. It's Patty Parot. My surname is spelled like the bird, but with a single 'r'.

EMILY: Great. And a telephone number?

PATTY: 020 2833 8924.

EMILY: Thank you. And have you decided yet when you will be travelling to Crete, exactly?

PATTY: We were thinking late summer, probably the end of August, or the beginning of September. We want to skip the mid-summer rush.

EMILY: That's a good idea. We'll have better availability then. So, which properties were you interested in?

PATTY: I like the look of the one by the old port in Chania.

EMILY: Is that the one-bedroom or the two-bedroom flat?

PATTY: I think it's the one-bedroom flat. The one above the jewellery shop.

EMILY: Yeah, that's the one-bed.

PATTY: So, what I was wondering was, what sort of facilities should I expect in the flat?

EMILY:	So, the flat is fully furnished, with a bathroom and a kitchen. It has an A/C in the bedroom, and a small <u>balcony</u> with a seaside view.
PATTY:	And how much does that cost?
EMILY:	That's £60 per night.
PATTY:	All right, not too bad. The next property I was thinking of is the maisonette in Old Town.
EMILY:	Is that the one in the east or the west part of town?
PATTY:	On the brochure it says "Maisonette in the Old Town", I don't… No, wait, yep, here it is. West.
EMILY:	Great, so that's also got one bedroom with a small kitchen and a bathroom. I'm afraid there's no oven in the property, so you won't be able to cook any hot meals there—and at the moment the <u>airconditioning is not working</u>, but I'm sure that will be fixed by the time you stay there.
PATTY:	And how much is that?
EMILY:	That's a little bit cheaper, £20 less per night than the first one—so <u>£40</u>.
PATTY:	Okay. And I was looking at one more in Chania, and then we can move on to the ones in Rethymno.
EMILY:	Excellent. Which one's that?
PATTY:	It's just called <u>'the loft'</u>, looks like it's also in Old Town.
EMILY:	Ah, yes. That's a really popular one.
PATTY:	So, I'm a little bit confused because the brochure says it can accommodate up to four guests, but I can only see one bedroom in the picture?
EMILY:	Yeah, there's one bedroom and a sofa that opens into a bed. Young people and students tend to prefer this property for that reason.
PATTY:	Oh. So, does it get noisy at night?
EMILY:	Oh, no, not at all. The Old Town is a lively area for sure, but nothing extreme. It's like the other two properties.
PATTY:	And what about the facilities?
EMILY:	So, there's the bedroom and the living-room as I mentioned, there's also a kitchenette and a bathroom with a jacuzzi—and, of course, the <u>rooftop</u>, where you can see the whole city.
PATTY:	And how much is it?
EMILY:	That one's a bit pricier, £75 per night.

PATTY:	Hm. I'll have to think about it. I think we'll go for the first one, but I'll have to discuss it with my husband, first.
EMILY:	Of course. Shall we go through your options for Rethymno as well?
PATTY:	Yeah, there's a property there…

Practice Test 5, Section 2 (Track 18)

Good morning, ladies and gentlemen, and welcome to the Hat Museum. I'll try to keep this introduction short, as I can imagine you're all quite keen to have a walk around the museum and look at our exhibits, but I would encourage you to pay attention to the information I'll be giving you, as it will make your visit smoother and more fun.

I'd like to start by apologising for the very short opening times this week. As you can see, part of the museum is being renovated at the moment, which is why certain sections are not open to the public—I'll get back to that in a bit. Our usual opening hours are 9 am to 5 pm, but due to the works, we'll be closing down a bit earlier at 3 pm today. Still, it's only 11 o'clock now, which means you have four hours to go through everything and soak in all the beautiful hats. You are welcome to leave and return any time you like, but please note that last admission is at 2.30 pm, half an hour before closing time.

Now, as you can see here, we've got a very large hall which serves as an introduction to the museum and which is where you'll find most of our extra facilities, such as the restrooms on your left and the shop and café on your right. Those of you with children are also welcome to visit our Recreation Office behind the shop, where you will find resources for your kids such as quizzes, questionnaires, sheets for drawing and other handouts. If we have any teachers in our midst today, you might also find this useful if you'd like to plan a future visit with your class.

The museum is not particularly large, but you'll find it has a very ergonomic design.

Starting with the room on our left, you will find the Ancient World section, with replicas of the types of skull caps and straw hats ancient Greeks and Romans wore. The next room jumps forwards quite a few centuries and transports you to 17th-century Britain, where we have a small but impressive collection of original headgear. The rest of the museum's left section continues in the same vein, moving through the centuries all the way to the present, with a very large section dedicated to 20th-century Europe. By the time you reach that section you'll find yourself halfway through the semi-circle of the row of rooms in the museum.

This is the part where I'm afraid your visit will be slightly disrupted due to the renovation works I mentioned earlier. The right-hand section of the museum is dedicated to the journey of specific types of hats throughout history, and the impact they've had on society. We've got a room dedicated to fedora hats, another to top hats and yet another to berets and quite a few more. Unfortunately, one of these rooms is currently closed and will remain so for the next eight months. This is because of the fire that broke out in the museum a few weeks ago, which I'm sure you all heard about in the news. Thankfully, most of the exhibits in the fedora room were salvaged but, still, we have had to shut the room to fix it. Since this was our most popular room, however, we decided to move the exhibits temporarily to the cowboy hat room.

What this all means for you is that when you reach the final room on the left-hand side of the semi-circle, instead of being able to continue straight ahead into the right-hand side you'll have to exit, skip the next room and move on to the second room on the right-hand side, the bowler hat room.

Now, just a few final words and then I'll let you be on your way. As you can imagine, most of our original hats are fragile and therefore exhibited in glass cases. Some of the replicas, however, are exhibited on mannequins. I hope this goes without saying, but trying on these hats is strictly prohibited, and we would greatly appreciate it if you carefully monitored your children. The hats should be out of reach for them, but we have had cases of children knocking down our mannequins to reach the hats, so please be extra vigilant. You will have the chance to try out hats in the shop if you wish to, and we have many different sizes, for adults and children alike.

Also, you are welcome to take pictures of the hats if you would like, but please *do not* use flash as this can damage our more fragile hats. If you've forgotten your cameras, fear not: there's a phenomenal selection of photos and postcards in our shop.

Finally, as some of you might know already, the Hat Museum is run entirely by volunteers. We do not charge an entrance fee, but you are encouraged to leave your donations in this box here by the entrance. Please be advised that we accept all currencies.

Now, enough of my rambling on. Time for you to go in and enjoy our magnificent…

Practice Test 5, Section 3 (Track 19)

TUTOR: Hi, Agnieszka. Have a seat.

AGNIESZKA: Hi. Thank you.

TUTOR: So, I take it you've finished your interviews for your dissertation?

AGNIESZKA: I have, yes.

TUTOR: And have you had a chance to analyse the data yet?

AGNIESZKA: Oh, yes. I've prepared a graph, as well.

TUTOR: Excellent, let's have a look. Wow, that's quite comprehensive, well done. OK, can you talk me through it a bit?

AGNIESZKA: Sure. So, like we discussed in our previous meeting, I decided to focus on just two nationalities rather simply questioning everyone. It made it a bit more difficult to find enough participants, but I'm glad

I took your advice because <u>it was much easier to identify patterns in the responses</u>. I did consider, briefly, going for three nationalities—one from continental Europe, one from Britain and one from further afield, but I don't think one European country would be representative of the whole continent, so I decided against it.

TUTOR: I'm glad you did. Remember: the narrower the scope, the clearer the results.

AGNIESZKA: Yeah, that's what I thought, too.

TUTOR: Did you go for Polish and English, then?

AGNIESZKA: I did, yes. I created a survey and passed it around to a couple of friends of mine: one from the UK, and one studying at university in Poland. I also got in touch with the Polish community in the area and asked my friends and acquaintances to pass the survey around to their parents, because I wanted to get answers from as many age groups as possible.

TUTOR: Very good. Did you use the internet to find people as well?

AGNIESZKA: I did, I posted the survey on my social media and on forums and pages for Polish immigrants in London.

TUTOR: So, what was the response rate?

AGNIESZKA: <u>It was actually quite good, much higher than I'd anticipated. I got about 200 responses from UK citizens and around 250 from Polish people in the 18–25 age group, then about 150 each from both nationalities in the 25–40 group and around 200 in total in the 41 and over group.</u>

TUTOR: That's quite impressive.

TUTOR: So, what did you find out?

AGNIESZKA: Well, unsurprisingly, the majority of respondents under 26 from both countries were far more positive about immigration. 45% of young Polish people and 59% of young British people said that immigration had a positive effect on London. Another 32% and 26% respectively said the effect was neutral, and only 23% of Poles and <u>15% of Britons said immigration was a bad thing for the city</u>.

TUTOR: What about the other two groups?

AGNIESZKA: The findings in the 25–40 age group were very similar, but the 41 and over group were massively different: only 28% of Poles and 31% of Britons said immigration was a positive thing, and a huge 35% and 38% said it was bad.

TUTOR:	Did you think about splitting the group into smaller categories, for example, 40 to 55 and then 56 and over?
AGNIESZKA:	I did think about it, but the thing is, that I asked people to write their exact age as well as ticking the age group category just to be able to check if there'd be differences between those closer to 40 and those much, much older, but <u>I didn't find any notable ones</u>—so I don't think splitting them would've made a difference.

TUTOR:	OK. And what were the reasons people gave, generally?
AGNIESZKA:	Well, unsurprisingly, the main thing younger people mentioned was that London is <u>culturally enriched</u> by immigrants, who bring their customs and their cuisine and their language with them, and this has contributed, in their opinion, to making London the <u>world city</u> it is today. People from other age groups agreed with this, but the problem they had with immigration was the perception that people arriving to the UK are often resistant to <u>change</u> and might not be willing to adapt to the existing customs, which they felt defined their nationality. Oh, unemployment was also a major concern for many, as well as a perceived rise in crime in certain areas.
TUTOR:	OK. Anything else?
AGNIESZKA:	Yeah, some people also mentioned that the city is getting overcrowded and that's having an effect on <u>housing</u>, but not many of them thought it would be much better if there was less immigration.
TUTOR:	And any other positives?
AGNIESZKA:	Well, actually there was something quite surprising in the 25–40 age group. About 20% said one of the things they loved about immigration in London was the fact that it contributed to creating many new <u>romantic relationships</u> between Britons and foreigners.
TUTOR:	Now that's interesting.
AGNIESZKA:	Yeah, and of course many of them also mentioned that the British economy has thrived thanks to the constant stream of skilled, tax-paying immigrants.
TUTOR:	Of course. Anything else?
AGNIESZKA:	Um, there are quite a few more things but I think those are the main ones. I have to say there were some very interesting <u>personal stories</u> that people contributed anonymously both in the online and the paper survey. I had a section at the end where I asked people

to write any positive or negative experiences they've had with immigrants or because they themselves were immigrants, and I've got a bank of fascinating examples.

TUTOR: Great! Are you planning to reference any of these in your presentation?

AGNIESZKA: Yeah, I've picked a couple of positive and a couple of negative experiences from each nationality. There are plenty more, but I'll add these to my dissertation because it would take too long to read more than four.

TUTOR: All right, then. Let's have a look…

Practice Test 5, Section 4 (Track 20)

Being left-handed was once seen as a sign of the devil, who was said to baptise his followers with his left hand. It was also thought to be a sign of <u>witchcraft</u>. Joan of Arc, who was famously burnt at the stake, was often depicted as left-handed in art. As a result, parents in previous centuries often tied their left-handed children's hands behind their backs and forced them to learn how to write with their right hand, leading, we now know, not only to bad handwriting but also to poor concentration, unruly behaviour, shyness, bad memory and reading difficulties, as well as fatigue and neuroticism.

But what do we actually know about left-handedness? For a phenomenon that has existed since the early days of humanity and even further back, surprisingly little. We know that we have been predominantly right-handed for at least <u>500,000 years</u>, at least according to research conducted by the University of Kansas, and we know that, contrary to popular opinion, being left-handed doesn't necessarily mean being <u>right-brained</u>: in fact, while 95% of right-handed people use the left half of their brain more, up to 70% of left-handed people actually do the same. We also know that there's a long list of advantages and disadvantages associated with being a "<u>lefty</u>"—by the way, that's spelt with a 'y' at the end, not an 'i-e'—as left-handed people are often called.

Let's start with the advantages, shall we? It might surprise you to hear that most of these advantages have to do with the fact that left-handed people grow up in a world that overwhelmingly favours and expects right-handedness. Take sport, for example: left-handed people are more likely to excel in sports with one opponent, but this is not generally due to a naturally higher sporting ability. It has more to do with how often they get to practise against their opponents: living in a right-handed world, left-handed people get a chance to play against right-handed people far more often, thus growing more adept at <u>anticipating</u> a right-handed opponent's moves than a right-handed person might with a left-handed opponent, as there are so few left-handed opponents out there.

Similarly, left-handed people recover from illnesses more quickly than right-handed people but, once again, this isn't some innate characteristic they're born with, scientists believe it's because left handed people often need to strengthen <u>both sides</u> of their brain in order to thrive in our right-handed world. While a right-handed person does not have to struggle to use a pair of scissors or drive in most countries, for example, a left-handed person will need to take that one extra step in order to teach their left hand to mirror the movements of a right hand.

Then, of course, there are those advantages which I personally do not find as strong or empirically proven, such as the idea that left-handed people tend to become presidents more often, or that they are more creative. It has indeed been proven that left-handed people are better at <u>divergent thinking</u>, but this just means they are better able to examine a situation from all points of view rather than that they possess more creativity. At any rate, as Professor Ronald Yeo suggests, it's incredibly hard to measure something like creativity.

And there are, unfortunately, plenty of disadvantages linked to left-handedness as well. As I mentioned before, driving is one. <u>The UK</u> is a notable exception here, as left-handed people tend to pass their driving exams more easily than right-handed people because the gear stick and the lever are both on the left-hand side in UK cars. Unfortunately, most Western countries drive on the right, which puts left-handed drivers at a disadvantage.

Moreover, an Australian study from 2009 found that left-handed children were more likely to have issues in reading and writing, but also in their <u>motor skills</u> and the way they develop socially. Most children, the researchers said, catch up with their right-handed classmates as they get older—but that's not always the case.

Then there's the 2013 study which was conducted at Yale University, and which discovered that left-handed people are more likely to suffer from schizophrenia or other <u>psychotic disorders,</u> as well as the score of studies suggesting a link between left-handedness and dyslexia, ADHD, PTSD, etc.

But, as I said before, it's not all bad for left-handed people. Setting aside the advantages and disadvantages, what most researchers now agree on is that whether you're left-handed or right-handed doesn't really affect you that much at the end of the day. Sure, you will often be met with curiosity and have to answer the pointless question of "Are you left-handed?" when someone sees you using your left hand to write, and you might get your left hand, as well as your writing, smudged if you decide to use a fountain pen, but overall, the differences between left-handedness and right-handedness are so subtle and so insignificant that they are not enough to create two distinctive categories of people. It does, however, accentuate the fact that humans are varied and diverse for reasons we often misunderstand.

Practice Test 6, Section 1 (Track 21)

WOMAN:	Good morning. South West Railway Transport Information. How may I help you?
MAN:	Hi, good morning. I'm hoping you can help me to organise my travel plans. I'm taking the 6.17 from Basingstoke to London next Wednesday, and then I need to get to Streatham. Could you tell me how to get there?
WOMAN:	Streatham, was it? Just let me have a look. Streatham is about 5 miles from London Waterloo, which is where the train from Basingstoke will terminate. Which station was it in Streatham? Streatham, Streatham Hill, or Streatham Common?
MAN:	Streatham Common.
WOMAN:	Okay. Now if you give me a second I can try to find the best route in our system. Here we go, even though it's only five miles away from Waterloo, apparently it will take you around 70 minutes to get there.
MAN:	Wow! Really? Why's that?
WOMAN:	It's crazy, I know, but the thing is, you'd have to take the underground to Victoria Station before you could take a train to Streatham Common Station. I suppose you could always take a cab, if you're in a hurry.
MAN:	Right. Well, I don't really want to spend the money. I thought it'd be cheaper if I booked the whole journey with you instead of paying for things separately, you know. I've done this before and it saved me a lot of money.
WOMAN:	Yes, it often can. Just let me have another look at our system to see if there's an alternative route. You said you're leaving from Basingstoke, correct?
MAN:	Actually, I'm in Chingham. But yes, the closest railway station with a service to London is Basingstoke. I thought I'd take the 6.17 because it's direct and I'd get to London just before rush hour.
WOMAN:	OK. So let's see what the route planner has to say. So departing from Basingstoke. Which day are you travelling?
MAN:	Wednesday, 22 March.
WOMAN:	Oh, so it's a weekday, then. And what time do you need to be in Streatham? I'm only asking because it would be much cheaper to use an off-peak service.

MAN:	Right. Let me think. As long as I get there by lunchtime I should be fine. <u>I'm meeting some friends for lunch at 1.00</u> so if I got there at around 12.00, perhaps 12.30, that would be fine.
WOMAN:	OK. Just bear with me for one second.
MAN:	No problem.

WOMAN:	So, how about this. You could take the 10.43 from Basingstoke to Clapham Junction.
MAN:	Clapham Junction?
WOMAN:	That's right. You don't have to go all the way to London Waterloo and then Victoria. You can change trains in Clapham Junction and go directly to Streatham Common from there, as it's closer to Stratham than Waterloo.
MAN:	That's good news indeed. And that should save me loads of time, right?
WOMAN:	I believe so. As I was saying, you could take the 10.43 from Basingstoke, and get off at Clapham Junction.
MAN:	Right.
WOMAN:	<u>You'd be getting to Clapham Junction at about 11.25</u>. There you'd have to change platforms to take the 11.35 to Streatham Common. You'd arrive in Streatham Common at 11.45, as it's only 10 minutes away.
MAN:	That's brilliant. So it'll take me just over an hour for the entire journey?
WOMAN:	Yes. And if you take the 10.43 it's also much cheaper than going early in the morning.
MAN:	Great. So how much is it going to be then?
WOMAN:	Are you looking to buy a single or a return ticket?
MAN:	Return, please.
WOMAN:	Day or open return?
MAN:	What's the difference?
WOMAN:	If you choose a day return, you'll have to return on the same day. If you choose an open return, you can return any day as long as you make the journey within <u>60 days from purchase</u>.
MAN:	I guess I'll go for an open return, then. I'm not really sure whether I'll be going back on Saturday or Sunday.

WOMAN:	Perfect. So it's the 10.43 from Basingstoke to Streatham Common and you're changing trains at Clapham Junction... Sorry, the system is a bit slow today.
MAN:	Don't worry.
WOMAN:	Got it. Are you travelling first or second class?
MAN:	Second, please.
WOMAN:	That will cost you £31.00, then.
MAN:	Wow! That's far cheaper than what I was about to pay just to get to Waterloo. Excellent! Thank you.
WOMAN:	You're welcome, sir. Would you like to book your ticket now?
MAN:	Yes, please. Can I use a credit card?
WOMAN:	Yes, of course. But you'll have to take this card with you to collect the tickets from the station.
MAN:	That's not a problem.
WOMAN:	So if I could take your full name and the long number on the front of your card…
MAN:	No problem. I'm Matthew Sheppard, and the number is… uummm… 3320 1010 4665 1224.
WOMAN:	Thanks. And the expiry date?
MAN:	10, 2020.
WOMAN:	Thank you. And the last three digits on the back of your card?
MAN:	442.
WOMAN:	Thank you. I'm now processing your transaction, I won't be a minute. Fantastic, that's all done for you, sir. Make sure you take this card with you when you collect your tickets at the station.
MAN:	Thank you very much. I really appreciate your help.
WOMAN:	I'm just doing my job. Is there anything else I can help you with?
MAN:	I think that's it. Thank you very much.
WOMAN:	You're welcome, sir. Thank you for choosing South West Railway and have a good day
MAN:	And you. Bye.

Practice Test 6, Section 2 (Track 22)

Hello and welcome everyone. I'm Paul Martens and I'll be your guide for this virtual tour of the Jurassic Coast. So without any further ado let's get started with our tour of this magnificent site which was designated as England's first natural World Heritage Site in 2001.

I'll start by giving you some general background information. As you can see from the 3D map on your right, the Jurassic Coast is about 96 miles long, stretching all the way from Exmouth in East Devon to Studland Bay in Dorset. Apart from the breathtaking views, its cliffs are formed by many layers of sedimentary rock, which reveal the history of Earth going back approximately 185 million years. These layers cover the Triassic, Jurassic and Cretaceous periods. The images you are about to see are all based on data collected from the continuous sequence of rock formation. At different times this area has been: a desert; and if you look at the slide you can see an image of the arid plains, or what we believe what they would have looked like; it has also been a tropical sea, and here are some of the species that would have inhabited these waters; later it became a sprawling ancient forest—this is an image of the species of birds which would have lived here then; and then also, believe it or not, a lush swamp, populated by these various reptiles and amphibians. It still blows my mind that the area I call home was once inhabited by tropical fish, crocodiles and snakes. There's just so much these rocks can tell us.

Now, to the sights. On the screen to your left you can see a satellite image of the Jurassic Coast. It is home to some of the most beautiful landscapes in the whole of the UK, if not the world. Firstly, it is impossible to talk about the Jurassic Coast and not mention the incredible Durdle Door.

Durdle Door is a world famous geological wonder. It's an impressive natural limestone arch located between Swanage and Weymouth in Dorset. It has a sloping beach, which is perfect for snorkelling, and also features dozens of caves to be explored and exciting rock strata to be marvelled at. And, it's only a short walk away from one of my favourite places in the world, Lulworth Cove. The cove is the prime tourist attraction in Dorset. Both the cove and the arch are believed to have been created after the collision of two formerly separate continents, similar to the formation of the Alps. This brings me on to the next part of the tour.

Around 25 million years ago, the European tectonic plate collided with the African plate. This huge impact actually folded rocks and created the mountain range we know today as the Alps. Ripples from that collision heavily impacted the rock layers, and as the sea broke through the hard limestone and washed away the softer rocks, Durdle Door and Lulworth Cove were born. Normally, layers of limestone are horizontal, but Durdle Door is formed from a layer of limestone standing vertically out of the sea. There's only one force strong enough to have arranged these rocks in this way; the force of tectonic plates. Another impressive feature of the Jurassic Coast, as you should now be able to see on the screen right behind you… so if you could just… yes, thank you. As I was saying, a very distinct feature of the Jurassic Coast is the number of preserved fossils that can be found there. It is possible to recreate vivid landscapes from the Mesozoic Era. All the images you can see now were created using the fossils found in the area.

Let's take a closer look at some. This is an early Triassic desert, and now you can see the first dinosaurs and mammals. Here, the <u>tropical Jurassic seas that dominated the area about 180 million years ago… if you look here you can see that there's a vast increase in the number of dinosaurs compared with the Triassic period, and even some birds.</u> This last reconstruction shows the landscape evolving into a Crustaceous swamp, look at these flowering plants… Astounding, isn't it? I've worked here for almost a decade now and it still amazes me.

Well, that's the end of the first section of your tour. I'm leaving you now in the very capable hands of my colleague, <u>Professor Rhoades. He'll be talking you through the methods involved in fossil hunting on the Jurassic Coast.</u> Those of you who won't be joining us on our field trip to Lulworth tomorrow can follow me to the shop instead, if you prefer. If we exit through the doors at the back and then turn…

Practice Test 6, Section 3 (Track 23)

MATTHEW: Hello. James Southgate, isn't it?

JAMES: That's right. Pleased to meet you.

MATTHEW: Nice to meet you. Matthew Forsyth. Please sit down.

JAMES: Thank you.

MATTHEW: Well. First of all, thank you for your interest. <u>We were all really impressed with your results in the admissions tests.</u>

JAMES: Thanks.

MATTHEW: Shall I call you call James?

JAMES: Please.

MATTHEW: So, James. As we explained in your letter, those who achieved satisfactory results in the admissions exam would be invited to an interview, and this is why you are here today.

JAMES: Yes.

MATTHEW: This is the first part of the interview and I believe everything was explained in the letter.

JAMES: Absolutely. If I am correct, <u>we will be discussing my application form and experience</u> in this stage of the interview.

MATTHEW: Absolutely. And in approximately 45 minutes, we'll go on to the group dynamics.

JAMES: Perfect.

MATTHEW: <u>So… your first degree was in Communications?</u>

JAMES: <u>Yes, but I also took extra modules in Media Studies for my final year.</u>

MATTHEW: And you graduated in 2005, is that right?

JAMES:	Yes, and I have been a teacher since then. <u>I worked as an assistant teacher in New Zealand</u> and I was there for about thirty months, or two and half years. From 2006 to… 2009.
MATTHEW:	That's interesting. Why New Zealand?
JAMES:	I'd always wanted to go there. My uncle moved there when I was seven… he and my cousins would always come and spend most summers with us here in the UK, but I never really had a chance to go and visit them. My aunt is a teacher, and once I got my degree, she managed to get me a job there.
MATTHEW:	And that was at Wellington University, if I'm not mistaken.
JAMES:	That's correct.
MATTHEW:	It's a big university. I've been there myself a couple of times. And what did you teach?
JAMES:	Oh, a variety of things. <u>I used to cover for some of the permanent teachers, so I had the opportunity to teach English as an additional language, writing for scripts</u> and, what else…? The history of radio and television.
MATTHEW:	Right. Quite a variety, then.
JAMES:	Yes, and <u>I also ran some video editing workshops.</u>
MATTHEW:	Oh, that sounds like fun.
JAMES:	It was great. Obviously, if I am honest with you, there were times I didn't really know what I had to do, or if what I was doing was right.
MATTHEW:	Why's that?
JAMES:	For instance, once I was told to step in right in the middle of an EAL lesson because the teacher was feeling sick—
MATTHEW:	Pardon my ignorance, but what's EAL?
JAMES:	Oh, excuse me. English as an additional language.
MATTHEW:	Right
JAMES:	So, I was asked to step in right in the middle of the lesson and I had no idea what was going on, <u>but because I had some experience teaching English in Argentina during my gap year</u>, they thought I'd be able to just stride right in and pick up where their teacher left off with their lesson.
MATTHEW:	Uh oh!
JAMES:	<u>Yes, but the problem was that they were all medical students</u>, and they'd been practicing very specific vocabulary, most of which I had never even seen before.

MATTHEW:	I see.
JAMES:	But in the end I did manage to explain the situation to the students. They were quite good about it and we ended up having an interesting conversation about the differences in public health in the UK and New Zealand.
MATTHEW:	It sounds like you handled it well after all.
JAMES:	Thanks.
MATTHEW:	And why is that you want to do an MSc in History?
JAMES:	Well, I've come to realise that teaching is what I want to do for a living. Although I did enjoy my time teaching English and media studies, history has always been my favourite subject…and when I had the opportunity to teach the history of radio and television, for example, I remembered how magical it was for me to explore the past in order to better understand where we are today, and how we got here… I used to love history at school.
MATTHEW:	Well, I have to say I am impressed with both your work experience and your passion. So, now I'll ask you to quickly take me through your studies, from…

Practice Test 6, Section 4 (Track 24)

Hello, everybody, and welcome to the first week of our Creative Writing course for beginners. This course looks like the busiest one yet! Believe me, it's so nice to see so many of you here. My name is Thomas Rugely and I'll be your teacher-slash-instructor for this course. Teacher, because I will be teaching you some of the most common writing strategies used by modern novelists and writers; and instructor, because I will also be coaching you on how to put these strategies into practice.

As you can see from the first page of your programmes, today is really just an introductory session. I'm going to be talking you through the course itself so we can make sure you know exactly what is going to happen during the two hours you'll be spending with us each Thursday for the next 12 weeks.

First, let's cover the basics. This is a creative writing course in the 21st century and as such, I don't expect any novelists to be *handwriting* their 300-page books.

Instead, the vast majority of our work will be done digitally. You're more than welcome to bring your own laptops to class if you'd rather, though we do also supply our own equipment here. Having said that, tablets and phones are not considered appropriate for this course, so if you want to use your own machines they have to be appropriate, portable computers with a relatively up-to-date word processor installed on them. If any of you are not that comfortable with your typing skills and feel that you might get left behind, just log onto our learning platform using your student details—you should have all received these by email, but anyway they should be in one of the forms in the welcome pack I'm about to give you—just log into our platform and download the typing trainer. You'll see that your typing skills will drastically improve in just a couple of hours. Also, if you're using your own equipment, it's a good idea to arrive half an hour earlier next week, so that you can copy over all the files we'll be using in the course.

This is a 12-week course, with the first week being a simple introduction and get together, and a formal exam in the last week. That then leaves us with 10 different modules to be covered during the term, over the remaining weeks.

The first module is all about character development. Next week, we'll be discussing and experimenting with various character development techniques. This is, in my opinion, the heart and soul of creative writing. A writer can have a very sketchy plot, and yet manage to produce a great book if their characters are strong enough. Not that I'm trying to belittle the benefits of a well thought out plot, on the contrary, and that's why they're the topic in the following week for module 2; I simply believe that you cannot have a good story without solid, plausible characters. Anyway, as I've just told you what our topic is for module 2, let's move swiftly on to module 3, which is all about 'points of view'. You need to understand that 'the speaker', or, the person you decide to tell your story through, has a crucial effect on the reader's experience. During this module, you'll be practising different techniques, such as writing in the first or third person, and writing from one character's point of view or those of several different characters within your books.

'Description Strategies' is the title for module 4, and here we'll be exploring how to depict the world of your story and the people who live in it. The following week, you'll revisit the characters you created in module 2. It is essential to keep revisiting, revising and adding depth to the relationships between your characters if you want to create realistic and interesting stories, so that's what we'll be doing in module 5, which is week 6. After that, we'll break for two weeks for half term. That should give you plenty of time to get the basics of your story together: main characters, plot and locations before we can move on to module 6.

After half term, we'll be discussing and experimenting with some basic principles of writing engaging dialogues, so this is where your workload will be more than doubled. Make sure friends, family, the dog and the cat know that you'll have no life as of week 8 of the course. 'Voice' is the topic for module 7. It's directly connected to module 3 as we'll be exploring how to give the narrator, or narrators, of your story lively compelling voices to engage and arouse the reader's curiosity and keep them reading. During module 8, 'setting', you'll have the chance to go through what I like to call 'the creators checklist'. It will help you master the art of devising a dynamic world full of interaction, struggles and conflict. Then we will move on to 'beginnings'—for me, this the one aspect which is more important than a good ending is a good beginning. It's your business card, the photo in your passport, the suit you wear to a job interview, and no one will continue to read a book if the beginning is not engaging. It's the rod, the line, the bait and the hook for the fish. So, in module 9 we'll be exploring what should be revealed, hinted at, or withheld in the first chapter of a novel.

Santosh Kalwar once said "every beginning has an end, and every end has a new beginning". In module 10 we'll be exploring how to <u>design endings that give readers a sense of closure without closing the doors on the possibility of a sequel</u>. And finally, drum roll please, your extended assignment in week 12. You'll be asked to write an extended piece of fiction based on specific circumstances which will be provided to you on the day of the exam. Those of you who look horrified now can relax; this extended assignment is worth just fifty per cent of the course marks, with the other fifty based on your performance throughout the course. We do believe in continuous assessment so don't worry if…

Answers and Explanations

PRACTICE TEST 1

Listening Section 1

1 Jane Schmilton
2 Swiss Cottage
3 16 February/16th February
4 continuous enrolment
5 ten weeks/10 weeks
6 once
7 £90
8 not necessary
9 comfortable
10 deposit/deposits

Listening Section 2

11 A
12 E
13 C
14 G
15 F
16 K
17 C
18 A
19 C
20 B

Listening Section 3

21 Fright Night
22 jazz
23 75
24 3
25 welcoming
26 started dating
27 logistics
28 privacy

29 penpals/pen pals

30 aggressive

Listening Section 4

31 Equality Act

32 hindrances

33 [established] practices

34 parking spot

35 ramps

36 delegate

37 [purposely] unclear

38 work flexibility

39 20%

40 effective, practical

Academic Reading Passage 1

1	**NO**	Text: Scottish poet Robert Burns wrote his 'Address to the Toothache' in which he described the malady as the 'hell of all diseases' (Paragraph 1)
2	**NOT GIVEN**	Text: There are actually more instances of tooth decay now than ever before, probably due to our high-sugar diets. (Paragraph 3)
3	**YES**	Text: … primitive forms of toothpaste that consisted of pulverised brick, charcoal and other dubious ingredients. (Paragraph 4)
4	**NO**	Text: … they also doled out detrimental advice on how to care for teeth and soothe an aching tooth— suggesting, for instance, that patients pick their gums with the beak of an osprey bird. (Paragraph 6)
5	**NOT GIVEN**	Text: … for the average person, the only solution to tooth decay would be extraction … (Paragraph 6)
6	**NO**	Text: … advances in dental health have continued into the 21st century. (Paragraph 8)
7	**modern practices**	Text: neither the physical pain nor the inconvenience inflicted through modern practices can compare with what our ancestors would have had to face when one of their teeth decayed. (Paragraph 2)

8	**tooth worms**	Text: In fact, a reference to tooth decay can be found in a Sumerian text (circa 5,000 BC), which attributed the disease to 'tooth worms' … (Paragraph 3)
9	**vinegar**	Text: … sometimes vinegar—which, any modern dentist will tell you, is highly acidic and can weaken your tooth enamel. (Paragraph 4)
10	**pliers**	Text: Though the thought of having healthy teeth removed with pliers and with no anaesthetic may seem alarming and incredibly unwise to modern readers … (Paragraph 7)
11	**G**	Text: … collapsible tubes of toothpaste, which were introduced in the 1890s, didn't become popular until the early 1900s. (Paragraph 4)
12	**F**	Text: Cinnamon, bay leaves, nutmeg and cloves were also used, as they were found to combat bad breath. (Paragraph 5)
13	**both D and E**	Text: … not only had the manufacturing process of silver fillings been standardised, but the x-ray had also been adapted for use in dentistry by G.V. Black and Edmund Kells. (Paragraph 5)
14	**C**	Text: … and for the average person, the only solution to tooth decay would be extraction … (Paragraph 6)

Academic Reading Passage 2

15	**B**	Text: … although it was one of the more successful methods employed to protect British civilians and their homes from German air raids by effectively making it more difficult for night bombers to navigate and pinpoint targets in the dark.
16	**H**	Text: … forcing the government to reduce the speed limit to 20 mph and paint white lines on the streets to guide pedestrians and drivers.
17	**C**	Text: Surprisingly, the measure was initially met with curiosity and excitement, and many civilians took to stargazing.
18	**I**	Text: Full lighting did not return until April 1945—more than five years after the blackout was first introduced …

19	**G**	Text: Several accounts from the *Mass Observation* journals (a sociological research project that sought to record everyday human activity) suggest …
20	**F**	Text: … under the floorboards of the recently bombed Vauxhall Baptist Chapel …
21	**brown paper**	Text: … and sealing any gaps with brown paper every single night. (Paragraph 3)
22	**[hefty] fines**	Text: … if one of the Air Raid Patrol wardens who monitored the streets saw even the smallest hint of light slipping through their covers, the owners were subject to hefty fines and, less often, court appearances. (Paragraph 4)
23	**second door**	Text: … many shops had to install a second door in order to prevent light from being visible outside when customers entered. (Paragraph 4)
24	**helmets/armbands**	Text: Gangs such as the infamous Billy Hill's raided jewellery shops and stores. As the men took to wearing Air Raid Patrol helmets and armbands to disguise themselves … (Paragraph 6)
25	**TRUE**	Text: It didn't take long for the novelty to wear off, however, as people soon realised the difficulties involved … (Paragraph 3)
26	**FALSE**	Text: According to figures collected by the Home Office, the reported cases of indecent assault on women in Britain almost doubled from 1935 to 1944 … (Paragraph 8)
27	**NOT GIVEN**	Text: People navigating the city in the dark sometimes fell off bridges into rivers and ponds. (Paragraph 9)
28	**NOT GIVEN**	Text: Full lighting did not return until April 1945—more than five years after the blackout was first introduced—with the symbolic illumination of Big Ben in London. (Paragraph 10)

Academic Reading Passage 3

29 **recent technological advances**
Text: ... recent technological developments, however, are beginning to change the way we view death. (Paragraph 1)

30 **online user agreements**
Text: ... the murky and often contradictory online user agreements ... (Paragraph 2)

31 **[online] afterlife services**
Text: ... why online afterlife services such as *The Digital Beyond, Legacy Locker* and *If I Die* have sprung up. (Paragraph 2)

32 **social media accounts**
Text: ... as Eterni.me offers the possibility to leave behind a 3D avatar version of ourselves after we've gone, equipped with knowledge taken directly from our social media accounts ... (Paragraph 3)

33 **mechanical challenge**
Text: ... the end goal of Terasem is similar to other religions, [...] but for us it's not simply a spiritual concept, it's a mechanical challenge. (Paragraph 4)

34 **ethical questions**
Text: For Graziano, this raises a host of ethical questions ... (Paragraph 5)

35 **online presence**
Text: To begin, let's look at virtual afterlife, that is, the personal information and online presence which remains on the internet after a person has died. (Paragraph 2)

36 **3D avatar**
Text: Eterni.me offers the possibility to leave behind a 3D avatar version of ourselves after we've gone ... (Paragraph 3)

37 **dreamscape look**
Text: ... aims to offer people the chance to meet and talk to deceased loved ones in a virtual-reality setting replicating a place with special significance to the deceased, adjusted in order to present a 'dreamscape look'. (Paragraph 3)

38 **digital backups**
Text: Technology could one day make this a reality through digital backups. (Paragraph 4)

39 **digital humans**
Text: What kind of human rights will we ascribe to digital humans? (Paragraph 5)

40 **speculation**
Text: Of course, unlike with virtual afterlife and digital reconnection, digital afterlives remain simply speculation for now. (Paragraph 6)

Academic Writing Task 1

The flow chart shows the typical journey of a fiction novel from the moment of its conception all the way through to its publication.

To begin with, a novel is just an idea in the author's head. Once the author puts pen to paper, that idea slowly transforms to the first draft of a novel, which is then edited and polished in preparation for submission. When ready, the author sends the novel off to agents, and those who find it worthy of publication contact the author.

Eventually the author signs a contract with an agent, and then the two work together to further improve the novel. Once the novel is ready, it is the agent's turn to submit it to editors in publishing houses. Interested editors then make an offer and, depending on the interest the novel generates, an auction might be organised.

Once the agent and author have selected a publisher, the agency negotiates a contract, which the author signs. The author and the publishing house editor then discuss potential changes to the novel and when the final draft is ready, it is copyedited and a design is prepared for publication. Meanwhile, the publishers get in touch with booksellers and also design a marketing campaign. When all of this is done, a publication date is set and the book is finally published.

(223 words)

Academic Writing Task 2

The amount of food available to people in developing and developed societies has seen a dramatic increase in recent decades. Unfortunately, so has the amount of food being thrown away, both by individuals and by businesses. In this essay, I am going to discuss a few of the reasons behind this phenomenon, and what we can do to address it.

Perhaps the biggest factor in food waste is poor education. Personally, I do my shopping once a week, after I've planned out all my meals and not only which ingredients I will use, but also how much of each I will need. Unfortunately, a lot of people in my social circle do not do this. Instead, they visit the supermarket after work and purchase what they need for their next meal, without any consideration for how much they're buying or how they can use their leftovers. As a result, a lot of the food they buy spoils and ends up in the bin.

Businesses are probably much better at planning how much of each product they need to order. However, it is impossible to predict how much food will go unsold—and as we live in a society where presentation and money are everything, companies would rather throw away blemished food or food past its best before date than offer it at a discount or give it away for free to charities.

The solutions to these causes, however, are quite simple. When it comes to individuals, government programmes aimed at educating people on how to 'buy smartly' might help to reduce waste. Indeed, plenty of my aforementioned friends bemoan the lack of such initiatives. As for businesses, perhaps the best solution would be to make a law forcing them to give away all their leftover food to homeless people and charities. Such a law was passed in France quite recently and has already proven a smashing success.

To conclude, food waste is a terrible issue that affects most civilised countries, and it is a direct result of consumerism and our poor food education. There are, however, many ways to tackle this problem, as long as everyone agrees to do their best to control how much food they personally waste.

(369 words)

General Training Reading Section 1

1	D	Text: I'm offering a finder's fee of £200 …
2	C	Text: Please let me know if you have any information by contacting Richard at richysutton@denty.com.
3	A	Text: Small, ginger kitten with no collar reading 'Buttercup' found …
4	B	Text: To claim, you must be able to correctly describe the keyring to us.
5	E	Text: To claim, visit the lost property office at the bus depot, Penrith …
6	(brown) bear/teddy	Text: My daughter misplaced her favourite teddy on a walk in Arnside last weekend. He's a brown bear with a yellow jumper …
7	Morecambe Bay	Text: I lost my smartphone last week in the vicinity of Morecambe Bay …
8	picture	Text: If this is your cat, please call 07700900174 and be prepared to provide a picture.
9	FALSE	Text: SHODDY FURNITURE FALLING APART? Let SOUTHWARK CARPENTERS help.
10	TRUE	Text: Or just want to replace your creaky floorboards?

11	NOT GIVEN	Text: (4) the timeline for the work to be completed. That generally gives us enough information to create a custom quote …
12	TRUE	Text: George was professional, friendly, and went the extra mile to finish the job on the same day.
13	NOT GIVEN	Text: Sarah was able to get the work done for half of our initial quote, and didn't skimp on the quality!
14	C	Text: Sarah was able to get the work done for half of our initial quote …

General Training Reading Section 2

15	managers	Text: As managers, it's your responsibility to maintain a healthy work environment …
16	openly	Text: Managers should address changes likely to cause unrest openly …
17	vacations/breaks	Text: Vacations should not only be encouraged, they should be mandatory …
18	working overtime	Text: In cases where employees are working overtime, ensure that they are taking time off to make up for this at a later date …
19	thoughts and feelings	Text: Make sure to have regular one on one conversations with your direct reports, and encourage them to share their thoughts and feelings with you about work.
20	manager's resources portal	Text: *If you'd like to learn more about creating a healthy workplace environment, you can access our manager's resources portal for further reading.*
21	B	Text: If they voice complaints, take what lengths you can to address these, and if they offer suggestions, consider implementing them.
22	G	Text: The Pomodoro technique was created in the 90s by the Italian entrepreneur Francesco Cirillo. As a student …
23	C	Text: When used consistently over a longer period of time, The Pomodoro Technique can even help to improve your attention span, and increase the rate at which you complete projects.

24	I	Text: If you finish your work before the timer goes off, end your pomodoro at this point …
25	B	Text: After you have completed 4 pomodoro cycles, take a longer break of 20–30 minutes. This is a good time to have something to eat if you're hungry …
26	F	Text: If you find you're competing work too quickly, try to make each chunk of work longer, or complete 2 different 10–15 minute chunks of work together, as one pomodoro.
27	A/D	Text: Using the technique can prevent procrastination, help you to keep working at a regular pace, and cause you to complete a number of items from your to-do list.
28	A/D	Text: Using the technique can prevent procrastination, help you to keep working at a regular pace, and cause you to complete a number of items from your to-do list.

General Training Reading Section 3

29	D	Text: Their colour makes them instantly recognisable due to the London Transport paint standards, first implemented at Chiswick Works Laboratory.
30	C	Text: This differentiates the colour from Post Office Red, which is for mail boxes.
31	B	Text: In the 1970s, paint producers started to use white in their mixes to reduce costs and to improve coverage. Lead was banned in paints at this time, which meant that buses had a slight pastel sheen …
32	A	Text: … the classic diesel-fuelled bus …
33	NOT GIVEN	Text: If you've ever visited the capital of England, you will know that the brilliantly red London Routemaster buses are a global icon …
34	NO	Text: However, the primary function of red British telephone boxes is to stand in tourist spots …
35	YES	Text: The London Transport Museum has stated that there are several paint tones available to the public, and have made the list available on request.
36	YES	Text: TfL has come under fire for allowing zealous religious and political groups to advertise, as well as permitting risqué jokes in ads for movies and plays.

37	NO	Text: … 'Green buses', which cut down CO_2 emissions through hybrid engines and particulate filters. Despite the name, these buses will continue to resemble the classic bus in style and colour …
38	controlled	Text: The paint colour of London buses was controlled by Chiswick Works Laboratory from the 1950s until around the 1980s.
39	colour	Text: There was no master colour for the paint being created at this time; instead the colour was mixed fresh for each bus. As a result, it was possible to detect slight discrepancies between the colours of London buses …
40	models	Text: … obsessive hobbyists writing in to find out how they can get hold of authentic Bus Red paint for their models …

General Training Writing Task 1

Dear Max,

I was so happy to read your letter telling me that you're coming to Berlin for the weekend. Berlin is a very fun city, especially in the summer. There are so many things to do and places to go. I'm sure you're going to have a great time.

In two or three days it's hard to fit in everything that's worth seeing here. One way to see a lot of the city in a short time is by boat. You can take a boat tour along the rivers and canals of Berlin and see the city from a unique perspective while learning about its history. I also recommend going to Alexanderplatz. There's a huge TV tower there that the locals call Alex. You can go up to a viewing platform near the top and see all of Berlin and beyond. Once you've done that, you should visit some of the shops and restaurants in the area. There are many to choose from.

In order to get around quickly and easily, I recommend buying a weekend ticket for Berlin public transportation. You can get these at any train station kiosk or download an app and buy your ticket on your phone. The trains and buses can be a bit tricky in Berlin, so I recommend using a navigation app on your phone to help you get around.

You have any questions or need some help you are welcome to call me on my mobile phone or send me a text.

Have a great time in Berlin!

Sincerely,

Fabian

(259 words)

General Training Writing Task 2

As long as students have been going to school, they have had homework to do afterwards. The older students get, the more difficult and time consuming homework becomes. It can be hard for students to balance their academic requirements with fun activities, which are also important. Perhaps that's why some people think homework should be banned. However, I believe that homework is a crucial part of students' education.

Some people believe that homework should be banned because students spend enough time studying while they're at school. In fact, most students spend all day at school, often starting early in the morning. They often experience a lot of pressure to learn the material and pass exams while earning good grades and following the rules. That's why some people believe students should be free to do whatever they want after school.

It is true that it can be hard for students to balance school and homework with other activities they might want to do, like play sports or hang out with friends. However, it is possible for students to do those activities and still complete homework assignments if they organise their time well.

Although students do spend a lot of time at school, the environment can be very distracting and it is often difficult for students to process all of the information they learn in a school day. Homework assignments are especially useful for reinforcing the lessons they learned at school. While doing homework, students can work at their own pace and in a more peaceful environment. This way, they are able to remember what they are studying, which will help them when they are in class the following day.

I believe that homework should not be banned, because it is an essential part of students' education. It gives them the opportunity to revise and remember what they've learned at school. If students are well organised, they can do homework and still have time for friends and extracurricular activities. That way, they can learn, relax and have fun too.

(337 words)

PRACTICE TEST 2

Listening Section 1

1 £20/20 pounds
2 10.15
3 Streatham High
4 opposite
5 events department
6 balanced diet
7 Smart Cooking
8 cooking strategies
9 Conscious Food
10 31

Listening Section 2

11 B
12 A
13 C
14 responsible
15 activities
16 (the) accounts department
17 of Operations
18 security arrangements
19 (local) police
20 Lunch Break

Listening Section 3

21 A
22 C
23 A
24 C
25 D

26 Email Mark a copy/email him a copy

27 The bigger picture

28 (He feels) (ridiculously) frustrated

29 Notes from the Underground

30 being human

Listening Section 4

31 practical progress

32 speaking (skills)

33 increasingly busy

34 interactive and detailed

35 leading publisher

36 enable teachers

37 B

38 A

39 C

40 B

Academic Reading Passage 1

1   **NOT GIVEN**

2   **NOT GIVEN**

3   **YES**   Text: despite the perhaps ironic efforts of some of the contributors to add an apolitical romanticised aura to the conflict. (Paragraph 2)

4   **YES**   Text: Philip Carson's remarkable drawings and paintings of aerial battles focus on the plastic beauty of one of the ugliest times in human history … (Paragraph 3)

5   **NOT GIVEN**

6   **NO**   Text: … interspersed with sympathetic images of young Italian women working for the British Army Service Corps … (Paragraph 5)

7   **C**   Text: … Carson first created these pieces while serving as a fighter pilot, which might explain his reputed emotional detachment from the more brutal aspects of the conflict. (Paragraph 3)

8	**A**	Text: … unfortunately, some of his portraits take on a strong resemblance to backstage shots from a period soap opera. (Paragraph 4)
9	**D**	Text: Despite the evident failings of some of the work, the collection does have its merits, and these come largely through the work of Peter Paul Carroll. (Paragraph 5)
10	**B**	Text: Carroll's work gives a true representation of what life would have been during and shortly after the conflict, without presenting sterile, emotionless images. (Paragraph 5)
11	**A**	Text: … *War in the Sunny Alps* offers very different perspectives on this final apocalyptical stage of the First World War … (Paragraph 6)
12	**D**	Text: … fought in what was undoubtedly one of the most formidable landscapes of the entire conflict. (Paragraph 6)

Academic Reading Passage 2

13	**x**	Text: Though the new 12-sided pound coin is still a charming novelty to most British people on the high street, for policymakers at the Royal Mint and the Bank of England, it may be the solution to a serious problem … (Paragraph 1)
14	**v**	Text: Counterfeit money has been in circulation for almost as long as legitimate currency. (Paragraph 2)
15	**iv**	Text: Today, counterfeiters are very rarely motivated by such political aims. Most forgeries are created simply in order to provide the counterfeiters with more disposable income. (Paragraph 3)
16	**xi**	Text: In total, there are around 30 million fake pound coins in circulation … (Paragraph 4)
17	**iii**	Text: In 2016, an East London gang were found to have created £16,000 worth of counterfeit money in only a month. (Paragraph 5)
18	**i**	Text: It is often possible to tell whether a pound coin is fake or not by looking at the edges of the coin to see whether they are rough. (Paragraph 6)

19	viii	Text: There are plenty of urban legends about other ways to tell a fake: for instance, it is commonly believed that a false pound coin will lose its colour if its surface is scraped with a copper 1p or 2p coin. In fact, this will only be the case with the shoddiest, least proficiently produced forgeries. (Paragraph 7)
20	vi	Text: since no replacement money can be given for these technically worthless items, it is perhaps unsurprising that few people who detect false coins ever hand them in. (Paragraph 8)
21	legitimate currency	Text: Counterfeit money has been in circulation for almost as long as legitimate currency. (Paragraph 2)
22	economic disaster	Text: … with the intention of lowering the value of legitimate American currency by flooding the market with forgeries, and causing an economic disaster. (Paragraph 2)
23	2.55%	Text: A study in May 2015 found that 2.55% of pound coins in circulation at that time were fakes … (Paragraph 4)
24	ingots	Text: The gang created their own counterfeit coin press and used ingots of metal to create one and two pound coins. (Paragraph 5)
25	urban legend	Text: There are plenty of urban legends about other ways to tell a fake: for instance, it is commonly believed that a false pound coin will lose its colour if its surface is scraped with a copper 1p or 2p coin. (Paragraph 7)
26	shoddiest	Text: In fact, this will only be the case with the shoddiest, least proficiently produced forgeries. (Paragraph 7)

Academic Reading Passage 3

27	C	Text: This collaboration marked the first time in Blackburn's career that her experiments began to focus on the real lives of individuals.
28	H	Text: Blackburn now believes that both a healthy lifestyle and emotional support help, but meditation is the most effective way of keeping levels of telomerase high.

29	B	Text: Elissa Epel, a postdoctoral student from UCSF asked Blackburn for help with a study she was carrying out …
30	G	Text: Currently, in collaboration with the care consortium Kaiser Permanente, Blackburn is concerned with measuring the telomeres of over 100,000 people.
31	J	Text: They believe that children are the age group most exposed to damaging behaviours from bullies, abusive parents, rough neighbourhoods, low socio-economic status, and environmental pollution.
32	E	Text: As soon as the paper was published, an explosion of further research was triggered.
33	TRUE	Text: Blackburn discovered an enzyme called telomerase. This enzyme is capable of slowing the shortening of telomeres, effectively providing a means of slowing the ageing process. (Paragraph 1)
34	FALSE	Text: … Elissa Epel, a postdoctoral student from UCSF asked Blackburn for help with a study she was carrying out, looking into the behaviour and health of mothers of chronically ill children. (Paragraph 2)
35	TRUE	Text: Many scientists regarded the findings with disbelief, so more evidence to either confirm or deny these findings was sought. (Paragraph 5)
36	FALSE	Text: The big question now is whether telomeres merely work as a unit of measurement for the ageing process, or whether they play an active role in age-related health problems. (Paragraph 6)
37	NOT GIVEN	Text: What most people don't know is that meditation—according to Sara Lazar, a Harvard neuroscientist—is even capable of changing brain structure. (Paragraph 9)
38	TRUE	Text: Studies have also reported a broad range of benefits such as depression relief and lowering of high blood pressure. (Paragraph 9)
39	NOT GIVEN	
40	NOT GIVEN	

Academic Writing Task 1

The first table shows how much of the total energy used by Sweden and the United Kingdom in the years of 2013 and 2015 originated from fossil fuels.

For both years, the largest percentage was used by the United Kingdom with more than double the percentage of Sweden. However, both countries reduced the use by 3% in a twenty-four-month period, which represents a significant drop of 10% for Sweden but only about 3.5% for the UK.

The second table illustrates electricity consumption per person in the same countries for the same period. It is possible to see that an average person in Sweden uses approximately three times more energy than the average British person. Figures for both countries dropped slightly from 2013 to 2015, which might reflect the use of more environmentally friendly technology. It might be possible that the Swedish population use more electricity per year due to their long winters and a more sustainable use of fossil fuel, which would make them feel less guilty about their electricity consumption than the British.

(174 words)

Academic Writing Task 2

Over the last 50 years, the routine of human beings has changed drastically due to scientific breakthroughs. These technological advances are completely changing the way we live our lives, which means that change cannot just be seen as a personal option these days. However, there is still a group of people who prefer to live their lives in the same way as they used to ten or twenty years ago. These individuals do not believe that change is inevitable and take pleasure in maintaining a stable, slow-paced routine.

One might say that those people who feel they gain a sense of security by always doing the same things are living in denial. They might resist change themselves, but they cannot stop the world around them from evolving, and evolution comes through change. It is only a matter of time until these people realise that their usual behaviour is no longer socially acceptable or that their jobs no longer exist.

On the other hand, the idea that change is always for the better can be a dangerous one. The capitalist world in which we live these days is constantly promoting changes, with the ultimate aim of making a profit. We live in a society where the 'elite' is capable of imposing changes for their own benefit. Large amounts of technological innovation will not necessarily make our lives easier.

In conclusion, I would say that everything in life needs to be done in moderation. Changes can be motivating and energising, but too much change can make people live in a constant process of adaptation and prevent them from ever being able to truly enjoy their lives.

(273 words)

General Training Reading Section 1

1	**accept payment**	Text: Bus drivers are no longer able to accept payment for travel.
2	**valid transport pass**	Text: You must have a valid transport pass, AVG card or a contactless credit or debit card to pay for your journey.
3	**£40/forty pounds**	Text: If fees are paid within 21 days, the penalty is reduced to £40.
4	**postal order**	Text: You may mail your payment in the form of a postal order …
5	**the station**	Text: The station where your journey began on that day
6	**accepted**	Text: If the evidence you provide is accepted, you will not have to pay a penalty fare.
7	**email**	Text: You will receive an email to notify you of the outcome of your appeal.
8	**TRUE**	Text: Have you been hearing your nurse use the term "Lamaze" but unsure what that means? Come to this introductory one-day course …
9	**FALSE**	Text: Drawing on the strength of the people in your community, this class will help expecting mums and their partners to prepare for a calm, peaceful childbirth.
10	**FALSE**	Text: this class will help expecting mums and their partners to prepare for a calm, peaceful childbirth.
11	**TRUE**	Text: Course delivered by certified paramedic.
12	**NOT GIVEN**	Text: These questions and many more will be answered in this course focused on skills you'll need as a new parent.
13	**TRUE**	Text: Classes are twice a week for four weeks.
14	**TRUE**	Text: Many new parents would prefer to have support in their own home. Our trained nurses visit your home …

General Training Reading Section 2

| 15 | **v** | Text: To avoid strain on your back, you should change your chair to make sure it is supporting your lumbar spine, or the part of your back above your bottom. |

16	**i**	Text: Your feet should be comfortably flat on the floor.
17	**viii**	Text: Adjust the height of your chair to accommodate your requirements.
18	**vii**	Text: Your keyboard should be approximately 4–5 inches away from you and at the height of your ribs.
19	**vi**	Text: Shift the position of your computer monitor to ensure there is no glare from sunshine or overhead lights. You can adjust the settings on your monitor to make it more or less bright.
20	**iii**	Text: You should not need to crane your neck in order to see your monitor clearly. It should be directly in front of you …
21	**iv**	Text: It is better to take more frequent, shorter breaks, than only one or two long breaks …
22	**B**	Text: Never ignore a customer complaint. All complaints should be resolved to the best of our abilities within 72 hours of the complaint being received.
23	**C**	Text: By listening carefully and recognizing the customer's feelings, this will help calm an angry customer and make it possible to find a solution.
24	**A**	Text: It is important that you don't try to give a solution to a customer's complaint until you have understood it well and the customer has given you the necessary details.
25	**B**	Text: You will be expected to ensure any offer you make to a customer is completed as you have agreed.
26	**A**	Text: While you are expected to be aware of standard operating procedures, in case of difficulty, do not hesitate to contact the manager on duty when you receive the customer complaint.
27	**(customer) notes**	Text: Customer notes include the customer's name, location, date of delivery, and details of the customer's complaint.
28	**for the inconvenience**	Text: When the manager is done speaking with the client, follow-up with the customer and apologise for the inconvenience before ending the call.

General Training Reading Section 3

29	H	Text: The sturdy design proved popular with working men, such as miners, ranchers and cowboys …
30	I	Text: Modern versions of denim include not just the original indigo colour, but all the colours of the rainbow.
31	E	Text: In the early 1800s, about half a century after denim was invented, a Frenchman called Guimet invented an artificial indigo dye …
32	C	Text: The word 'jeans' also comes from the history of denim. The French word for Genoa, Italy, where the serge fabric the French weavers imitated came from, is Gênes.
33	D	Text: India began to grow plants especially to create indigo dye and the country became a major exporter of the dye.
34	G	Text: At the same time in Reno, Nevada, another immigrant from Latvia received an order to sew a pair of tough work pants.
35	F	Text: Levi Strauss followed the Gold Rush to San Francisco …
36	FALSE	Text: The name dungaree is believed to come from the Indian town Dongri …
37	FALSE	Text: … weavers attempted to recreate a material called 'serge', a tough cotton corduroy made in Genoa, Italy. They were unsuccessful …
38	TRUE	Text: The indigo colour which was used as the dye when denim was invented was incredibly cheap thanks to the busy trade routes that brought the plant leaves the dye is made from into Europe.
39	NOT GIVEN	Text: He asked Levi Strauss, who supplied his fabric, to provide the financial backing for the patent, which they were granted in 1873.
40	FALSE	Text: … 30% less waste to produce a pair of jeans.

General Training Writing Task 1

Dear Mr Evans,

I am writing to you regarding my neighbours, in Apartment 22, in Erasmus House. The people who live across the hall moved here approximately three months ago.

Recently, every day when I arrive home around from work, I can smell cigarette smoke coming from under my neighbour's door. This is a problem because I live directly across the hall, which means the smell of smoke also comes under my door. Some days, I can smell the cigarette smoke in every room in my apartment. It is very unpleasant. I have also asked them to turn their music down several times.

I know the building has a no-smoking rule and I believe that my neighbours are breaking that rule. Could you please remind them about the rule and ask them to smoke outside?

Thank you very much for your assistance. I look forward to hearing from you about this issue.

Best wishes,

Emily Read

(155 words)

General Training Writing Task 2

The role of celebrities and the roles that parents and teachers play are all important for children. Children can be impacted by the people close to them and people they see on tv or read about online. Who should be a role model is a question all parents and teachers face.

Some of the advantages of celebrities using their positions to influence young people is that celebrities are able to reach many people with their message. Celebrities can become leaders for important causes. Children can learn that they should use their own position to help others. Another advantage of celebrities is children may see someone they admire and decide that they want to work hard to be like them. A celebrity doesn't have to be just a movie star or a musician, but a celebrity might be a famous scientist or politician.

The main advantage of parents or teachers being role models for children is that teachers and parents know the child personally. They can help the child to choose the right path in life by offering advice or using situations to teach the child. Parents and teachers can also see what talent a child has and help to nurture that talent, so the child feels they have support of the people close to them.

In my opinion, the best role models for children are the people closest to them. Parents and teachers can love and support a child to help them grow up healthy and make good decisions.

(249 words)

PRACTICE TEST 3

Listening Section 1

1   Andrews

2   Westminster / University of Westminster

3   postgraduate certificate

4   12 Meymott

5   SE1 8NZ

6   evening work

7   workshop[s]

8   21 February / 21.02 / 21st February / 21/02 / 02/21

9   of address

10 originals/photocopies **NB:** *in either order, both required for 1 mark*

Listening Section 2

11 12/twelve

12 1870

13 modernist vision

14 functional

15 **horses/servants NB:** *in either order, both required for 1 mark*

16 (intricate) woodwork

17 Universal

18 (count's) daughter

19 world heritage (site)

20 Catalan artists

Listening Section 3

21 B

22 A

23 C

24 B

25 A

26 B

27 C

28 D

29 G

30 H

NB: *26–30 in any order*

Listening Section 4

31 A

32 C

33 B

34 instinctive reactions

35 overestimate

36 heart disease

37 [incredibly] frightening

38 beneficial

39 never

40 worse

Academic Reading Passage 1

1   viii

2   i

3   iv

4   x

5   vi

6   iii

7   v

8   xi

9	NO	Text: although that might have more to do with the average age of a student rather than a person's inclination towards academia. (Paragraph 2)
10	YES	Text: In German, the mare who was said to cause it was known as the *Nachtmahr* … (Paragraph 4)
11	NOT GIVEN	Text: Sleep paralysis has been heavily documented in art, too: Herman Melville's novel *Moby Dick* is a notable example … (Paragraph 5)
12	NO	Text: sleep paralysis is completely harmless—though it certainly might not feel that way for the sufferer. (Paragraph 6)
13	YES	Text: Sleeping in your side is also less likely to trigger a sleep paralysis episode than lying on your back, so this is also often recommended to sufferers. (Paragraph 8)

Academic Reading Passage 2

14	C	Text: If it's the cover-subsidence kind, the bedrock will become exposed and holes will appear on it, which will then turn into ponds. (Paragraph 3)
15	E	Text: Some areas, such as Florida in the USA, are more prone to sinkholes … (Paragraph 3)
16	F	Text: … as with the sinkhole that swallowed a whole building complex in Guangzhou, China, in January 2013. (Paragraph 4)
17	D	Text: Over the decades, dams built along the river Jordan by surrounding Middle Eastern countries to produce hydroelectric energy and divert water for irrigation have reduced the volume of water that flows into the lake … This causes a rapid drop in the water level. (Paragraph 2)
18	A	Text: The sinkholes in occurring in the Dead Sea are formed by the dropping sea level leaving behind layers of salt underground … As these layers dissolve, they leave behind unstable chasms under the ground. (Paragraph 5)
19	I	Text: while one of the widest sinkholes is the Qattara Depression in Egypt … (Paragraph 6)

20   **holes/ponds**   Text: If it's the cover-subsidence kind, the bedrock will become exposed and holes will appear on it, which will then turn into ponds. (Paragraph 3)

21   **solubility**   Text: Some areas, such as Florida in the USA, are more prone to sinkholes due to the solubility of the bedrock they've been built on. (Paragraph 3)

22   **rainfall**   Text: This is usually due to poor drainage systems combined with heavy rainfall … (Paragraph 4)

23   **rainwater**   Text: … plenty of the most recently collapsed sinkholes occur near constructions where rainwater is concentrated on a particular patch of land … (Paragraph 4)

24   **localised/localized**   Text: This is because most sinkholes tend to be localised. (Paragraph 8)

25   **acidic**   Text: They are the result of what is known as the karst process, where soluble bedrock (such as limestone or chalk) is dissolved by acidic rainwater. (Paragraph 3)

26   **sandstone**   Text: … which means that some types of ground, such as sandstone, will take longer to disintegrate as they are more consolidated … (Paragraph 7)

27   **governments**   Text: Many experts are now pushing for more research. Given how sinkholes are becoming widespread both in urban and rural settings, perhaps governments will soon be more inclined to listen to these pleas. (Paragraph 8)

Academic Reading Passage 3

28   **E**   Text: Such a tactic, however, would not only be time-consuming and impractical, it would also be impossible for larger-scale problems than the Königsberg one. (Paragraph 5)

29   **G**   Text: It is thanks to graph theory, for example, that we can now tell with certainty which order of moves a knight on a chess board should follow in order to land on each square once and return to his original square. (Paragraph 7)

30   **F**   Text: … and graph theory, or geometry of position as Gottfried Wilhelm Leibniz had earlier called it, was born. (Paragraph 6)

31	**D**	Text: Euler had published a paper, *Solutio problematis ad geometriam situs pertinentis*, that not only gave a definitively negative answer to the famous Königsberg Bridge question … (Paragraph 4)
32	**F**	Text: To simplify things, then, Euler drew a diagram ('network', or 'graph') which represented the four landmasses ('nodes', or 'verteces') … (Paragraph 6)
33	**H**	Text: Nowadays, very little remains of the original city in Kaliningrad besides a few restored historical buildings such as the Dom or Sackheim Gate. (Paragraph 8)
34	**trading centre/center**	Text: Back in the Middle Ages, the city of Königsberg was an important trading centre and the capital of the German province of East Prussia. (Paragraph 1)
35	**four districts**	Text: Between the two sides of the city were two large islands, thus dividing the city into four districts … (Paragraph 2)
36	**mathematical proof**	Text: … at the same time, Ehler theorised that one could not be certain there was no solution without solid mathematical proof. (Paragraph 3)
37	**banal**	Text: Euler was at first dismissive of the Königsberg Bridge problem, describing it as "banal"… (Paragraph 4)
38	**network/graph**	Text: To simplify things, then, Euler drew a diagram ('network', or 'graph') … (Paragraph 6)
39	**D**	Text: In the case of Königsberg, all four nodes had an odd degree, as one land mass had five bridges touching it and the remaining ones had three … (Paragraph 6)
40	**C**	Text: Following this, the city was also targeted by Soviet troops who arrived in January 1945 and left in April, slaughtering thousands of people and leaving behind them nothing but ruins. (Paragraph 8)

Academic Writing Task 1

The two maps demonstrate the developments that took place on the island of Petrichor in the thirty-year period between 1987 and 2017.

In 1987, Petrichor was a relatively unspoiled, green island with a significant number of trees and a few individual houses in the west. By 2017, however, most of the trees had been cut down except for a small number in the east. Houses in the west were demolished and replaced with blocks of flats, and a shopping centre and hospital were constructed in the southwest. In the north, there were further developments in the form of a large shoe factory and an airport.

The old ruins in the southeast remained untouched, but a few individual houses were built in the vicinity. New bus transport links were also introduced to connect the old ruins, the airport and Petrichor's city centre to each other, as well as with the shoe factory.

Overall, the two maps suggest that in the given thirty-year period Petrichor underwent a series of drastic changes that not only modernised it, but also industrialised it.

(178 words)

Academic Writing Task 2

The concept of alien life which is intelligent and comparable to human life has fascinated us for over 100 years. The majority of books, films and T.V. programmes in the science-fiction genre include alien life forms, and many scientists are currently engaged with trying to find evidence of life on other planets within our solar system.

If scientists are able to successfully prove that alien life does exist, the implications for us would be literally astronomical. Finding proof that life could survive outside of Earth not only suggests that one day humans might be able to live on other planets, but it would also suggest that many more planets contain alien life, and would suggest that somewhere in the universe, beings comparable to humans could exist.

However, as yet there is no proof that alien life exists. Some people claim to have been visited by aliens, but as these people never have any verifiable evidence to support their claims, merely anecdotal stories and conjecture, such stories seem unlikely to be true.

Some people believe that, as the universe is unimaginably large, with countless planets observed in other solar systems which seem to have the potential to harbor life, probability alone should suggest that alien life must exist in the rest of the universe. They argue that, given so many different possibilities for life, how can Earth possibly be the only planet to actually contain life forms?

Other people argue that, as the universe is so vast, and so old, and human beings are an extremely recent addition to the solar system, if intelligent life existed on many other planets, a large number of these aliens should have existed for much longer than humans, and would therefore be more evolved, more intelligent and have better technology than us. If this were the case, many of these alien beings should have discovered how to travel faster than the speed of light, and how to identify other planets which contain life, and have discovered a method to communicate with these life forms. Clearly, this has not yet happened on Earth, as we have no evidence of having been visited by alien life.

(359 words)

General Training Reading Section 1

1	**(or download) any**	Text: watch or download any BBC programing, including BBC iPlayer.
2	**homes and businesses**	Text: These costs are the same for both homes and businesses.
3	**1/one**	Text: A TV licence covers all televisions, computers or other devices used to watch or download content in one property.
4	**DVDs or videos**	Text: You do not need a licence to watch DVDs or videos or clips on some websites.
5	**hearing or vision**	Text: If you have severe hearing or vision impairment you may also been able to apply for a reduced fee.
6	**live programing**	Text: The fine for watching or recording live programing, watched at the same time as it is being broadcast, not at a later date, is up to £1,000.
7	**valid**	Text: The TV Licensing Agency may perform unannounced home visits to check that you have a valid TV license.
8	**declare**	Text: If you are not watching live programming ... you do not need a TV license, and you should declare this fact.
9	**TRUE**	Text: Some runners who plan to run in more than one Park Run may pay £10 to have their barcode transferred onto a fob that is easy to lace onto your shoe.

10	**NOT GIVEN**	Text: We provide water at the finish line of every Park Run …
11	**TRUE**	Text: but to reduce the number of plastic bottles we use, we ask runners to bring their own reusable water bottles. There will be stations at the finish line where you can refill your water bottles.
12	**FALSE**	Text: If you know that you will complete the 5K race in under 20 minutes, please position yourself closer to the starting line. If you know that it will take you 30 minutes or longer to finish, please place yourself closer to the back. This ensures that there is less crowding as the race begins.
13	**TRUE**	Text: When you pass the finish line, your time will be recorded, based on the official start of the race.
14	**FALSE**	Text: Final times will not be given until after the race is completed by all participants.

General Training Reading Section 2

15	**D**	Text: This should also reflect best practice and the post-holder may manage plans with individual departments.
16	**C**	Text: This will include working with leads of other departments to prepare and deliver updates for rolling out new policies. The Senior Accountant will be responsible for reporting on plans and policy implementation in meetings held every quarter.
17	**F**	Text: In the interview, the successful applicant will be expected to show interpersonal skills, including strong leadership qualities.
18	**E**	Text: The applicant should also be able to demonstrate up-to-date knowledge of financial regulations in the private sector with recommendations for the organisation.
19	**B**	Text: The Senior Accountant will be responsible for ensuring that the organisation follows all legal requirements for accounting …
20	**A**	Text: To lead and manage the Accountancy Team, ensuring delivery of effective and timely accountancy services to all departments within the organisation.

21	**2.2 days**	Text: In you first year of work with the organisation, you will accrue, or earn, your holiday by 2.2 days each month.
22	**first quarter**	Text: However, you must use these five days within the first quarter of the new year, which means you must take these days of leave before June 30th.
23	**iv**	Text: Every full-time (working 35 hours per week) member of staff is entitled to 25 days of annual leave every year.
24	**iii**	Text: Our company works on an April–March calendar for annual leave.
25	**vii**	Text: If you are not able to take all of your annual leave, you may carry over five days onto the next calendar year.
26	**i**	Text: Firstly, before applying for annual leave, check with your line manager.
27	**vi**	Text: Once you have informed your manager, log on to MyHR.com and complete the required information.
28	**ii**	Text: If you feel that your annual leave request has been denied unfairly or you are finding it difficult to organise your work responsibilities, please contact the Human Resources Manager.

General Training Reading Section 3

29	**thick soot**	Text: Before the invention of the stove, a fireplace was used several times a day for cooking as well as heating. This meant chimneys were often coated in grease from cooking as well as thick soot from wood or coal.
30	**house to house**	Text: After the Great Fire, households became acutely aware of the dangers of a dirty chimney, and knew just how easily fire can spread from house to house in a crowded city like London.
31	**flue**	Text: (a flue is a passage for smoke and gases from a fire).
32	**knock down**	Text: The child would go down inside the flue and use their feet to knock down the clumps inside the chimney.

33	**tradesmen/chimney sweeps**	Text: These children would be hired by tradesmen, called chimney sweeps, who would clean chimneys for a few coins.
34	**gather wood**	Text: Children are often expected to gather wood, which is time that they lose on studying or play.
35	**TRUE**	Text: Before the invention of the stove, a fireplace was used several times a day for cooking as well as heating.
36	**FALSE**	Text: During this period of British history, dirty chimneys also caused pollution in the nearby atmosphere such as smog as well as devastating fires from burning ash lingering in the air.
37	**FALSE**	Text: The original flue cleaners were made of a long cane made of a substance called Malacca, imported from the Caribbean, and a brush made of whalebone. These brushes were initially used by children working in the chimneys …
38	**FALSE**	Text: It wasn't until 1864 that the House of Lords banned the use of Climbing Boys by chimney sweeps in the UK with an Act of Parliament.
39	**NOT GIVEN**	Text: Nowadays, some people continue to have fireplaces or wood-burning stoves in their homes for heating or because they like the cozy smell and feeling of a fire indoors.
40	**TRUE**	Text: It is also a common cause of death of young children …

General Training Writing Task 1

Dear J&R Builders,

I live in the Saversen Building, next to the office building where you have been working.

Because of your work, the back exit to my building is closed. I have to walk for several blocks out the front entrance to the parking lot behind the building to get my car. This is extremely inconvenient.

I believe the exit has been closed because some materials are put behind the door. These materials should be moved to another part of the parking lot and the exit could be opened. Is it possible to make those changes?

Occasionally, the workers are very loud during the night. I have asked them to be quiet but please remind them residents may be sleeping.

Thank you for your attention and your solution to this problem. Please feel free to contact me if there are any questions. My email address is at the end of this letter.

Sincerely,

Joel Silverstein

(157 words)

General Training Writing Task 2

More and more people find themselves in jobs that do not have the same structure as full-time work. There are pros and cons of this type of informal or freelance work, which I will describe in this essay.

Informal work has several advantages. One advantage is that work without a fixed contract allows people to work the hours that are the most convenient for them. People who take care of children or who have another full-time job can do this work alongside their other commitments and earn more money. This work may also be done at home or in your own car, like drivers hired by popular app companies. The flexibility and convenience of this work makes it attractive to many people.

The main disadvantage of this work is that it is not very stable. Sometimes the work might not be available when you need it, for example if you make and sell a product from your home. When you are not able to get customers, you do not earn, which can be very difficult if you need to pay for food for your children. Moreover, if you are sick, or unable to work for some reason, you also cannot earn money.

Overall, the disadvantages of this work far outweigh the advantages. Workers need protection to be able to miss work for illness and also to be able to enjoy holidays. This kind of work may add extra income for the family but it should not replace formal full-time employment.

(251 words)

PRACTICE TEST 4

Listening Section 1

1 100
2 178
3 black
4 £170
5 £500
6 £550

7   Thornton

8   38 Dean Park

9   police station

10 8.15

Listening Section 2

11 founder and president

12 every term

13 5 pounds / £5

14 (at) 5 pm / o'clock

15 B

16 A

17 C

18 C

19 A

20 B

Listening Section 3

21 emissions

22 global warming

23 B

24 C

25 C

26 A

27 thermal radiation

28 carbon dioxide

29 fossil fuels

30 ice caps

Listening Section 4

31 families changed

32 New Mexico University

33 straightforward

34 appropriate

35 immediate / nuclear

36 realities

37 acceptable

38 wealthy

39 divorce

40 A

Academic Reading Passage 1

1	TRUE	Text: As we continue to finds new ways to store more data on a smaller scale, we are able to create faster, more detailed computers … (Paragraph 1)
2	NOT GIVEN	Text: Data storage took off as a result of the invention of magnetic tape. Fritz Pfleumer patented the first brand of such a tape that fused oxide with paper or film. Sometime after its initial creation, magnetic tape began to be used as a medium through which music and video could be recorded and preserved. (Paragraph 2)
3	FALSE	Text: Magnetic drums were created in the 1930s, but did not become widely used until the 1950s. These drums were used in early computers to provide a similar function to RAM in modern computers. (Paragraph 2)
4	FALSE	Text: Floppy disks as a form of magnetic data storage were first devised in 1967, but weren't available commercially until 1971 with the 8 inch 'Diskette 1'. (Paragraph 3)
5	TRUE	Text: The disk, fabric and casing were created with a hole in the middle, allowing a spindle in the disk drive to be inserted in order to spin the disk. (Paragraph 3)
6	TRUE	Text: The fabric sleeve used in floppy disks performed two functions: to remove any dust that settled on the exposed magnetic disk, and to reduce friction as the disk was spun in the drive. (Paragraph 4)
7	NOT GIVEN	Text: In fact, the common name 'floppy' arose because these 8 inch disks were very flexible and could easily be bent. (Paragraph 4)
8	flexible	Text: In fact, the common name 'floppy' arose because these 8 inch disks were very flexible … (Paragraph 4)

9	**corruption**	Text: There was also the risk of data corruption if the disks were ejected while they were still spinning … (Paragraph 4)
10	**aperture**	Text: In addition, the aperture through which the disk was read ... (Paragraph 6)
11	**protected**	Text: In addition, the aperture through which the disk was read was at this point protected by a spring-loaded metal slider, which would be automatically pushed aside when the disk was inserted into a floppy disk drive. (Paragraph 6)
12	**sectors**	Text: Before the disks could be used for the first time, each had to be formatted, a process where a series of concentric rings (called tracks) and sectors (or, the angular blocks in a track) were created … (Paragraph 7)
13	**1.44Mb**	For a 1.44Mb 3½ inch disk, this involved creating 80 tracks on each side, each track having 18 sectors, each sector holding 512 bytes of data. (Paragraph 7)
14	**B/E**	
15	**B/E**	

Academic Reading Passage 2

16	**ii**	
17	**vi**	
18	**iv**	
19	**vii**	
20	**infrequency and unpredictability**	Text: The infrequency and unpredictability of tsunamis makes them very difficult to study. (Paragraph 2)
21	**not all tsunamis**	Text: A common misconception is that all tsunamis are formed by earthquakes. While earthquakes are indeed responsible for about three-quarters of all tsunamis, the caving in of giant icebergs, the eruption of underwater volcanoes, and even meteorites hitting the ocean have all been known to produce giant waves in the past. (Paragraph 3)
22	**shallow**	Text: In addition, shallow earthquakes are more likely to cause tsunamis than earthquakes occurring closer to the Earth's core. (Paragraph 3)

23	**wavelength**	Text: We can measure the size of tsunamis by calculating the difference between the crests the highest points of the waves. This measurement is called the wavelength. (Paragraph 5)
24	**tracking system**	Text: Following the invention of the tsunami tracking system, scientists are able to forecast when and where one could hit the coast. (Paragraph 6)
25	**Electronic buoys**	Text: Devices at the bottom of the ocean can measure any increase in pressure and send this information to the electronic buoys on the surface. Data is then passed to satellites and transmitted to monitoring stations on land. (Paragraph 6)
26	**drastically**	Text: Tsunamis can achieve speeds of up to 850 km/h at sea, but they slow down drastically and somewhat erratically on their approach to shore. (Paragraph 7)
27	**column of water**	Text: … a tsunami in open sea can be thought of as nothing more than an enormous column of water shifted from a large and sudden displacement of the sea floor. (Paragraph 8)
28	**natural barriers**	Test: It is also known that coral reefs and mangroves can reduce the wave energy and act as natural barriers. (Paragraph 9)

Academic Reading Passage 3

29	**chemical stability**	Text: Limestone is used in order to provide chemical stability … (Paragraph 2)
30	**colour**	Text: Other ingredients, such as iron and carbon may also be added in order to provide colour to the glass. (Paragraph 2)
31	**cullet/recovered glass**	The amount of cullet, as recovered glass is known by glass manufacturers, used can vary considerably, with as much as 40% being used in some areas of glass production. (Paragraph 3)
32	**furnace**	Text: These batches are then fed into a glass furnace to be melted in a stage known as the 'hot end' process. (Paragraph 4)
33	**red hot liquid**	Text: When the materials are mixed in the furnace, the extreme heat produces a liquid substance called molten glass. This red hot liquid glass … (Paragraph 4)

34	**gobs**	Text: A shearing blade is used to cut and form the glass into cylindrical shapes called gobs. (Paragraph 5)
35	**Press and Blow**	Text: (Paragraphs 4/5)
36	**Blow and Blow**	Text: (Paragraph 6)
37	**parison**	Text: There it assumes the mould's shape and a rounded mass of glass, called a parison, is formed. (Paragraph 5)
38	**annealing**	Text: This process is known as annealing and it reduces the amount of stain in bottles, which makes them more resistant. (Paragraph 7)
39	**pieces of stone**	Text: the bottles are inspected for cracks or pieces of stone that might compromise the quality of the final product. (Paragraph 8)
40	**beverage**	Text: the bottles are packaged and delivered to various beverage factories, where they are filled up with liquid, sealed, and sent out … (Paragraph 8)

Academic Writing Task 1

The chart compares the unemployment rates between the UK and the US in January from 2008 to 2015. The general trend which can be seen to occur in both countries is that unemployment rate rise then fall between 2008 and 2015, giving similar rate of unemployment for both countries in 2008 and 2015. It can be said that the figures represent the end of a cycle which saw unemployment rates peak in 2010 before correcting to more usual numbers in 2015.

In January 2008, both the US and Britain had very similar unemployment rates in the region of the 5 percent mark. For the twelve months that followed both rates rose, however, the unemployment rate in the US suffered a sharper rise surpassing the British rate by approximately one percent. The same trend occurred in the following twelve months when the American rate reached a staggering ten percent. Even though numbers also increased in Britain, they did not exceed the eight percent mark in January 2010.

The scenario changed after January 2010 when the rate in the US began to fall, dropping to eight percent in January 2012, catching up to the British rate for the first time in four years. Both figures remained stable until January 2013 before a decrease taking the American unemployment rate below the British for the first time since 2008. Both rates suffered a further drop in the following twelve months, reaching approximately 5.2 and 5.6 percent respectively in January 2015.

(246 words)

Academic Writing Task 2

Music used to be much more simple to access than it is today. You could enjoy it on the radio for free, even if you didn't get to pick what would be played. If you went to a concert, you paid for it. If you bought a CD, you paid for it. Stealing music would have meant shoplifting a CD from a shop, and everyone knows that that type of theft is wrong. The invention of technology has changed the way we access music. Is there a difference between listening to a song on a licensed website and illegally downloading music?

Illegally downloading music is wrong because it is against the law, however, it is also true that many more people engage in downloading content illegally than those who commit theft of physical objects. It is often difficult to compare the two forms of theft, as stealing a physical object has a direct negative impact on the person you steal from; they have lost the item you have taken. Illegally downloading music, on the other hand, does not have an immediate negative impact on the person you are stealing from—you have provided yourself with a song without paying for it, but the owner of the song still has the song, too, and can continue to sell the song indefinitely with others.

The main issue with illegally downloading music is that, if everyone continues to illegally download songs instead of purchasing them (as a very large proportion of the population currently do), this leaves the artist with less money for their music, which makes it more difficult for an artist to make a career out of their music, and in turn, limits the amount of good music being produced.

Many people do not feel that illegally downloading music is wrong, because they are quite far removed from the effect of illegally downloading on the artist, but I feel it is wrong because if you appreciate a musician's music enough to want to download it, you should be actively trying to support that artist, in order to help them to make more music you like.

(355 words)

General Training Reading Section 1

1	**NOT GIVEN**	Text: A foundational course that teaches the basics of yoga …
2	**TRUE**	Text: taught by our professional training staff.
3	**FALSE**	Text: Beginners and experts welcome!
4	**FALSE**	Text: a fun workout in this new group course …
5	**NOT GIVEN**	Text: … please reserve a spot in advance.
6	**NOT GIVEN**	Text: Location: Cycling Studio

7	**ecologically responsible**	Text: marketing solutions for ecologically responsible businesses.
8	**maintain**	Text: Maintain a high standard of organisation in the office
9	**external service providers**	Text: Coordinate appointments with external service providers
10	**appliances**	Text: Maintain office supplies (stationery, appliances, etc.)
11	**team members**	Text: Act as the go-to source of service and office information for team members
12	**English and Spanish**	Text: Strong written and verbal communication skills in English and Spanish …
13	**2/two years**	Text: Minimum 2 years proven office management experience
14	**current environmental issues**	Text: Knowledge of current environmental issues is a plus

General Training Reading Section 2

15	v	Text: At Galonzo Inc., we strive to maintain a working environment that is safe and fair for all employees … our company philosophy.
16	x	Text: It is crucial that all full-time employees at Galonzo, Inc. maintain a 40 hours per week schedule.
17	i	Text: All part-time and freelance employees are eligible for specific exclusions …
18	ii	Text: Occasionally, full-time employees will be requested to work some overtime hours …
19	ix	Text: All full-time employees are entitled to 14 days of vacation leave during their first two years of employment.
20	vii	Text: Galonzo, Inc. employees are entitled to paid sick leave.
21	iii	Text: Strict adhesion to these policies and procedures by the company employees and administration will ensure that everyone at Galonzo, Inc. has a productive experience while maintaining their well-being both during and beyond office hours.

22	**consequences**	Text: The legal, social and psychological consequences of discrimination can be severe.
23	**behaviour**	Text: Unlike prejudice, discrimination involves behaviour.
24	A	Text: Prejudice refers to the attitude a person may have about a person or group of people.
25	C	Text: Unlike prejudice, discrimination only involves behaviour. Discrimination in the workplace occurs when an individual is treated unjustly due to a variety of factors.
26	B	Text: A more serious form of this is called harassment, which can include jokes, slurs, cyberbullying, or threatening behaviour like physical intimidation or verbal abuse.
27	D	Text: Direct discrimination occurs when an individual is treated unfavourably or unfairly by someone else because they have a certain characteristic, like age or skin colour.
28	E	Text: Indirect discrimination occurs when rules or requirements that are presented as neutral and universal actually create disadvantages for a certain person or group of people.

General Training Reading Section 3

29	G	Text: The monkeys have been portrayed on Gibraltar's five-pence coin since 1988. They are also feature into a number of novels and films, including a 1987 James Bond film.
30	D	Text: Currently, the Gibraltar Ornithological and Natural History Society (GONHS) and the Gibraltar Veterinary Clinic care for and monitor the island's monkey population.
31	C	Text: DNA links them to being the last survivors of a general European population that spread as far as the UK …
32	A	Text: … the locals refer to them simply as "monos", which is the Spanish word for monkeys.
33	F	Text: Due to the improvements here, the Barbary Macaque population in Gibraltar is increasing at a steady rate. This puts pressure on the environment, which must also be carefully monitored.
34	B	Text: The apes are recorded as appearing on the Rock of Gibraltar long before the British occupation in 1704.

35	**E**	Text: Macaques are caught regularly in order to monitor their health.
36	**tourist attractions**	Text: Macaques have become one of the most popular tourist attractions in Gibraltar.
37	**troops**	Text: approximately three hundred monkeys in five troops …
38	**pickpocketing**	Text: This means that the monkeys are very bold and sociable, and now have inherent pickpocketing skills …
39	**illegal**	Text: However, encouraging the monkeys carries a fine of up to £4,000, and is illegal.
40	**British rule**	Text: the local belief that as long as there are monkeys on the Rock, it will remain under British rule.

General Training Writing Task 1

Dear Sir/Madam:

I saw your job advertisement at your bookstore and I believe I am a strong candidate for this position.

I am a recent graduate of Jameson College, where I majored in literature and creative writing. I have always loved reading, especially classical Japanese literature and poetry. I also enjoy reading modern novels, and can almost always be found in a park or café with a book in my hands when I have some free time. In addition to reading, I love to write and hope to someday publish a book of my own.

While I was in school I had a job at the campus library, where I was charged with shelving books, processing inventory on the computer and helping students find the books they were looking for. So not only do I have experience with organizing and locating books, but I have some customer service experience as well. I love working with people and helping them find the books that they need or recommending books if they are not sure what to get.

This job is of particular interest to me because it combines my two favourite things: books and people. I have visited your bookstore before and have always had very pleasant experiences there. I believe I would be an ideal addition to your team.

Please feel free to contact me with any questions or for further information. I look forward to hearing from you.

Kind regards,

Martin Kemper

(243 words)

General Training Writing Task 2

At a time when obesity is on the rise, people have been struggling to come up with solutions for encouraging the population to make healthier choices. Advertisements for gyms and diets can be found all over the internet and on television. And yet, the problem shows no signs of disappearing or even slowing down. One idea some governments have proposed is to add a tax on unhealthy foods, like chips and sugary drinks. I believe this idea could be effective, but only if it is executed in the right way.

The argument in favour of the tax on unhealthy foods is simple. If people have to pay more for unhealthy food, they are less likely to buy it. If people buy less unhealthy food, they will eat less of it and therefore lose weight and have healthier lifestyles. But is this actually the case? How much impact would a tax like this actually have? The idea has not been around long enough to know whether or not it would really work. People might just end up spending more money on food and then have less to spend on other necessities, like their households, healthcare, or leisure activities.

Nevertheless, it is possible that the money generated from taxing unhealthy foods could be used for community programs that promote fitness and healthy eating. One reason that many people live unhealthy lifestyles is that they lack nutritional education. Many people also do not have the time or resources to exercise, or even just to get outside and spend time on physical activity. This tax could raise money that could then be spent on promoting healthy lifestyles in ways that are far more effective than commercial advertisements.

I believe that taxing unhealthy foods could be very beneficial, as long as the revenue is used to address the growing health concerns that are inspiring this proposal in the first place. Otherwise, the tax could end up doing more harm than good. It is up to government officials to decide how to proceed, but I think there is the potential for this tax to have a positive impact on the overall health of the population.

(359 words)

PRACTICE TEST 5

Listening Section 1

1   B
2   C
3   Parot
4   020 2833 8924
5   one bedroom
6   balcony
7   air conditioning
8   40
9   loft
10 rooftop

Listening Section 2

11 3 (pm)
12 2.30 (pm)
13 Recreation Office
14 (very) ergonomic
15 Europe
16 fire
17 fedora
18 glass
19 Flash
20 donations

Listening Section 3

21 C
22 A
23 B
24 B
25 [culturally] enriched
26 world city
27 change
28 housing

29   romantic relationships

30   [personal] stories

Listening Section 4

31   witchcraft

32   500,000 years

33   right-brained / right brained

34   lefty

35   anticipating

36   both sides

37   divergent thinking

38   the UK

39   motor skills

40   psychotic disorders

Academic Reading Passage 1

1	**unhealthy**	Text: Twenty years ago, if you described symptoms of nostalgia to a doctor, you would have been told that it's unhealthy to focus on the past. (Paragraph 2)
2	**[Swiss] mercenaries**	Text: Hofer created the term to refer to the often debilitating homesickness Swiss mercenaries endured in foreign battlefields … (Paragraph 2)
3	**cowbells**	Text: … the 'disorder' was ascribed as a symptom, by various military physicians, to brain or ear damage caused by the clanging of cowbells. (Paragraph 2)
4	**fundamental**	Text: One of the first things Sedikides and Wildschut discovered was that the experience of nostalgia is fundamental to human existence and present among all major human civilisations. (Paragraph 4)
5	**cold room**	Text: Bizarrely, we are more likely to become nostalgic in a cold room than a warm one … (Paragraph 5)
6	**coping mechanism**	Text: … Wildschut was contacted by a concentration camp survivor who reported that one coping mechanism people used in the camps was remembering the good times of the past in an attempt to alter their perception of the present. (Paragraph 5)
7	**helpful**	Text: Still, not all forms of nostalgia are helpful. (Paragraph 6)

8	**TRUE**	Text: Indeed, though little research had been conducted on the neurological origins and effects of nostalgia, psychologists generally agreed that it was a mental disorder. (Paragraph 2)
9	**NOT GIVEN**	Text: The symptoms of this nostalgia were described as fainting, fever, death—and, of course, a longing for Alpine landscapes. (Paragraph 2)
10	**TRUE**	Text: … not only that, but nostalgia can also make us feel as if our environment is warmer than it actually is. (Paragraph 5)
11	**FALSE**	Text: Reflective nostalgia, according to Boym, focuses on 'longing and loss, the imperfect process of remembrance.' This type of nostalgia accepts that the past is irretrievably gone, giving the experiencer of this type of nostalgia a feeling of empathy and bittersweet consolation. (Paragraph 6)
12	**NOT GIVEN**	Text: In addition, restorative nostalgia can manifest in sinister ways, such as with the 'national and nationalist revivals all over the world, which engage in the anti-modern mythmaking of history' (Paragraph 6)
13	**FALSE**	Text: What's more, in countries where nostalgia is more prevalent, people are more likely to volunteer, be free thinkers, and build strong bonds with their peers … (Paragraph 7)
14	**D**	Text: Recently, nostalgia, or the act of looking wistfully back into our past, has become increasingly common. (Paragraph 1)

Academic Reading Passage 2

15	**vii**	
16	**x**	
17	**iii**	
18	**i**	
19	**v**	
20	**ix**	
21	**ii**	
22	**iv**	
23	**creativity and knowledge**	Text: Intellectual property (IP) is an ethical system that values human creativity and knowledge. (Paragraph 2)

24	**recognition**	Text: These benefits will often include recognition for their IP and the ability to earn money from their IP … (Paragraph 2)
25	**(training) workshop**	Text: To combat these views, the World Intellectual Property Organisation (WIPO) hosted a training workshop for basket weavers in Kenya … (Paragraph 6)
26	**sisal plant**	Text: Their baskets are laboriously crafted from the hand-twisted fibres of the sisal plant. (Paragraph 6)
27	**(wooden) spatula**	Text: First, the women peel the sisal leaf with a wooden spatula to extract the fibres … (Paragraph 7)
28	**2 / two months**	Text: As the women weave in spare moments between farm work and housework, it can take anywhere from two weeks to two months to make a single basket. (Paragraph 7)

Academic Reading Passage 3

29	**D**	Text: It was this exact question, interestingly, that triggered the establishment of a prediction tournament by the Intelligence Advanced Research Projects Activity (IARPA) in 2011 … (Paragraph 4)
30	**A**	Text: Tetlock, a professor of psychology at the Wharton School of Business who famously made the assertion (following another prediction tournament that ran from 1984 to 2004) that a chimp throwing darts at a board labelled with every possible outcome would predict as many future events correctly as the average political expert. (Paragraph 4)
31	**B**	Text: … those new to prediction training, Tetlock says, have to be taught how to watch out for confirmation biases which can create false confidence … (Paragraph 5)
32	**D**	Text: … the team still hopes that governments will take notice and use their methods to improve the way they make decisions. (Paragraph 8)
33	**NOT GIVEN**	Text: While we've known that predicting the future is impossible since at least the 18th century, psychic mediums and clairvoyants continue to abound today. (Paragraph 1)

34	**TRUE**	Text: It was this exact question, interestingly, that triggered the establishment of a prediction tournament by the Intelligence Advanced Research Projects Activity (IARPA) in 2011, to determine whether our predictions of how uncertain future events will unfold could be enhanced. (Paragraph 3)
35	**NOT GIVEN**	Text: As it turns out, you need neither be a political connoisseur nor possess a Mensa-calibre IQ to be a good forecaster … (Paragraph 5)
36	**FALSE**	Text: … superforecasters are foxes, more open to a wider range of experiences and less attached to a specific viewpoint or mental framework. (Paragraph 5)
37	**uncanny**	Text: … except, perhaps, their uncanny ability to predict global events with sometimes frightening accuracy. (Paragraph 1)
38	**chimp**	Text: … that a chimp throwing darts at a board with possible outcomes would probably predict as many future events as the average political expert. (Paragraph 4)
39	**Political**	Text: As it turns out, you need neither be a political connoisseur nor possess a Mensa-calibre IQ to be a good forecaster … (Paragraph 5)
40	**Tracking**	Text: Finally, and this is something that applies not only to the superforecasters but also the organisations they belong to, there is tracking. (Paragraph 7)

Academic Writing Task 1

The two tables demonstrate how many books library members took out in different genres per week in two libraries in London in 2016. Overall, it can be seen that thriller and horror were the most popular genres in both libraries, whereas literary fiction was among the least popular in the North London Library, and the least in South London Library. Science fiction was also not very popular in North London Library, but was slightly more successful in the South.

Looking at the graphs in further detail, thriller and horror stood at 45 books per week in the North and South London Library at the beginning of the year. That number grew consistently for the North London Library, peaking at 60 per week in the September–December period. In the South London Library, however, it dropped to 41.

Young Adult was the second most popular genre in the North London Library by the end of the year, having briefly enjoyed the top spot mid-2016. By contrast, in the

South London Library, YA numbers were consistently low at 10 to 12. General Fiction started out near the bottom in the South London Library, but by the end of the year it had reached 30 per week, close to North London's 34. Literary fiction, finally, was similarly unsuccessful in both libraries, while science fiction was at least thrice more popular in South London than the North London Library, with numbers ranging from 15 per week (January–April) to 23 (September–December). The numbers of books borrowed in other genres were relatively similar throughout the year in both libraries.

(262 words)

Academic Writing Task 2

When mobile phones began to be more widely used in the 1990s, no one could've predicted the enormous impact they would eventually have on our day to day lives. It is now near impossible to find anyone in the western world, many children included, who does not own a mobile phone. I firmly believe, however, that the demerits of young children owning phones eclipse the merits.

The reasons parents buy their children phones are varied: some believe that mobile phones provide safety, for example, as they allow you to track, at any given time, where your child is. My parents were an example of this when I was young: while applications like "Find My Friends" did not exist at the time, I was expected to reply to all calls and texts and give them my location whenever required—something that arguably kept me safe, although not necessarily out of trouble. What's more, modern mobile phones are often presented as having the ability to teach: there are all sorts of apps and games that children can learn from, and a mobile phone is also helpful in introducing technology to kids.

However, none of these arguments are strong enough, in my opinion, to outweigh the negatives when it comes to children younger than twelve. While teenagers often go out on their own and it is useful for a parent to be able to contact them, young children should always be accompanied by an adult. Moreover, while it's true that mobile phones have a plethora of useful applications, they are also a gateway to danger, as they have access to the internet. Granted, you can set most mobiles up with parent control, but chances are that children will find ways to get around these barriers, as younger generations are generally far more knowledgeable than their parents when it comes to technology. In addition, mobile phones can be a distraction for children when they are supposed to do their homework, and can even prove a distraction from socialising with their peers and playing outside.

To conclude, there are several advantages and disadvantages to mobile phones, and I strongly believe that all teenagers and adults should own one. In the case of *young children, though, the benefits are overshadowed by the drawbacks, and I think that parents should think twice before purchasing a mobile phone for their child.*

(394 words)

General Training Reading Section 1

1	B	Text: At Hard Core Climbing, our instructors are all highly experienced climbers and trainers, certified by the National Association of Climbing Professionals.
2	F	Text: We offer three types of membership: Silver, Gold, and Platinum.
3	C	Text: When you buy one of our weekend passes for £40 from now until 30 May, you'll receive a free weekday pass redeemable for the rest of the year.
4	A	Text: Book a party package now for only £50!
5	E	Text: Don't have the right equipment? Don't worry— you can rent some from us at a flat rate of £20 per course.
6	G	Text: Gallery seating available for £15–£30 each, and a limited number of private boxes are also available for only £50.
7	D	Text: (An initial 15-minute golf cart training course is required for all new members.)
8	TRUE	Text: Copying and printing unnecessarily use valuable paper, toner, electricity, and cause wear and tear to equipment
9	NOT GIVEN	Text: Please use appropriate recycling bins for all paper, plastic, and other recyclable waste.
10	FALSE	Text: Please check this list carefully and remember to rinse out all liquid containers before depositing them in the appropriate bins.
11	FALSE	Text: Consult the attached list of equipment that must always remain plugged in and turned on, even when not in use.
12	TRUE	Text: … all lightbulbs in the building have been switched to low-energy alternatives …
13	NOT GIVEN	Text: Employees can ask at reception for a discount voucher at Connelly's Bike Shop on Arthur Ave.

| 14 | TRUE | Text: Paper and plastic cups at water coolers and in the breakroom will be discontinued throughout the building as of the end of the month. |

General Training Reading Section 2

15	x	Text: At MegaCo, our remote work policy provides guidelines for employees who qualify to work from home or from a location outside our offices.
16	vi	Text: Only employees who have worked for the company full-time for a minimum of 1 year can qualify.
17	i	Text: Qualifying office-based employees will be permitted to work remotely up to 3 days a week or up to, but no more than, 12 days per calendar month.
18	ix	Text: Employees who work from home are encouraged to maintain a suitable working environment.
19	ii	Text: When working from home, employees are free to wear whatever they find comfortable and appropriate.
20	v	Text: Even when working off site, it is essential that all employees maintain company standards of discretion, data protection, and confidentiality.
21	vii	Text: These regulations are outlined in the company's code of conduct, which is reviewed and signed by all employees during the onboarding process.
22	managers and employees	Text: Annual Employee Reviews are an essential practice that help managers and employees align expectations …
23	human resources	Text: They also give workers the chance to address human resources concerns.
24	goals and expectations	Text: Take this opportunity to share your annual goals and expectations with employees …
25	list	Text: Provide employees with a list of these goals, so they can refer to them throughout the year.
26	ahead of time	Text: Annual reviews are successful only when the manager prepares feedback ahead of time.

27	self-evaluation	Text: A few weeks before annual reviews, ask your employees to write a self-evaluation. This will give them an opportunity to consolidate their thoughts ahead of time, as well as some time to consider their performance throughout the previous year.
28	open-ended	Text: Ideal evaluation forms include questions that are open-ended.

General Training Reading Section 3

29	A	Text: Pencils have been used to make marks on paper since Roman times, when lead rods were used by scribes to write with.
30	C	Text: When locals tried to use it like a lead pencil, they found that it was too soft …
31	B	Text: the more clay used in the mix, the harder the pencil.
32	D	Text: while in China, pencils are painted yellow …
33	D	Text: The Welsh author Roald Dahl wrote all his books using yellow pencils on yellow paper.
34	C	Text: In order to avoid any accidents on set, these pencils were created with erasers on both sides.
35	A	Text: However, given the emphasis on damage caused by the timber industry to the planet, manufacturers are looking to find sustainable materials.
36	beer	Text: The villagers went graphite crazy, putting graphite in and on everything, including using it to mark their sheep, and even adding it to their beers!
37	string	Text: Before wood, string was used, wrapped around the graphite and unwound as the pencil wore down.
38	hardness and blackness	Text: Most makers in Europe assign their pencils with H ("hardness") and B ("blackness") with a number to show how intense the hardness or blackness will be.
39	environmental laws	Text: Traditionally, Chinese linden wood has been used, as this is a good solid grain, and can be chopped from forests on the borders with Russia without much regulation, because the environmental laws are more lax.
40	newspaper	Text: Some recycling plants are currently using pressurised recycled newspaper to create planet-friendly pencils.

General Training Writing Task 1

Dear Sir/Madam,

I have just returned from a holiday at San Giacomo beach, during which time I stayed at your hotel, the Seashell Resort. I had been looking forward to this trip for months and had to work very hard to save enough money to afford such luxurious accommodations.

Based on the photos and descriptions on your website, I was expecting the Star Suite to have a balcony with an ocean view and a king-sized bed. Perhaps the pictures you have online are of another Star Suite, because my room did not have any of these features.

The "balcony" was, actually a plank of wood with a railing that was too small and seemed too precarious to support even a child. There was an ocean view , but only if I stuck my head out the window and looked to the left. Even then, I could only see a sliver of water in the distance. As for the king-sized bed, I had to make one myself by pushing the two single beds in my room together. Nevertheless, I had to sleep on one side or the other in order to avoid lying on the uncomfortable crack down the middle of this makeshift bed.

I feel it is reasonable for me to request a 20% refund of the price I paid for my stay. Additionally, I encourage you to redesign your website so that it does not raise anyone else's expectations as it did mine. I will also be posting reviews of the Seashell Resort online. Hopefully this will help future guests avoid making the same mistakes that I made when booking accommodations at your establishment.

Sincerely,

Lana Moore

(276 words)

General Training Writing Task 2

It seems that everywhere people go these days, there are security cameras watching and recording their every move. In banks, office buildings, grocery stores, even in some schools—people are constantly being monitored for potential breaches of security. In many countries, like the UK and China, CCTV cameras monitor and record everything that occurs on city streets and sidewalks. While there have been some incidents during which these cameras were used to solve serious crimes, they also constitute a serious breach of public privacy.

It is a well-known fact that CCTV camera surveillance has helped law enforcement officials solve crimes. Security professionals have used camera footage to identify suspects, and to help them get a better understanding of what happened during a crime or violent incident. However, one of the central arguments made for installing so many CCTV cameras in public spaces has been that they deter criminals and prevent crime from happening in the first place. And yet, is there any evidence that this is actually the case? Crime statistics fluctuate in different parts of the world, but there is no way to prove that public surveillance has any influence on them.

Because of the rise in CCTV cameras and public surveillance in the name of public security, privacy has become a privilege of the past. Unless someone is in their own home with the curtains drawn, it is impossible to know whether they are being watched. We have all sacrificed our dignity and privacy for the sake of a security system that may or may not effectively protect us.

In my opinion, CCTV monitoring is an invasion of privacy, and should be more tightly regulated. Although public surveillance has the potential for helping solve crimes, there is no evidence that it deters criminals. The sacrifice of privacy seems like too high a price to pay for a system that does not necessarily live up to its promise.

(319 words)

PRACTICE TEST 6

Listening Section 1

1   6.17
2   Common
3   underground
4   Wednesday
5   13.00 / 1.00 / 1 / one
6   11.25
7   purchase
8   credit card
9   Matthew
10   2020

Listening Section 2

11 natural

12 layers

13 species

14 swamp

15 limestone

16 C

17 C

18 A

19 B

20 B

Listening Section 3

21 admission tests

22 application form

23 Communications

24 assistant teacher

25 scripts

26 video editing

27 gap year

28 medical students

29 favourite subject

30 work experience

Listening Section 4

31 instructor

32 (an) introduction session

33 12 / twelve weeks

34 tablets and phones

35 (the) typing trainer

36 heart and soul

37 (different) techniques

38 experimenting with

39 (dynamic) world

40 sense of closure

Academic Reading Passage 1

1	**ten times**	Text: The Highway Code warns drivers that in rainy weather, stopping distances are twice the length they would be on dry roads. On ice, this stopping distance becomes ten times greater. (Paragraph 1)
2	**skidding**	Text: Similarly, in heavy snow, most road vehicles struggle to grip adequately, making steering and braking less controlled, causing skidding and leading to many road accidents. (Paragraph 1)
3	**legal obligation**	Text: In 2003, the 1980 Highways Act was amended to place a legal obligation on local councils to keep their roads clear. (Paragraph 1)
4	**dispersing**	Text: This brownish substance is dispersed along roads and motorways in cold weather by vehicles known as 'salt spreaders' or 'gritters', which are large trucks and lorries equipped with grit dispersing apparatus. (Paragraph 2)
5	**aid traction**	Text: … the grit being there simply to aid traction and tyre grip on the asphalt. (Paragraph 3)
6	**−10°C**	Text: Any lower than −10°C and the rock salt has no effect at all. (Paragraph 3)
7	**dissolve**	Text: … the rock salt needs to be crushed by vehicle tyres into smaller particles to allow it to dissolve into the moisture on the road. (Paragraph 3)
8	**the continent**	Text: … in times of need, rock salt is also imported from the continent. (Paragraph 4)
9	**2 million tonnes**	Text: In total, over 2 million tonnes of salt is used on Britain's roads every year, at a cost of some £150 million. (Paragraph 4)
10	**meteorology reports**	Text: Councils install weather monitoring stations across their region, and also keep an eye on meteorology reports in order to be aware of current and future drops in temperature. (Paragraph 5)
11	**air drafts**	Text: … if a stretch of road is gritted too early the road will still be dry, and the rock salt will just be blown away by air drafts from passing vehicles. (Paragraph 5)
12	**less effective**	Text: As the rock salt itself would still need to be crushed by tyres to allow it to dissolve, salting

roads which are already too dangerous to drive on is significantly less effective at not only dissolving the ice already on the road, but also from preventing more ice from forming. (Paragraph 5)

13	**chloride**	Text: Over all lakes in the US, the concentration of chloride ranged from 0.18 to 240 milligrams per litre. This is still quite low (seawater, for instance, contains around 35 grams of chloride per litre), but the levels of salt are certainly rising. (Paragraph 6)
14	**imperfect precaution**	Text: Still, gritting remains an imperfect precaution against ice roads, though at the moment, it remains the best solution to an impractical issue. (Paragraph 7)

Academic Reading Passage 2

15	**camera obscura**	Text: The British aristocrat William Henry Fox Talbot is an important figure in the history of photography. He is remembered today for his discovery in 1839 of the negative-positive process, inspired by the camera obscura … (Paragraph 1)
16	**upside-down**	Text: Through this process, objects seen scatter and reform by the law of optics, and the object appears upside-down to the viewer. (Paragraph 2)
17	**inaccurate**	Text: Henry Fox Talbot's desire to create a mechanism to photograph scenes and objects began during a visit to Lake Como in Italy, where he became frustrated with his inaccurate attempts to sketch the scene. (Paragraph 3)
18	**numerous (photographs)**	Text: Talbot found that repeating the process of developing the photograph into a negative would allow him to print numerous positive photographs from the negative sample … (Paragraph 3)
19	**photographic**	Text: what is less well known is that there were a number of photographic processes developed by different people in the first half of the 19th century … (Paragraph 4)
20	**first**	Text: It is now widely accepted that the first photograph was created, not by Talbot, but by a French inventor named Nicéphore Niépce, of the view outside his window in the late 1820s. (Paragraph 4)

21	**commercially**	Text: It was in fact Daguerre, rather than Talbot, who created the first commercially successful form of photography … (Paragraph 5)
22	**daguerrotype**	Text: … named the daguerreotype. (Paragraph 5)
23	**reliable**	Text: The daguerreotype was reliable and relatively cheap to produce … (Paragraph 5)
24	**calotype**	Text: Talbot, on the other hand, found it much more difficult to profit from his invention in its early years. At first it seemed as though his negative-positive method, also known as the calotype … (Paragraph 6)
25	**superior**	Text: … superior to Daguerre's, because instead of creating a single image, it produced a paper negative from which unlimited positive copies could be made. (Paragraph 6)
26	**standard**	Text: As daguerreotypes sank into obscurity, the principles established by Talbot became the standard … (Paragraph 7)

Academic Reading Passage 3

27	**NOT GIVEN**	Text: The area in north-west Venezuela where the Catatumbo river meets Lake Maracaibo (Paragraph 1)
28	**TRUE**	Text: The area where the Catatumbo river meets the lake attracts an average of 28 lightning strikes per minute, which is about 1.2 million lightning flashes in a year. (Paragraph 2)
29	**NOT GIVEN**	Text: The area has recently been declared by NASA to be the lightning capital of the world, and has even earned a place in the 2005 edition of the Guinness Book of World Records … (Paragraph 2)
30	**FALSE**	Text: In the areas surrounding Lake Maracaibo, 1 to 3 people are struck by lightning every year. (Paragraph 3)
31	**TRUE**	Text: For hundreds of years, travellers have been captivated by these incredible light shows from 'Maracaibo's Lighthouse' … (Paragraph 4)
32	**TRUE**	Text: Indigenous tribes once believed that the lightning storms were triggered by encounters between fireflies and ancestral evil spirits that were believed to have inhabited the area—the lights produced by the lightning showed the efforts of

a fight between good and evil. Such tales are still popular today … (Paragraph 4)

33	TRUE	Text: There is also the theory that humidity plays an important role in the lightning activity since the longest hiatus between events happened during Venezuela's severe drought in 2010. (Paragraph 5)
34	TRUE	Text: When this hot moist air meets with the cooler air from the Andes, it is forced upwards. This is when large amounts of vapour begin to condense, forming clouds that discharge electricity in the form of lightning bolts. (Paragraph 6)
35	FALSE	Text: The scientist says that the lightning storms do not happen near the shore of South America's largest lake, but about 40–70 miles far from the observers … (Paragraph 8)
36	NOT GIVEN	Text: The flashes appear in a wide variety of colours ranging from blues and purples to reds and oranges. Dr Cybil attributes the colour change to the presence of dust particles: 'As white light passes through varying amounts of dust particles and moisture, it gets absorbed or diffracted making it appear as different colours …' (Paragraph 8)
37	minute	Text: The area where the Catatumbo river meets the lake attracts an average of 28 lightning strikes per minute … (Paragraph 2)
38	Caracas University	Text: Dr Cybil from Caracas University, however, has asserted that none of these theories are correct. To counter them, she has put forth a theory of her own to explain the large amount of lightning present in the area. 'The area is surrounded by the Andes with its high mountains trapping the warm winds …' (Paragraph 6)
39	15/fifteen miles	Text: It is practically impossible to hear thunder if you are 15 miles or more from the spot where lightning is striking. (Paragraph 7)
40	white light	Text: As white light passes through varying amounts of dust particles and moisture, it gets absorbed or diffracted making it appear as different colours. (Paragraph 8)

Academic Writing Task 1

The table compares the amount of beef, pork, poultry and lamb consumed in four different countries in the year 2015.

Paraguay is the country which consumes the most beef with approximately 26 kilograms per capita. This is a very high number compared to the other figures, since it is only slightly below the beef consumption of the other three countries combined.

South Korea and Paraguay are the countries with the highest consumption of pork with 28.4 and 21 kilograms per capita respectively. Compared to these countries, South Africa consumes very little pork with only 3.4 kilograms per capita each year, whereas Turkey consumes no pork.

As for poultry, South Africa gets through almost 31 kilograms a year followed by Turkey with 16.5 kilograms and South Korea with slightly more than 14 kilograms for each person. Though Paraguay is a significant consumer of beef and pork, it only consumed 6 kilograms per capita in 2015.

Overall, it can be said that Turkey does not consume anywhere near as much meat as the other countries, with a total meat consumption of 28.9 kilograms per capita each year.

(185 words)

Academic Writing Task 2

The existence of natural talent is a frequent topic of discussion when people try to explain the successful careers of musicians, artists, and sports people.

Firstly, we need to understand that the whole educational system in most countries is based on the belief that skills can be acquired. Another important aspect to be taken into consideration is the number of hours people spend practicing their skills. During the two and a half years they spent in Hamburg, the Beatles performed for about 5 hours a night, six nights a week, which adds up to approximately 4,000 hours of practice. Perhaps this is how they honed their performance skills, leading on to their first recording and ultimately to becoming the biggest rock band in history.

However, some people might argue that the Beatles dedication to practicing would all have been in vain if not for their natural talent. In other words, all those hours of practice could have helped them become very good musicians, but they would never have been able to become extraordinary without their natural abilities. Many believe that innate talent is the difference between world class and average. For instance, footballers who play for the same club and undergo the same amount and type of training would all be at the same level if not for differences in natural talent.

I personally think that both talent and practice play important roles in the creation of talent. If a child with an innate talent for music only gets to play their favourite musical instrument for a couple of hours a month, they will not develop their skills as much as the other, perhaps even less talented children who practice their instruments every day.

In conclusion, I believe that anyone can be taught a particular set of skills, but how proficient they become employing those skills will always depend on a combination of innate talent and practice.

(317 words)

General Training Reading Section 1

1	B	Text: Savings can be applied to up to 5 dairy items at checkout.
2	E	Text: Expires 22/11/19.
3	E	Text: Buy 2 get 1 free on FreeMilk chocolate products.
4	A	Text: Coupon cannot be used in conjunction with any other offer.
5	D	Text: To use in store, simply hand coupon to cashier. To use online, use code SHOP20 at checkout.
6	C	Text: £10 gift voucher redeemable online only, following your friend's first purchase.
7	2/two years	Text: you were supplied with 4 water filter cartridges, which should last you a total of 2 years.
8	generic (brand/water)	Text: DO NOT attempt to replace the water filter with a generic water filter. Using anything other than an official Doodle water filter will void your warranty.
9	6/six months	Text: label your water filter with a date 6 months into the future, to help you to remember when you will need to change your water filter.
10	plastic film	Text: remove the plastic film on the bottom of your new filter (if your new filter is not covered, DO NOT USE and contact your supplier for a replacement).
11	(the) arrows	Text: Place the new filter in the canister, making sure the arrows on the sides of the filter are pointing upright.

12	**D**	Text: Remove the existing filter by snapping off the lid of the filter canister …
13	**C**	Text: press and hold the ice and water buttons for 10 seconds, to reset the filter schedule.
14	**B**	Text: Fill and discard two to five large glassfuls of water, as many as needed until the water runs clear.

General Training Reading Section 2

15	**TRUE**	Text: Full-time employees are entitled to take up to 3 days of paid leave … following the death of an immediate family member (… parent, grandparent, child or significant other).
16	**NOT GIVEN**	Text: Full-time employees are entitled to take up to 3 days of paid leave … following the death of an immediate family member … (parent, grandparent, child or significant other). Leave for death or illness of other family members and close friends may be granted upon consideration.
17	**NOT GIVEN**	Text: Occasionally, employees may be entitled to longer periods of leave.
18	**FALSE**	Text: Any compassionate leave provided after the first 3 days will be unpaid.
19	**TRUE**	Text: Dependants can include: parents, grandparents, children, spouses and others who depend on you for their primary care.
20	**D**	Text: **DRD Compassionate Leave Policy**
21	**B**	Text: Any compassionate leave provided after the first 3 days will be unpaid.
22	**form**	Text: To be eligible for the above scheme, employees must first complete the Eye Care Scheme Form, and have it signed by both a partner of this firm and an optician.
23	**£25**	Text: Up to £25* per eye test
24	**additional**	Text: If employees would like to purchase a more costly appliance, they will need to pay the additional cost …
25	**invoice**	Text: To claim money back after your eye test or purchase of spectacles, please complete an invoice and submit to the finance team with approval from your line manager.

26	A	Text: If eye problems persist with CMS using employees, Edmonds and Partners are willing to consider reasonable requests for further eye tests.
27	C	Text: All employees who use a Computer Monitor Screen (CMS) for 5 hours or more per day are entitled to a free eye test and/or sight test by an optician.
28	B	Text: Up to £25* per eye test

General Training Reading Section 3

29	E	Text: Some individuals have even managed to make money from their amateur photographs, by selling images of celebrities to newspapers and gossip magazines for a small fee.
30	A	Text: The term *paparazzi* was reportedly coined by the Italian film director Federico Fellini as an onomatopoeic reference to the sound of a camera shutter operating. In Italian, the word means 'those who pap'.
31	D	Text: powerful telephoto lenses have led to scandals in which celebrities and royalty are photographed without their consent from over a kilometre away.
32	B	Text: Paparazzi are not artists … As such, paparazzi are classified as a form of journalists.
33	G	Text: celebrities have been given a greater control over what to share and what to keep private in their lives
34	C	Text: Though the actual term first arose in the post-war era, many identify photographer Erich Salomon, active in the twenties and thirties, as the first paparazzo.
35	F	Text: Unlike the photographs obtained by the paparazzi, such phone-hacking actions are illegal …
36	D	Text: The term *paparazzi* was reportedly coined by the Italian film director Federico Fellini as an onomatopoeic reference to the sound of a camera shutter operating.
37	G	Text: … as Rome, and especially the cafes of the famous Via Veneto, became a hangout for globally famous

38	A	Text: … they could earn much more money by photographing the stars and selling these images to the international press.
39	F	Text: At the same time, a number of celebrities have successfully resorted to court orders to ban paparazzi from gathering outside their homes, and been awarded damages in response to particularly egregious invasions of their privacy.
40	B	Text: However, it is likely that as long as the public appetite for salacious photographs of celebrities continues, paparazzi, along with other methods which expose the private lives of those in the public eye, will continue to exist.

General Training Writing Task 1

Dear Sonya,

It is with regret that I must inform you that I will be resigning from my current role of Operations Manager at Grandos Ltd. Following a talk I gave about Motivational Management Styles, I was offered a job as senior Opeations Director with Haweson IT.

As you know, I am very keen to further my career development, and have always wanted to work at a larger company. Having said that, I thought long and hard about resigning from my current post before making my decision, as I have learned so much from the team, and have enjoyed working with and getting to know everyone here.

I am extremely grateful for all you have taught me over the years, and I hope you will support my decision.

I will be able to work for a further 6 weeks, which should hopefully give you enough time to find my replacement, and provide me with enough time to train the new employee and finish all of my current assignments.

If you would like to discuss this further, we could schedule a meeting at some point this week.

Best wishes,

Octavio Montoya

(188 words)

General Training Writing Task 2

The number of vegetarians is steadily rising in England, as people are abandoning more traditional English diets consisting of meat and vegetables, for entirely meat-free food. Some people argue that eating meat-free diets is not natural, though many other civilizations have not eaten meat for many years, and many animals are naturally vegetarians.

Other people argue that it is healthy to eat meat, and not eating meat will be bad for people, but actually the opposite seems to be true. People who do not eat meat tend to live longer, and those who do not eat meat or any other animal products (a diet called veganism) are thought to have even longer life expectancies than vegetarians.

People who do not eat meat generally have a variety of reasons for abstaining. Some people do not eat meat for religious reasons. Some people do not eat meat because they believe that it is cruel to kill animals. Other people believe that, as the environmental impact of growing animals to slaughter for meat is much greater than the environmental impact of growing vegetables to eat, it is more environmentally friendly to be a vegetarian.

Many people find the idea of not eating meat unsettling, because they are used to eating meat, and they like the taste. These days there are many vegetarian alternatives that people can use to replace meat in their diets.

I believe that eating meat is wrong, as it is not only possible but also quite easy to eat a vegetarian diet, and as such it does not seem worth the environmental impact and the cruelty of breeding and slaughtering animals.

(268 words)